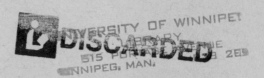

Kings at Arms

GENERAL SIR RICHARD *Nelson* GALE

Kings at Arms

The use and abuse of power in the great Kingdoms of the East

 HUTCHINSON OF LONDON

HUTCHINSON & CO (*Publishers*) LTD
3 Fitzroy Square, London W1

London Melbourne Sydney Auckland
Wellington Johannesburg Cape Town
and agencies throughout the world

First published 1971

*This book has been set in Plantin type, printed in Great Britain
on antique wove paper by Anchor Press, and
bound by Wm. Brendon, both of Tiptree, Essex*
ISBN 0 09 107950 0

Contents

Illustrations

Acknowledgements: Nos. 1, 2, 4, 10, 11, 12 are from the Radio Times Hulton Picture Library. Nos. 5, 7, 8, 13 are from the Mansell Collection.

Maps

1   *The Use and Abuse of Power*

Bacon in his *Essay on Great Place* remarked how strange it was that a man in seeking to gain control over others should in the process lose control over himself; yet such is the attraction of power that in spite of this man will seek to gain it. Indeed, it is the very lure of power that will drive many to great achievement, each success forcing them on to further efforts; but, for others, power has appeared to come more as by-product of success than as the result of ambitious intent and they have ended with something they had, as it were, not necessarily sought. Some have abused power for selfish motives and others have used it for good. There is, perhaps, no surer yardstick by which to measure true greatness than the use to which power gained has been put.

The issue is as old as history and at the same time contemporaneous. Hitler and Stalin used power as does Mao Tse-tung today. While Hitler's abuse of power led to his downfall ultimately, Stalin's use of it enabled him to consolidate a form of rule in Russia that, in spite of minor changes in emphasis, pertains in that country now. Others have used power for what they believed to be the betterment of their country, witness Franco in Spain and Salazar in Portugal. Nkrumah tried and failed in Ghana. Even with elected governments there is from time to time displayed the use of the power that authority gives; bureaucrats can use it as ruthlessly as emperors. 'These little monarchs reigning for a year, seeing the limit of their powers so near' will impose their petty will.[1] Politicians, having a majority, will abuse the power they temporarily wield and there is probably less brake here than there was with Jenghiz Khan, who, when he went against the wishes of the quriltai, had to pay the price, learning a lesson that even he never forgot. Some of these dictators have rested their position on fear and the ruthless oppression of any form of resistance, while others have relied on mass hysteria. In China today this may well be the case and it is probably true to say that in 1971 the foreign visitor there has less freedom and liberty of movement than in the times of Qubilai Khan.

If we examine the use to which the great conquerors who ruled in the far-off East put the power they wielded we may, therefore, find lessons that are applicable now. When kings rode in Asia, long before the days of democratic systems of government as we know them, there was splendour, romance, chivalry and a remarkable degree of stability of government in the areas over which they held sway. If at these times there were evils, in Europe and the Christian world there were shortcomings also. At the time when small European States were emerging from a morass of petty wars, court intrigues and the ambitious exploits of princes, while the Empire of Constantine was sinking to its inevitable end and when Roman and Protestant Churches were in open conflict, historic movements were convulsing Asia. Kings were riding; kings who ruled over vast areas and whose subjects numbered many millions were building empires, some of which endured for centuries. These kings had qualities of greatness.

Their achievements were the products of their philosophies and a chronological account of these achievements does little to disclose the forces that drove these men on. The interesting thing about any great man, be he soldier, statesman or poet, is not so much what he did or wrote or the irrelevancies of his daily life but rather the essential keys to open the door to his character and personality. Sometimes with these kings the key lay in antecedent influences, sometimes in the circumstances of early experiences, sometimes in religious philosophy and sometimes merely in innate character. Wherever it lay, one thing they had in common: they all achieved great power. Was this due to an inexorable chain of events or was it due to greed?

One of the easiest pegs on which to hang their motives is, of

[1] Anatole France: *Les Opinions de M. Jérôme Coignard.*

course, the inborn desire of man to conquer for gain and for conquest's sake. Ambition undoubtedly feeds on success and the determination to amass great wealth grows as the accumulation of treasure increases. Conquest can become a habit and, fed by the flames of ambition, success may lead the victor on to further aggression. On the other hand, power and the desire for power may stem from fear, the fear of a known or imagined enemy. Religious fervour may be either the cause of an aggressive war or merely the excuse for robbery and looting. Which of these factors drove Jenghiz Khan or Tamerlane, Saladin or Babur, Mahmud of Ghazni or Qubilai Khan?

In endeavouring to answer these questions there is always the danger of applying a Western philosophy or mental approach to what is essentially an Asiatic matter. Much of the perspective of history depends upon the point from which one views it which in turn may depend on the accident of birth. The Hindu or Chinese for instance, would look at the United States of America or Great Britain and their histories somewhat differently from the average American or Britisher. Although the adoption of a universal outlook should transcend the limitations of race and locality, the historian can find himself on the horns of a dilemma when he tries to unravel the relations of historical fact and sociology. The problems presented are difficult but should not be impossible of solution, provided one is prepared to cut across some cherished customs and accepted beliefs. For example, Western historians have described the Mongols as people addicted to drunkenness, as being brutal and treacherous, as a race believing that might was right and as men who were as savage in their behaviour as they were remorseless in their lust for blood and loot. Yet it was a Chinese religious devout who, when passing through their territory at the time of Jenghiz Khan, wrote that there was much that was pleasing about these people. Although they had no writing, he said, their contracts were sacred. Whatever they had they shared and if any was in trouble the others hastened to his or her assistance. Finally, he remarked that they seemed to him to have preserved all that was best in simple primeval life.[1]

Undoubtedly the conduct, philosophies and attitude of people have been deeply affected by religion. Thus, the teachings of Buddha have accounted for much in Chinese culture, their way of thinking

[1] Li Ch'ih-Ch'ang: *The Travels of an Alchemist.*

and of acting; the character of the Arab and Turkish races have been affected by the tenets of Muhammad; and the Vedic epics and the cult of Hinduism have moulded the characters of both priest and soldier in India. In Europe the philosophy of the Greeks and god-worship of the Romans vied with the teachings of Christ and, although much is owed to Roman Law, much also is owed to the New Testament. At first sight the adoption of a creed or belief by a particular people would appear to be the outcome of geography, yet on more close scrutiny the most important factor would seem to have been racial character and natural predilection. Thus, in the West Christianity was embraced; the inscrutable Chinese delighted in the subtle teachings of Buddha and of the Taoists; Hindu India, in spite of invasion upon invasion and years of persecution, remained loyal to her gods and legendary past; and the stern, rugged and puritanical teachings of Muhammad gripped the imagination of Arab and ancient Turk alike.

Towards the peoples of the East, if not so much today certainly in the past, the Western attitude has been one of patronising condescension. Nevertheless, when the Mongol Emperors of India were practising tolerance in religious matters, a bloody struggle was being carried on in Europe. Church fought against Church, and in the name of Christianity the Inquisition was performing horrors of torture. Within thirty years of the death of Tamerlane the English burned Joan of Arc at the stake. At the time of Qubilai Khan Christian Nestorians lived in peace beside fierce Mongol tribes and travellers were free to move throughout Asia to far-off Cathay, to Bengal and deep into Arabia.

Today in many countries presidents have taken the place of kings and the electoral system has supplanted the hereditary; but there is nothing new in the idea of election. Qubilai Khan, though some may say he rigged the election, a not unknown device today, was in fact elected by the quriltai. In medieval Europe the kings were hereditary but the kingdoms over which they ruled were small. After all this passage of time one might well ask whether anything is to be gained by examining the lives and motives of those who ruled so long ago and in such far-off lands. I think this story will show there is. The greatness of nations and empires depends on the people; yet the people themselves depend on wise government and understanding leadership. Power and the lust for power can be as dangerous now as it was in the medieval period. Wisely used it can bring strength and prosperity. Abused it can be followed by misery, oppression and bondage. How wise were these kings in Asia, who from design or from sheer strength of character found themselves in control of events over enormous areas that in some cases dwarf the greatest kingdoms of the world in which we live today? The period I shall cover is contemporaneous with that from Richard I to that of Elizabeth I of England and in considering oriental acts, motives and philosophies one should bear this in mind.

2   *Mahmud of Ghazni and Muhammad Ghuri*

Two men whose greed led to invasions carried out in the name of religion were Mahmud of Ghazni and Muhammad Ghuri. The country they ravaged was India, whose suffering at their hands was as cruel as it was real.

There is a proverb that runs, '*Dilli dur ast.*' It is indeed a long way to Delhi, to the Plain of Panipat, where the Holy River Jumna meanders through an arid rock-strewn country. Here, within a few miles of the present capital of India, are the ruins of at least seven old cities, all capitals in their time. Here, too, a thousand years before Christ, the mythical war between the Kamavars and Pandavars was fought to its bitter and bloody conclusion; and here, today, the name Indrapat preserves the tradition that it was in this vicinity that the Pandavars founded their city of Indrapatha.

Something seemed to draw men to this spot. It was far away from the traditional homeland of either the priestly Brahmins or the fighting Rajputs; so one might ask why it was that here most of the consequential battles in India's chequered history were fought. The magnets that drew men to this hot uninviting and parched area were two; the one political and the other geographical, the former deriving largely from the latter. The Plain of Panipat lay on the most direct route into the country from the north. There were two main roads into Hindustan, that via the Khyber Pass on to Lahore and that from Kandahar via Multan, and both met at Delhi. He who wished to forage south or east or west must cross the Plain of Panipat where the roads to all parts of the land met.

The political significance of Delhi is almost as old as history, though much of its early story is based on little more than legend. The first reliable date is in the eleventh century when Anagapala, Chief of the Tomaras, built the fort to which he transferred the Asoka Pillar and where now stands the Kutb Minar. Since then there have been eight cities of Delhi, though many existed under other names.

The Muslim invaders with which this story is concerned were of Turkish origin. These Turks had moved down from the Altai Mountains of Central Asia, spreading across the fertile land between the Syr-Darya and Amu-Darya rivers into Khorasan and beyond. One such migration settled in the fortress city of Ghazni. Although they were little more than bandits these people founded what later was the great Ghaznavid kingdom. In the year 997 one Mahmud was Chief of Ghazni. He had succeeded his father, Sabuktagin, who had invaded India and defeated a large Hindu army under Raja Jaipal. Sabuktagin had, nevertheless, contented himself with the loot he gained and had never attempted to penetrate or conquer the country; but it was his exploits that fired the imagination of Mahmud.

Mahmud's character was a strange mixture of the religious zealot and the miser, which he combined with a restless activity and a ruthless ambition. Quick to realise his potential strength as a pillar of Islam, the Caliph of Baghdad invested him as the rightful Lord of Ghazni and Khorasan, applauding him for his devotion to Islam and welcoming his desire to spread the faith. Mahmud was flattered and, to mark his appreciation, and no doubt recalling the ease with which his father had defeated the Hindus, he vowed he would every year lead a campaign against the idolators of Hindustan.

In this way commenced a series of at least sixteen invasions. The first was confined to the frontier towns near the Khyber where Jaipal, again in vain, tried to defend Peshawar. These raids, for they were little more, went deeper and deeper into the heart of the country. Although they were ostensibly crusades against infidels the zeal of the missionary was amply rewarded by the acquisition of booty. Nothing succeeds like success and the victories of Mahmud brought many willing soldiers to reinforce his army. For his followers there was the lure of untold wealth in gold, in silver, in precious stones and in exotic jewels to be had as fortresses and cities fell.

Mahmud was personally neither cruel nor vicious; if he slew idolators by the thousand it was always in battle, and he never massacred in cold blood. Nevertheless, the loot he took back to Afghanistan was so great that it is difficult not to conclude plunder had been his principal motive. When, in 1030, he died, he left prodigious wealth. He never sought to occupy India and the only part where he attempted to retain any grip at all was in the Panjab where, at Lahore, he left a governor. Mahmud was a man of learning, a philosopher, a patron of the arts and, when in his palace, there was little to indicate the ruthless warrior. Though a great soldier, personally brave and a man of limitless energy, he was not far-seeing, nor was he a statesman. He left no laws, no institutions and no machinery for government even to span the gap that followed on his death. He achieved an outward order which was no façade, but which was entirely dependent on himself. Thus, on his death, although his Ghaznavid kingdom did last for a century and a half, it tended to diminish with every decade.

Glorious as his victories in India may have been for the holy cause of Islam, for Hindustan they were intolerably cruel. The Hindu losses in life, in treasure and in holy temples and other buildings, were immense. Yet, strangely enough, their culture and religious faith remained intact; these were things that no man could, it would seem, filch from them. It is indeed a most remarkable fact that, whereas the invasions by Muslims of most countries of the world had resulted in the latter's adoption of the Islamic faith, Indian religious customs and beliefs have remained to this day inviolate.

This is perhaps strange, for in contrast to the simplicity of the Muslim religious dogma, that of the Hindus was intricate and involved. In spite of the fact that they accepted one supreme heavenly being called Brahma, through the course of time they had become polytheistic as, more and more, they felt the need for some outward and visible object which they could venerate. They were subdivided into innumerable groupings into which they were born and from which they could not in their lifetime break away. This was the caste system. This complexity and fragmentation in both their deity and social structure tended to preclude political hegemony. The masses looked to two sects for leadership: in matters religious to the

Brahmin priests and in matters of security to their rajas who for the most part belonged to the Kshatriya or fighting castes. Such were the Rajputs.

These Rajputs were valiant and, while possessing great attributes, were also bedevilled by inherent weaknesses. Their name gives some clue to this apparent contradiction. Rajputra, from which their name is derived, means 'The King's Son'. Thus, by definition, all were princes; they knew no class distinction, and the poorest was a gentleman and equal in status to the greatest. Among equals the exercise of authority is not easy and calls for great strength of character on the part of the leader. There was no overall political entity among the many states, some large and some extremely small. Between all there were jealousies that stemmed from their different origins. At the period with which we are concerned the Tuars of Delhi claimed the kinship of flame with the Chauans of Ajmir and the Rathors of Kanauj were loyal to their cousins of Gujerat. With their origins wrapped in romance some claimed to have sprung from the sun, some the moon and others fire.

They were an attractive people, chivalrous and generous with a code of honour that was strict. They were quixotic, courteous, honourable and utterly disinterested in personal gain. They cherished their ideals, prided themselves on bravery, which was a reality and no mere guise. Their women moved freely among their menfolk, shared their sports and even rode with them to battle. They would face the horrors of death with their husbands and, if this did not come to them on the battlefield, they would burn themselves alive rather than fall into the hands of an unclean foe.

The country in which they lived was largely dry, arid plain or, as in the south, rocky mountainous uplands. Rajasthan was bounded on the north by the Sind Desert, on the east by the Jumna River, in the south by the Vindhya Hills and on the west by the Indus and the Arabian Sea. Such were the Rajputs and such their country. Militarily their position was or should have been a strong one, for their numerical strength was great. They were well equipped, had excellent cavalry and staunch infantry and large numbers of war elephants; they were also well trained and individually as brave as lions. They were deeply religious and determined to preserve their way of life. Wherein then did they fail? Their fierce spirit of independence, though it could have been a source of strength, stemmed too often

B

from selfish jealousy; jealousies that, even when the enemy was knocking at the door, they failed to overcome. United they could have and
at times did succeed. Divided they fell. However, after the passing of
Mahmud there came a century of easing tension and the gradual
decline of the Ghaznavid gave them opportunities they grasped.

Eight years after the death of Mahmud his successor had lost
Khorasan. At Ghazni, as ruthless and unprincipled son followed
son, while brother murdered brother, the wealth of the treasury was
dissipated. The grip on the Panjab and the control of affairs in that
area became more and more slack, only the actual city of Lahore
remaining loyal. This gave opportunities to the Rajputs which they
eagerly seized. As early as 1048 the Raja of Delhi took council with
his neighbours the Rajas of Ajmir, Kanauj and others, all of whom
declared their unity, proclaiming themselves no longer in any way
dependent on Ghazni.

The fate of Ghazni was sealed when Ghiyas-ad-din, chieftain of
Ghur, seized the citadel. There then followed a remarkable reign of
this man and his brother, Shihab-ad-din, known to posterity as
Muhammad Ghuri, who ruled jointly for a period of fifty years; the
one reigning in Afghanistan while the other, based on Ghazni, embarked on a series of campaigns which in the end culminated in the
establishment of Muslim rule in northern India, a rule that was in one
form or another to last for six hundred years. This was the difference
between him and his predecessor, Mahmud of Ghazni; the invasions
of the latter were punitive and opportunist while those of Muhammad Ghuri were systematic and in their effects long term.

It has been said that these two men were so curiously alike that
when reading of them one has to rub one's eyes to discern the one
from the other.[1] However, beyond the fact that both were Muslims,
both great soldiers and that both waged war against what they called
the idolators, and each sought plunder, there is little to support this
idea. There was a far greater ruthlessness about Muhammad Ghuri
and, whereas Mahmud's object had been to proselytise and plunder,
that of Muhammad was to subdue and to absorb. In seeking
power he was not animated by mere greed, he had a longer vision,
the subjugation of Hindustan. First, however, he had to eradicate
the remnants of the Ghaznavid kingdom in Sind and in the Panjab.
His opening campaign, on which his armies set out in 1175, was

[1] F. A. Steel: *India Throughout the Ages.*

directed against Multan and the surrounding areas. This was only completed after some seven years of heavy fighting, but in the end he was master of the whole of Sind down to the Arabian Sea. While this was in progress, at the head of another army he attacked the Panjab and had, by the winter of 1184, taken Lahore and Sialkot. This marked the end of Ghaznavid power in India and Muhammad Ghuri was free to embark on his war on Hindustan.

His aims were clear; these were to destroy all the Hindu religious strongholds, of which Benares was one of the most important; to seize the fabulously rich lands in Bengal; and, in the west, to subdue the Rajput strongholds in Ajmir and Mewar. But first Delhi lay in his path and it was here that a battle was inevitable, the results of which could be of vital consequence. Nevertheless, he knew he had certain advantages; he was undisputed king and the supreme commander of a united army; his men were bound by the common faith of Islam; his communications were secure; past experience of fighting a Hindu army had shown them to be inferior; and in addition to the lure of loot all his men knew that if they were killed fighting the infidels they would go to heaven.

For the Hindus it was a war the consequences of which could be horrifying; yet there were factors which, if they could only be exploited, were to their advantage. Numerically their combined strength was superior to that of the Muslims; they would be fighting a defensive battle in their own country and on ground of their own choosing; they had known leaders who were capable generals; and, finally, they knew they were to fight for all they held most dear.

Both sides had, therefore, much to gain and everything to lose if beaten; both would be fighting for something in which they believed and that they held to be precious; both were led by intrepid generals, skilled in war and as brave as the men whom they led. But, whereas the Muslims were united under one supreme commander, the Hindus were an alliance of individual states, each with its own king and its own commander-in-chief. The teaching of history has, however, shown that sometimes alliances can be capable of winning against a united enemy.

In their first main battle against Muhammad Ghuri's Turko-Afghan army the Hindus were brilliantly successful, the Moslem leader fighting an action that might well have been his last. The road to Delhi lay across Sirhind, the name by which that stretch

of country between the Sutlej and Jumna rivers is known, and
whose southern edges merge into the Plain of Panipat. Across
the hot and dry area, about one hundred and twenty miles south by
east of Lahore, lay the big pink and white fortress of Bhatinda. The
women had just picked the flowers of the great dakh trees for their
dyestuffs when news came that, with the migration of the winter
birds, the terrible 'Toourkhs' were on the march. At Bhatinda the
will to resist was weak and so the fortress fell, proving once again
that the strength of a position lies not in bricks and mortar but in
the will of the men defending it. With Bhatinda in his hands and
the hot weather approaching Muhammad Ghuri was anxious to get
back to the better climate of Afghanistan, and so, after leaving a
detachment to hold Bhatinda, he commenced his return march. Before he had gone many miles he heard that the King of Delhi with
Ajmir and several other princes had assembled a large army at or
near Karnal, some hundred miles east of Bhatinda and about the
same distance north of Delhi.

Determined to give battle, disregarding the weather, he turned
in his tracks. The spirit of his men was high; they had everywhere
been successful and much booty had come their way; and all were
anxious to close with the infidels whom they had no doubt they
could easily defeat. They had overcome with little effort the Hindus
serving with the Ghaznavids in the Panjab, and Bhatinda had fallen
like a ripe pear in their hands. They had, therefore, contempt for
the fighting qualities of their enemy. This can be a dangerous and
even a fatal frame of mind.

They were now to face a different enemy. Their own army, a
mixture of Afghans and Turks, were well acquainted with the Seljuks
and people of Transoxania. Their tactics were essentially offensive,
beating their enemy by the sheer ferocity of their attack and their
ruthlessness and their perseverance. Filled with religious zeal they
were eager now to close with the idolators for whom they had so little
regard, and of whose fighting prowess they had no opinion. But up to
now they had not met the real Rajputs and the lessen they were to
learn was both salutary and lasting.

When Muhammad Ghuri's army reached Narain, which lay a
few miles to the north of Karnal, it found the Rajput army of
Prithivi Raj and his compatriots drawn up in battle array ready to
meet them. The sight was imposing. In sheer numbers the Muslims

were faced by something they had as yet not encountered. The Rajputs, drawn up in divisions, with their coloured gay head-dress, their swarthy lean faces, their dark and fearless eyes, stood like a wall before them. In the sun their spears gleamed and shimmered in the dazzling light. In the rear, protected by the lines of infantry, stood the war elephants, each with a wooden tower erected on its back and a brightly dressed mahout sitting between the great animal's ears, giving a stamp of pomp as well as an impression of immense strength. Standing in the howdahs on the elephants' backs were the warriors with brightly polished spears and drawn swords. On the flanks of this great host, but drawn back in rear, were the Rajput horsemen whose steeds, chafing their bits and pawing the ground, were restless to be let loose on the Turk and Afghan ranks. Never had the Plain of Panipat witnessed a more impressive spectacle than this. Indeed, this army, drawn up on ground of Prithivi Raj's own choosing, was an awe-inspiring sight. It seemed to exude confidence and even to invite attack in the certainty that it would thrash any enemy that would dare to challenge it.

Muhammad Ghuri must and surely should have had doubts whether his normal tactics would succeed against such a foe. Perhaps he had left it too late to change or perhaps over-confidence and past successes had blurred his judgement. Whatever the reason was he committed his army to a thoughtless attack. All the dash of his brilliant and experienced cavalry was powerless against the Hindu army whose soldiers stood firm and whose ranks remained unbroken. The Muslims were now in their turn charged by Prithivi's horse, who, in a skilful outflanking manœuvre, turned discomfiture into chaos. In the mêlée that ensued Muhammad Ghuri found himself cut off from his shattered army and hemmed in by the Rajput squadrons. His own personal gallantry was phenomenal, he himself charging through the Hindu ranks up to the standard of Phithivi's brother, the Viceroy of Delhi, whom he killed by ramming his spear down his throat. This all but cost him his life, which was saved by the bravery of a Khalji retainer, who, mounting behind his master, cut his way though and carried Muhammad off the battlefield. Seeing this the Muslim army lost confidence and fled in panic. They were pursued by the Rajputs for over forty miles and neither Muhammad nor his men paused until they were safe across the Indus, not even halting at Lahore. It was for Prithivi Raj a victory indeed.

The defeat was bred of over-confidence, a gross underestimate of the enemy, coupled with a rigid tactic quite unsuited to the situation. The cost was not as great as it might have been; yet never before had a Muslim Army suffered defeat at the hands of the Hindus. Muhammad and his men had wounds to heal and vengeance to nurse.

When Saladin suffered defeat at the hands of Baldwin he did not vent his spleen on his subordinates, he concentrated on reforming his army. But Muhammad punished those he considered had failed him, when the fault lay in truth with his generalship. Perhaps there is no better way of assessing greatness than to observe the general's reaction to defeat. Muhammad said he had many sleepless nights and well he might have had. Those whom he considered had failed him he paraded round the city in disgrace, with their noses thrust into bags of barley like so many mules, after which they were thrown into prison. Nevertheless, he was determined to avenge himself on Prithivi and within twelve months he was again ready to march, this time with a force of one hundred and twenty thousand men. He confided neither his plan nor his objective to his followers. When, however, his army reached Peshawar there could be little doubt of his aim: another holy war against the idolators with all the prospects of loot. It was here that an old warrior from Ghur, prostrating himself before Muhammad, told the Sultan that the soldiers all had faith in his leadership, but where was the army marching to and what was his design? Take, your men, he pleaded, into your confidence. When Muhammad told him of his vow to wipe out his defeat of last year and recover his lost honour or die in the attempt, the old man replied that those whom he had disgraced and put into prison should be released so that they, too, should be given the opportunity to wipe out the stain on their reputations. Muhammad released the disgraced officers and all, anxious to retrieve their reputations, lost no time in flocking to his standard. Reinforced, he advanced on Lahore and from here sent ambassadors to Prithivi summoning him to accept Islam or meet the true believers in battle.

Let us for a moment follow Prithivi Raj after his great victory of the previous year. We have seen how he followed the beaten army of Muhammad for some forty miles. Keeping a tight control over his headstrong followers, he did not press the pursuit too far. Rallying them and reorganising them he laid siege to the city of Sirhind which quickly fell. Then, returning to Narain, he commenced preparations to meet another attack by Muhammad, which he knew he must expect. He had heard of the size of the new Muslim army and this gave him great concern. This time he would want badly the assistance of every Rajput state and particularly that of Kanauj and Gujerat. But, in the event he did not get it. Why was it that, knowing the threat that beyond all doubt existed, the Rajputs could not put up a united front? The reasons were as petty as they were real. The story here is analogous to that of the Crusaders and Saladin, where disunity and jealousy among the Christians was the cause of their ultimate defeat.

Prithivi Raj's grandfather, the last Tomara King of Delhi, had no sons, and so when he died he left his kingdom to his eldest grandson, Prithivi of Ajmir. By doing this he united the Chauans of Ajmir and the Tomaras of Delhi under one head, Joya Chandra, the Raja of Kanauj, and the son of another daughter of Tomara, had hoped that Delhi might be joined to Kanauj and that it was not, embittered him. Unfortunately his resentment was fanned when Prithivi succeeded in performing the Aswameda or Horse Sacrifice, the details of which legendary custom need not concern us here. However its reward does. The winner was by custom accepted by all as sovereign lord of all Rajputs. The final humiliation came when Joya Chandra's daughter, the Princess Sanjogata, against her father's wish, chose Prithivi for her husband.

Thus, when Prithivi called for all Rajputs to join him in meeting Muhammad Ghuri, Kanauj and her ally Gujerat, refused. In the end this split, as it was bound to, resulted in the Rajputs being defeated in detail; first Delhi, then Kanauj and finally one by one all fell. Great as were the Rajputs, valiant in battle as they also were, their fierce individualism was their undoing.

Prithivi's misgivings were, therefore, not without good reason and he confided them to his wife. Her words were prophetic and her sentiments worthy of her state. Victory, she said, would surely be his; but to die was honourable for to die well was to live for ever. He must think not of himself but of immortality. If he should die she would be one with him in the hereafter. When eventually Sanjogata heard of his death and defeat, decked in her bridal jewels, she mounted the pyre and keeping her promise went to meet her husband through the flames.

When Prithivi replied to Muhammad he displayed neither his fears nor his misgivings. He pointed out his numerical superiority and even offered to allow the Muslims to withdraw to safety if they repented of their rashness in coming against him. Muhammad returned a courteous answer, saying that, as he was only the general of his brother, he could not retreat without leave, but he would report the offer to the King and until an answer should arrive he asked that there might be a truce. The Rajput assented and his men now passed the time in games and revelling, until one night, violating the truce that he himself had proposed, Muhammad crossed the Saravati River before the break of dawn and fell on his unsuspecting opponent.

Although they were at first thrown into confusion, the Rajputs quickly rallied and held the enemy until their main body had formed for battle. The fight raged throughout the day until Muhammad, learning from his previous experience and knowing something of the Rajput impetuosity, feigned withdrawal. As he had hoped, the enemy thundered in pursuit and, forgetting everything in their delight at riding down the fleeing Muslims, laid themselves open to the counter-attack Muhammad had planned. His reserves, consisting of twelve thousand men in steel armour, he led himself into the now disorganised Rajput ranks. Confusion turned into rout and, as a great building will shake to its foundations in an earthquake, so did the Rajput army totter to its fall, lost in its own ruins. Although of Prithivi Raj's fate many stories have been told, nothing is known for certain of the real details of his death. The defeat accomplished the Muslim conqueror was at liberty to tackle the other Rajput states in detail. Ajmir and Hansi fell; hundreds of temples, idols and great buildings were destroyed and sacked. The result of this victory was the annexation of Ajmir and Hansi, but the former was left in the charge of the son of the late raja as a vassal of Muhammad. The Sultan now returned to Afghanistan after placing his favourite slave, Kutb-ad-din Aybak, as viceroy at Delhi. This was a wise decision, as history was to show. However, in the following year he returned and overran Kanauj. After a crushing defeat of the Hindus on the Jumna River between Chandwa and Etawa the city of Benares fell and become part of the kingdom of Ghur. Muhammad advanced on into Bengal, while detachments under Kutb-ad-din were despatched to reduce those Rajput strongholds that still held out further to the west.

Muhammad's heart had, however, always hankered after the old Persian possessions of the Ghaznavids, and so, not content with his stupendous successes in India, he now invaded Khwarazm. Here he met failure for the first time. His campaign was disastrous and ignominiously he was forced to flee, burning his baggage and only narrowly escaping with his life. Revolts against him now broke out in all the surrounding country and only in India did the strength and the loyalty of Kutb-ad-din save the situation. In spite of all the apparently insurmountable difficulties he fought back, regaining control over Afghanistan and even of Persia. He was, however, denied the fruits of these successes when tragically he was murdered in his tent. Was this a just retribution for a man who had been not much better than a successful brigand? Surely not; for, though no patron of the arts and certainly not a man of letters, he had none the less left his mark on history. He had gained great power and had undeniably fed on ambition; but to do him justice he had been impelled by a sincere religious conviction. Having achieved power there is little evidence that he abused it. The series of invasions that he had led into India had been inspired by religious fervour. He was undoubtedly a great general who was quick to learn from experience, and he was a ruthless opponent. Nevertheless, it is interesting to note that, although a devout Muslim, his bigotry did not prevent his leaving a Hindu prince as his vassal in Ajmir. It was his genius that selected Kutb-ad-din as his viceroy, and surely the selection of the right man in the right place is a hallmark of greatness.

In striking contrast to him stood Prithivi Raj, a man of great moral stature who, though defeated and killed, left an indelible mark on the pages of his country's history. Six hundred years after his death during the Indian Mutiny in Delhi the cry was heard, '*Prithivi Raj ki jai*'—'Hail to the kingdom of Prithivi'. This cry was again heard after the final departure of the British Raj. There was something of the King Arthur about this man around whom half-truths and many myths have been woven. Prithivi sought no battles for the sake of conquest or to exterminate those whose religious beliefs differed from his: his military exploits were all defensive in nature. Power came to him because of his birth and on account of his chivalrous leadership, power which he never sought and certainly never abused.

These two men, Muhammad Ghuri and Prithivi Raj, though

so strangely different had much in common; both were religious, devout and sincere in their beliefs; but Prithivi was a mystic, born of the sun and a Rajput patriot, while Muhammad was a fanatic. If Prithivi's name in India is revered, that of Muhammad Ghuri is detested; and yet it was the latter who laid the foundations for a rule in India that was to last until the Mutiny.

3 Saladin—Egypt and Syria

The story of the twelfth century in Eastern Europe and the Mediterranean is coloured by the romance that is attached to the Crusades. Of the princes who moved across this stage, the best known and most romantic were Saladin and Richard Cœur-de-Lion. Each in his own way epitomised an ideal, and, although there were other great men, it is these two who are best remembered.

Abdul Mozaffar Yusuf Salad-ad-Din, known to history as Saladin, was of Kurdish extraction. A Kurd, one might have expected him to be recalcitrant, but this was not so. Born in 1137, he was, when we first hear of him on his visit to Egypt, twenty-six years of age. His home had been in the citadel of Takrit on the right bank of the Tigris between Mosul and Baghdad, where he was brought up in a religious Sunni household. Throughout his life he adhered strictly to the five tenets of the Muslim faith. Of simple tastes and disliking all forms of coarseness or ostentation, he commanded the respect of both friend and foe. In physical stature he was a smallish man, slightly built and of gentle manner. He was always courteous and, except on rare and justified occasions, kind. In an age of perfidy and intrigue he stood like a pillar of integrity in the sordid world surrounding him. He was single-minded and strong of purpose. His word was his bond. Brave himself he esteemed bravery in others and it was this characteristic in Richard that first drew these two remarkable men together.

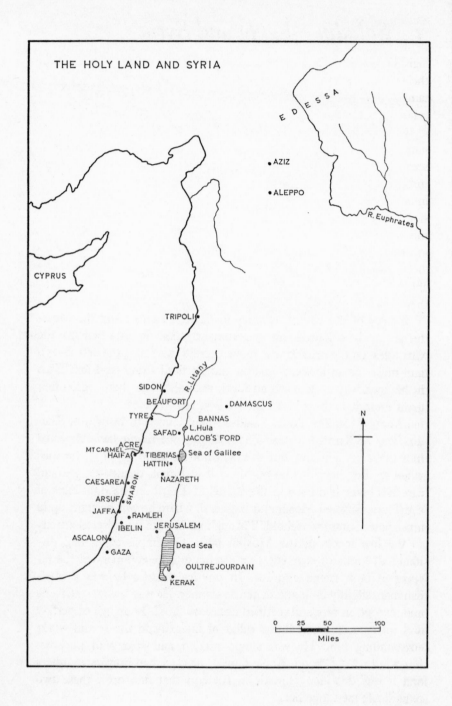

THE HOLY LAND AND SYRIA

E D E S S A

• AZIZ

• ALEPPO

R. Euphrates

CYPRUS

TRIPOLI •

R. Litany

SIDON •
BEAUFORT
TYRE •   • DAMASCUS
                    BANNAS
        SAFAD •   ○ L. Hula
                    JACOB'S FORD
    ACRE •
MT CARMEL
HAIFA •   • TIBERIAS   Sea of Galilee
        • HATTIN
CAESAREA •   • NAZARETH
         SHARON
ARSUF •
JAFFA •   • RAMLEH
    • IBELIN   JERUSALEM
ASCALON •
    • GAZA   Dead Sea
                    OULTRE JOURDAIN
            • KERAK

N

0   25   50   100
            Miles

His career fell into three distinct phases, though each followed logically on the other. The first commenced with his service in Egypt; the second concerned his subjugation of Syria and Upper Mesopotamia; and the third was the Holy War which culminated in his conquest of Palestine.

Opportunities and the fate of nations are the outcome of circumstances. What were the circumstances that predominated in the scene at this time? Both Christians and Muslims were passing through a critical period in their evolution, and each suffered from internal conflicts and deep schisms. In the Christian Church the division was between the schools of Rome and of Constantinople, and the arguments were bedevilled by such issues as the doctrine of the incarnation and the human or divine nature of Christ. These conflicts, had they remained at the council table, were both understandable and laudable, but they did not and, spreading far and wide, they developed into open war and bloody conflict.

The followers of the Prophet had their divisions also; there were the orthodox Sunnis who received the Sunna as of equal importance with the Koran, and whose name implied 'those of the faith'. Then there were the Shias who, while accepting the Koran, did not accept the Sunna. These divisions sometimes spelt fierce conflict, and so distinct had they become that each had adopted as a visible mark of their loyalty their own colour. The Fatimites, who ruled in Egypt and were Shias, adopted green, and the Abbasids, who were Sunnis and based on Mesopotamia, wore black. To these divisions were added the problems that came from the tribal tradition. There is little doubt that this inability to pull together was the principal cause of the success of the early Crusaders, and that it increased Saladin's difficulties, successful though he ultimately was.

When this story commences a typical example of Muslim confusion occurred in Egypt. It had for some time become customary in the weakening Fatimite kingdom for all to submit to anyone successfully revolting against the vizier, logical enough, as the powers of government rested with the army which the vizier controlled. Abu Shawar as-Sadi, the governor of Upper Egypt, raised such a revolt and seized the vizierate. However, one Abu al-Ashbal Dargham, refused to acknowledge this and himself revolted against Shawar who, forced to flee the country, sought the protection of the Abbasid, Nur ad-Din, at Damascus. In the light of certain promises made by

Shawar, Nur ad-Din sent Asad ad-Din Shirkuh with an army to Cairo with instructions to maintain the rights of Shawar, and also to look into and report on the general conditions prevailing in Egypt. Asad ad-Din took Saladin, his nephew, with him. Saladin disliked the idea and tried to avoid the assignment, which in the light of his future association with the Egyptians is interesting. He certainly was not showing any ambitious tendencies at this time. The expedition, mounted in 1163, was successful and in the fighting that ensued Dargham lost his life. Asad ad-Din was quick to realise the great potential wealth of the Delta and from now on cherished the hope that one day he might become the master of a land whose government was palpably ineffectual and whose army was demonstrably inadequate.

After his return to Syria he learned that promises Shawar had made were not being kept and this provided an excuse for a second expedition on which he again took Saladin. Shawar now called on the Franks in Palestine to assist him. To Amalric, the King of Jerusalem, the lure of Egypt, as well as the fear of the consequences resulting from the Syrian Abbasids becoming too powerful in the Delta, were sufficient to decide him; but, although he marched at once, he failed to intercept Asad ad-Din. The latter, on arriving in Egypt, made a strong appeal to Shawar as a Muslim to unite against the infidels; yet, typical of the discord in the Muslim world, the offer was refused.

When Amalric's knights arrived, Asad ad-Din found himself outnumbered, so, feigning retreat, he withdrew up the Nile, which later he crossed, and then, turning about, advanced upon the other bank. He met the combined Egyptian-Frankish army at el-Babria where he won a noteworthy success in which Saladin played an important part. Under him the centre feigned retreat, a subterfuge that drew Amalric's knights into a trap. Asad ad-Din's cavalry, poised for the event, now closed in on the exposed flank of their enemy and succeeded in surrounding Amalric's force, the King only escaping capture by a miracle.

Asad ad-Din now advanced on Alexandria which, with the apparent concurrence of the population, he entered. Still numerically weaker than his enemy he soon found himself besieged. Leaving Saladin to hold the city, he managed to withdraw the bulk of his army to Upper Egypt in the hope that he would lure the Egyptians after him. In this he failed, the enemy preferring to concentrate their efforts on the relief of Alexandria. Saladin thus found himself in dire straits and was forced to appeal to Asad ad-Din to return, and this he did.

In the meantime Amalric was becoming concerned about conditions in Palestine where Nur ad-Din had attacked several towns and was at that moment threatening Tripoli. Therefore, when Asad ad-Din on reaching Alexandria suggested that peace talks should be started on the basis of both his and Amalric's forces quitting Egypt, he found a ready listener. A peaceful solution was reached, prisoners were exchanged and Saladin's troops were permitted to march out of the city.

For several days Saladin was honourably entertained by King Amalric and his knights. He was impressed by the dignified pomp and ceremony of the knights as well as by their discipline and general behaviour and this, there is little doubt, left a mark on him. It was then that he formed a friendship with Humphrey of Toron, a knight well known to the Muslims among whom he had many friends. The meeting has suggested to some that Saladin received a Christian knighthood, but there is no evidence to support the story and neither at that nor at any other time did this happen.

Uncertainty as to Shawar's conduct and a belief that the Franks intended to return to the Delta, coupled with the obvious ambition of Asad ad-Din, decided the Syrian to stage yet a third expedition to Egypt. They arrived at the gates of Cairo in December 1168 where Asad ad-Din was received by the Fatimite Caliph, this time as a friend and deliverer. Shawar was arrested by Saladin and later executed. Asad ad-Din was invested with the robes of vizier; but, early in the following year, he died, to be succeeded by Saladin. Thus commenced the first phase of this man's remarkable career. A devout Sunni, Saladin found himself vizier to a Shi-ite caliph, an anomaly that was resolved when within two years the Caliph died and Saladin became Sultan of Egypt.

During the next four years the new sultan consolidated his position. He gained the confidence of the people by his wisdom, his justice, his simple and unselfish life and by his forthright dealing with dissidents. He settled the coast of North Africa as far as Tripoli and Gebez; he pacified the Yemen; and to the south he quelled an insurrection among the Sudanese. He dealt successfully with an attempt by the King of Sicily to capture Damietta. Nevertheless, he was continuously preoccupied by his anxieties over the machinations of Nur ad-Din, who now seemed to be jealous of his success and from whom he was as a consequence becoming more and more estranged. Only the wisdom of his father and his own natural caution saved him from an open break. The situation was, however, unexpectedly relieved by the death of Nur ad-Din in May 1174. Saladin immediately rode to Damascus to demonstrate his loyalty to Nur ad Din's son and he was installed with general acclamation as mamluk of the young king. The King, al-Mamlik as-Saleh Ismail, was a boy of eleven years.

True to the Arab custom, rival factions in Nur ad-Din's old kingdom soon started to rear their heads and breakaway movements formed, while conditions in the country grew more and more unsettled. Saladin's first task was to unite the Muslims, for only with a united Islamic world could he ever hope to prosecute his ultimate intention, a Holy War for the liberation of Jerusalem. The task took him many years; his annexation and settlement of Syria, which he commenced in 1174, was only completed in 1186. Of the many engagements and incidents throughout this period three only will be mentioned; one, because it indicated the chivalrous side of his nature; another, as a record of two aspects of his generalship which later were to stand him in good stead; and the third because it was the prelude to the Holy War.

The first incident occurred in 1175 when he took Aleppo, close to which lay the citadel of Aziz to which he laid siege. The place fell only after very heavy fighting lasting some thirty-eight days, during which he was wounded. It was while the parleys that followed were taking place that he received an unexpected visit. A little girl, none other than the sister of the young king, entered his camp and the Sultan received her with all honours. As he enquired what it was that she wanted, she replied, 'The castle of Aziz,' for, she said very simply, it was her home. This amazing request was granted and, bestowing presents on the child princess, Saladin personally escorted her back to the gates of the castle.

The second was when he suffered a severe reverse and it was here that Saladin displayed his best qualities as a leader. He had embarked on a raid from Egypt into the coastal areas of Palestine and had sacked Ascalon, Ramleh and Lydda; his troops, ravaging over the country, had even reached the outskirts of Jerusalem. Feeling secure in his strength and underestimating his enemy, he took risks which were unjustifiable and, with his forces widely dispersed, he allowed himself to be surprised by King Baldwin in the vicinity of Tel Jezet, close to Ramleh. Here he suffered a humiliating reverse and only by taking to a fleet-footed riding camel did he escape with his life. The remnants of his army fled with him to Egypt and, of them all, only a few survived. In the Delta he immediately set about reorganising his forces and within three months with a new army he was ready to march north again. By the spring he was encamped as far north as Edessa. This incident showed something of his character, for in defeat he was able to hold the confidence of his troops. Of all the qualities of generalship this is not the least important and certainly it is one of the most difficult to achieve. The incident further showed the degree of control he had gained over Egypt, where his wise rule had earned for him respect that would stand the test of defeat. As a general he realised that an essential to military success was to have a reliable base and this Egypt then, as indeed later, showed she could and would provide.

The circumstances which brought about the Holy War were the outcome of the rapacity and treachery of one man, Raynald of Châtillon. But first we must consider the relationship at that time between the Muslims and the Christians in Palestine. After his success at Ramla, Baldwin was inclined to underestimate his opponent. Across the River Jordan to the north of the Sea of Galilee was a grazing area known as the Plain of Banias that had in a friendly manner been divided between the Christians and the Muslims. Here caravans were free to move unmolested and grazing went on uninterrupted. At Jacob's Ford, just to the south of Lake Hula, was an old disused fort; this fort commanded the approaches to the plain and had not been occupied by either Arabs or Crusaders. Baldwin decided to restore it and to place a garrison there. In the light of the understanding that existed between the two peoples Saladin resented Baldwin's act. He did his best to deter the King, even going so far as to offer him a large sum of money to abandon the plan, but Baldwin was adamant. The Sultan laid siege to the place and on 30th August 1179 it fell. Baldwin, arriving too late to relieve the garrison was appalled at the devastation that met his gaze, for nothing but blackened stones and burning rubble was to be seen. Beginning now to

c

realise his mistake, Baldwin sued for peace. This Saladin agreed to and a treaty which was to last for two years was signed by which neither side would under any pretext attack the other. Saladin's attitude to the Crusaders is interesting. Although his biographers make much of his hatred of the Frankish kingdom, to what lengths he would have gone to exterminate this is very much open to question. He did not object to and, in fact, had no small admiration for many of the knights of the Hospitallers and the Templars. Some of these who had come with the First Crusade had settled in the land to which they had become very attached. They spoke Arabic and had developed friendships with many of the local Muslims. One of Saladin's biographers, Osman, referring to these settlers called them his friends. Indeed, amicable agreements had been reached on many issues, like the division of the Plain of Banias or in other areas, the free and unmolested passage of pilgrims and caravans. The two-year truce with Baldwin was a further case. However, the whole picture was to become distorted by the acts of one man, Raynald of Châtillon.

This filibustering knight came to Palestine with Louis VII's crusade. He was an adventurer by nature who, when Louis returned to France, had stayed behind to make his fortune. Unlike the earlier settlers, he neither liked the country nor its people and was as much mistrusted by his own as he was disliked by the Muslims. His marriage to Constance of Antioch had made him a prince, a position that he utilised to satisfy his greed. He earned for himself the unedifying sobriquet of the 'Fox of Antioch'. Though he had to pay the price for his outrageous behaviour, he seemed quite incapable of learning from experience. One day he robbed a band of shepherds peacefully moving their flocks from the Taurus as was their custom. However, when he returned laden with booty he was ambushed and captured, and for his crime was forced to spend many years in prison. On his release he then married the beautiful Stephanie, heiress of Oultrejourdain, and thus became the lord of an extremely important strategic area. All caravans coming from Egypt and Mecca had to pass through Oultrejourdain. Raynald's fortress at Kerak stood on a promontory in the Hills of Moab at the southern end of the Dead Sea and commanded the routes from both Egypt and Mecca.

In spite of the truce between Baldwin and Saladin, Raynald robbed a caravan on its way from Damascus. Saladin, at the time in

Egypt, complained bitterly to Baldwin, who admitted the breach and at the same time made strong representations to Raynald to make amends which the latter flatly refused to do. Saladin took hostage a Christian caravan which he offered to release as soon as Raynald returned the merchandise he had seized. Again the Fox refused to comply. The final breach came when he raided yet another caravan in which it was said Saladin's sister was travelling. When asked to release her his only reply was that since the Muslims put their trust in Muhammad, let him come and save her.

The die was cast and outright war was now inevitable. Saladin swore an oath that with his own hand he would avenge this outrage.

4 The Holy War

Secure in Syria and with a firm base in Egypt, Saladin was ready to wage the Holy War. Tribesmen from afar rallied to his call; Arabs came from Syria and Arabia, Turks and Muslims from Khorasan and Persia came in their thousands. In the spring of 1187 Saladin had assembled a vast army dedicated to expelling the infidels from Jerusalem and all Palestine. He had, however, two anxieties: one for a band of pilgrims from Mecca and the other for a caravan from Egypt. Both of these he knew would be vulnerable to attack from Kerak where his arch-enemy Raynald was. As a precaution against this he despatched a force to Oultrejourdain. When they heard both caravans were safely through his men returned to the Plain of Banias, rejoining the main army there.

By 26th June he was ready to move into Galilee and on 1st July he crossed the Jordan. Moving to the high ground at Hattin, some five miles west of Tiberias, Saladin waited to see what the Crusaders under Guy, now King of Jerusalem, would do; seeing that they appeared to have no settled policy he decided to invest Tiberias. Although he successfully stormed the city, the castle, commanded by the Countess Eschiva, wife of Raymond, Count of Tripoli and Prince of Galilee, still held out.

At the time that Saladin had crossed the Jordan Guy was at Acre, where he held a council of war at which there were two divergent and unresolved opinions. One, held by Raymond[1] was that in view of the excessive summer heat the attacker would be at a serious disadvantage, and concluded that the Crusaders should adopt a defensive posture. The other, sponsored by the headstrong Raynald of Oultrejourdain, calling this a cowardly policy, advocated attack. Only in this way, he claimed, could the Crusaders keep the initiative. Favouring the defensive concept, but without much enthusiasm, Guy decided to move to Siffurieh, some four miles to the north of Nazareth. The place was well suited to defence, which Guy now believed the wiser policy. However, just when his mind seemed to have been made up, news came in of the fall of Tiberias and of the Countess Eschiva's plight.

Raymond, in spite of the fact that it was his wife's life that was at stake, still contended that to attack could only lead to disaster. Though Tiberias was his city, as was the fortress, he would prefer to risk the losses here than that the very kingdom should be destroyed. His argument prevailed. But during the night the Grand Master of the Templars approached Guy to say that the Templars would sooner abandon their order than sacrifice Tiberias and the brave countess. Always influenced by the last who spoke to him, Guy gave way and commanded that the army should advance at dawn. In view, it is said, of his local knowledge Raymond was given the task of leading the army. He chose to march via Lublich where he believed there would be water; but, in the event, this proved to be a fatal mistake, for when the Crusaders reached the area parched in the heat of the July weather they found that although the wells were indeed there, they were dry. The result was a breakdown in discipline and ultimate disaster.

Saladin, hearing from his reconnaissances of the Crusaders' movements and the route they were taking, was content to remain concentrated at Hattin, for here he would be fighting on ground of his own choosing. Although some of the details of the battle may be conflicting, in general outline the reports by both Muslim and Christian eyewitnesses are reasonably consistent. From these it is clear that three factors decided the day. The first was the ill-discipline of the Crusaders' infantry, who, separating themselves from the knights, invited defeat in detail; the second was the tactical skill of

[1] Raymond III, Count of Tripoli, Prince of Galilee. See Stephen Runciman: *History of the Crusades*, Vol. II, for this discussion.

Saladin; and the third was the Crusaders' decision to adopt the offensive in circumstances that were so utterly unsuitable for such tactics.

Let us now trace the main outline of this battle. Parched in the heat and finding the wells at Lublich empty, Guy's infantry dispersed in search of water. Their sufferings, which were real, were accentuated by fires that swept across the dried grass over which they toiled; but hard though things were they were as nothing to the punishment of defeat which their ill-discipline brought on their heads.

Saladin, quick to observe their fatal mistake, attacked the disorganised and isolated infantry, who were by now incapable of contributing anything to the conduct of the battle. Now isolated the Frankish knights were forced to fight without either the aid or protection of their foot soldiers. In order to extricate themselves from a bad position they charged into a gap that Saladin had purposely left in his line. Thus they entered a trap from which they could not escape and were as a result virtually annihilated. Raymond has been accused of treachery in that he was said to have known that there was no water and that he was aware of Saladin's trap; there is, however, not a shred of evidence to support either charge.

This battle, fought on Friday, 3rd July, so frighteningly decisive in its results, was a classic example of misjudgement on the issue of the advantages and disadvantages of offensive as opposed to defensive strategy. The far-seeing Raymond had advocated a defensive policy in order to force Saladin to attack and to do so on ground of the Crusaders' choosing. Raynald, on the other hand, had been obsessed by the fear of losing the initiative. But where, in fact, did the initiative lie? Surely to hold one's hand and force the enemy to attack in conditions suited to the defence does not imply loss of initiative? This is what Saladin did and this, as much as anything else, was responsible for his victory. His strategical thinking is graphically told by his biographer, Baha ad-Din, who was present at the time. He describes how his master, playing on his hope that the enemy would advance and attack him, to this end took up a defensive position at Hattin, and how in the event the battle went as he, Saladin, had planned it. Whatever tactical mistakes were made by the Crusaders, Saladin took immediate advantage of them; this is generalship.

Guy and most of his knights were taken prisoner and Jerusalem lay bare with scarcely a man capable of bearing arms available for its defence. Saladin's capture of the Holy City was a mixture of quixotic chivalry and assiduous materialism. When the burghers came out to sue for peace he offered to leave them with freedom to fortify the place and to cultivate the land within five miles of the walls. His only condition was that if by the following Pentecost they had not been relieved they must surrender and he, in his turn, would guarantee their safe conduct out of Palestine to other Christian soil. In spite of their wretched weakness this offer was without hesitation refused.

However, help came from an unexpected quarter. One Balian, Lord of Ibelin near Ramleh and Constable of Jaffa, a refugee from Tyre, appealed to Saladin for permission to enter the city in order to relieve his wife, Queen Maria, and his children. He promised not to spend more than one night there, but when he saw the wretched state of the people and the almost complete lack of fighting men, he decided to stay. He wrote to the Sultan telling him frankly why he felt it his duty to break his word. Saladin respected Balian and, forgiving him, went so far as to give safe conduct to the Queen and her own as well as other children. It is said that when Saladin saw this pathetic party pass through his lines he wept.

Nevertheless, Jerusalem had to be taken. He first intended to assault the city on the western side opposite David's Tower; but, realising the difficulties of this approach, he withdrew and went round to the Mount of Olives. Seeing him depart, the defenders thought he was going away and rang the bells in glee; but on the following day they were disillusioned, for, developing his attack from the new direction, he delivered a hail of stones and arrows on the city while his sappers, covering their approach with shields, mined the walls. Against these odds the weak garrison was incapable of continuing the defence. Balian, in Saladin's camp, appealed to him to stop the fighting at the very moment when the breach was made and the Muslim flag was hoisted on the ramparts. Saladin, having sworn to take Jerusalem by sword, was unwilling to stop at the moment when victory was within his grasp; yet at the same time he wished to spare the inhabitants further suffering and Balian's vivid stories of their grim determination to fight to the death filled him with horror. Jerusalem, he said, if it surrendered would be saved from further

fighting on condition that a ransom was paid. This was accepted and there then commenced a tragic exodus.

First came Balian with thirty thousand gold besants, followed by seven thousand poor who were ransomed by money from King Henry of England's treasure. After these came the burghers with money in hand. For forty days this melancholy procession dragged its weary way through the Gate of David. Finally only those who could not be ransomed were left, the very poor and the aged; these were to be slaves. Something of the innate chivalry of the Muslim character now displayed itself in a quite remarkable way. Saladin's brother asked that a thousand slaves should be allotted him, and, immediately he received them, he set them free. The Patriarch and Balian each begged for a thousand slaves and when Saladin gave them these they, too, were set free. Then Saladin said that, as his brother had made his alms and the Patriarch and Balian had made theirs, he would make his. With this he proclaimed throughout the city that all the old people who could not pay their ransom should go free. The shocking sequel to this story is that when these poor refugees, whom a Muslim had released, arrived at the gates of Tyre and Tripoli the Christians there refused them entry and in one case a Christian baron even robbed them of their goods. Not until they reached Antioch did some find a resting place.

Before the outbreak of the Holy War Saladin had sworn to avenge the conduct of Raynald of Châtillon. The circumstances in which the 'Fox of Antioch' paid the price of his conduct have been recorded by more than one historian. The Sultan, after the battle at Hattin, commanded that King Guy and Raynald should be brought before him. With customary Muslim courtesy he gave a bowl of sherbet made with iced water to Guy who was suffering from thirst. When Guy had drunk a little he passed the bowl to Raynald. Saladin said to Guy that it was he and not Saladin who had given Raynald a drink. By Muslim custom he who sits to eat or who drinks with his captor will neither be molested nor killed. The Sultan now ordered the prisoners to be taken away to a meal that had been prepared for them, after which they were brought back to his tent. Telling Guy to be seated, he called upon Raynald and reminded him that he had said those who placed their trust in Muhammad could call on Muhammad to succour them. Did he, the Sultan asked, now embrace Islam? On Raynald refusing to do so, Saladin drew his sword and struck him down. Thus died the man whose raids and deprivations had sullied the order to which he belonged; who justifiably had earned the hatred of the Muslim people; whose advice had led to the ill-conceived attack at Hattin; and who, above all, caused the Holy War.

With the recovery of Jerusalem, one of Saladin's chief duties had been accomplished. It was now only necessary to reduce Tyre and those Crusader fortresses that remained; yet these operations proved to be more difficult than he had anticipated. Tyre, the most important city holding out against him, was his first objective. The inhabitants had, however, been working night and day to improve the defences of the city, whose moats they had both extended and deepened until the place was like an island approachable only by a narrow easily defended strip. The Muslims' attempts to storm Tyre were ineffectual, and Saladin, feeling that he must rest his troops, raised the siege. There is little doubt that Saladin had to handle his army with kid gloves. Enthusiasm quickly evaporated and the desire of some of his followers to get back to their flocks could not be ignored. Saladin's hesitancy on more than one occasion was attributable to this cause.

In the new year he commenced operations against Crusader fortresses. Long-drawn-out sieges he wished to avoid and it was this factor that in all probability encouraged him to offer reasonable terms for capitulation. It was by this method that the almost impregnable Kerak fell, as did the fortress of Belvoir and the stronghold at Safad. Saladin unquestionably displayed a remarkable tolerance and if he could get the besieged to capitulate he would not attack. Furthermore, those who surrendered were always permitted to go free. He seemed more intent on healing wounds than on prolonging conflict. This was typified by his release of Humphrey of Toron, even before the agreed submission of the fortress of Kerak by his mother, Stephanie of Oultrejourdain, and his release of Guy, though Ascalon had failed to honour the Frankish king's word. In contrast to Saladin's behaviour, in spite of his undertaking to leave the country and never again to take up arms against Islam, when released Guy joined the army at Tyre. Also there were the relations between Saladin and Reynard Garnier, Lord of Sidon. The story is as follows.

In the spring of 1189 Saladin invested Beaufort, a strong fortress

close to the border of the present State of Israel and Lebanon. The
fortress belonged to Reynard, Lord of Sidon, who was one of
those knights who spoke fluent Arabic and who had studied the
Koran. The castle of Beaufort, the ruins of which can be seen to
this day, stands at the top of a precipitous cliff several hundred feet
above the river bed. The spot is beautiful and the river, which cas-
cades over a stony bottom, is now, as it probably was then, flanked
by flowering oleanders. The approach by the west side was up a
more gentle slope, but here the walls were high, strong and protected by a moat. An ample water supply came from a well at the
top of the hill where the villagers even today toil up to draw their
water.

Like others, Reynard Garnier decided to capitulate. His relationship with Saladin was intriguing and, though at times he was
with justification mistrusted, he nevertheless always seemed to get
the Sultan's ear. When he came down from the fort and presented
himself at the entrance to Saladin's tent he was immediately
admitted and treated with every mark of respect. In their conversations Saladin was fascinated by his understanding of and interest
in Islam. An agreement was reached whereby he should be permitted to move his family and dependants to Tyre, and a respite
was granted him to make the necessary arrangements before handing
over the castle. As the days passed it became obvious that Reynard
was merely playing for time and he was seen to be actively strength-
ening his defences. When convinced of this Saladin had him placed
in custody in Banias, from whence he was later removed to Damascus. In spite of this it was this same Reynard who, as a free man, was
negotiating with Saladin no less than three years later. In the short
term Saladin sometimes paid dearly for his generosity; yet, in the
end, perhaps, he gained more than he lost.

While all this was going on the news of the fall of Jerusalem and
the loss of the Holy Cross, with the capture of most of the knights
at Hattin, had reached the capitals of Europe. Feelings ran high and
in France, England and Germany the Crusade was vigorously
preached. Richard, then a Count of France, received the Cross at the
hand of the Archbishop of Tours and Philip of France raised an
army, as did the Emperor Frederick Barbarossa, then in his seventieth year. Thus was the Third Crusade born. Nevertheless, in spite
of all this apparent enthusiasm, differences of opinion, conflicts of

purpose and petty jealousies between France and England caused endless delays.

News of these activities reached Saladin. He heard of the arrival of a German contingent in Constantinople and of the landing of a small force of knights under King William of Sicily. Whilst he was besieging Beaufort news also reached him of Guy's activities at Tyre, who was rumoured to be about to march on the Muslim stronghold at Acre. At first he believed this to be a subterfuge to draw him from Beaufort; but, as the evidence concerning the strength of Guy's force came in and of the route he was taking, he decided to move quickly to succour Acre. Marching via Tiberias he covered his flank with a strong detachment at Nazareth to which he gave implicit instructions to watch and report on Guy's movements.

The Crusaders reached Acre on 28th August, two days ahead of Saladin. They established themselves on the high ground overlooking the city and its approaches. On arrival Saladin posted his forces in a semicircle around the Crusaders with his left on the Tel Karuba and his right at Aiadiya, some five miles to the south. He later extended this flank to the coast and was thus able to open communications with the beleaguered garrison, which he visited. The Crusaders were themselves now besieged by Saladin.

However, in October Guy was able to take the offensive. Advancing on a front of some two miles, with archers in the van, his main body closed with the Muslims and the fighting was soon intense. The commander of Saladin's right ordered a backward movement, thereby hoping to entice the Crusaders on this flank away from their main body far enough to enable him to give a punishing blow to them. At this moment occurred an error of judgement on Saladin's part, for, believing the withdrawal to have been due to enemy pressure and not by design, he reinforced this flank from his centre. Seeing this movement, Guy attacked the weakened centre which gave way before the assault by the Crusader infantry. The path being cleared, the knights charged and the confusion in the Muslim ranks was complete. Headstrong as usual, the knights pursued the flying enemy as far as Saladin's camp which they sacked. The Sultan saw this and realised his mistake. Holding his left in check, he waited the return of the knights, then, charging in from both flanks, he turned what looked like a victory for Guy into a rout. Very much depleted in strength, the Crusaders were beaten back on to their camp, where they found shelter. Their losses were reliably reported to have been of the order of four thousand, while by comparison those of the Muslims were slight, most of these being accounted for by those who had fled from the centre. Their flight, a sorry story, was not checked until they reached the Jordan. With success within his grasp, Saladin now withdrew and Guy was permitted the time he so sorely needed to reorganise his defences.

Saladin has been criticised for his failure to reap the full bene-fits of his tactical success. What, in fact, were the circumstances? It is true that his losses were considerably less than those of his opponent, but his troops had been stretched for many months and there comes a time when a commander has to judge how much more his men can stand. Yet the root cause lay deeper. One of the in-herent Muslim weaknesses was that their forces were composed of a heterogeneous collection of tribes who would fight with great *élan* for a short period, but who, when operations were drawn out over many months, would grow impatient. The men of his centre who had fled the field had shown what could happen and the Sultan wanted no more of this. Also, it is of interest to note that when his council met it was they and not Saladin who counselled withdrawal. As an example of the general state of morale Baha ad-Din's report is ger-mane. He described clearly how soldiers of both sides, becoming accustomed to meeting one another, would stop fighting to talk. Here, surely, was the writing on the wall.

The rainy season was now commencing and with it fighting died down. As the Muslim host melted away, the Crusaders were left to wallow in the mud surrounding their camp. However, the spring of 1191 heralded two important developments. First, the Crusaders received considerable reinforcements, of which a contingent of some ten thousand fighting men under Henry of Champagne was the most vital, particularly so as the fighting character and leadership of this man were of inestimable value. To the tired and dispirited Cru-saders this was tonic indeed. The second factor was the hesitant generalship of Saladin. If Saladin wished to relieve Acre, delay could only make this more difficult; but delay he did. He seemed obsessed by rumours of large reinforcements arriving via Anatolia and to intercept these he sent a big detachment to the north. This was done when the relative strength of his force and that of the Crusaders could hardly permit such dissipation of strength. It is always easy to be wise after the event and to pass judgement when one has full knowledge of all the facts, many of which would be unknown to and only matters of conjecture for the General on the spot. Nevertheless, Acre was the prize and it should have been to this that his eye turned. Saladin paid heavily for his mistake. A year was wasted and, as another winter drew on, once again his army dispersed.

5 Saladin and Richard I

In 1191 the Third Crusade was on its way and this saw the turn of the tide. Among the first to arrive were the Germans, who had lost many of their men on the journey, including their gallant leader, the old Emperor Frederick Barbarossa. It is a strange commentary on the disunity of the Christians that both the Emperor Isaac of Constantinople and the Christians of Armenia should have been in correspondence with Saladin, telling him of the Crusaders' movements and what they knew of the latter's plans.

The German contingent was followed by those of France and England whose progress by sea had been inexplicably slow. However, by Easter, King Philip of France's ships lay off Acre and by the beginning of June the English fleet with Richard arrived from Cyprus. With odds now heavily against it, Acre could stand out no longer and on 1st July the garrison that had withstood siege for so long was forced to capitulate. Philip, a sick man, now departed and the full command devolved on Richard.

Whatever Richard's failings as a King of England might have been, he was an able general and a brave man. He has, in English history, been scathingly criticised, but what did the Muslims think of him? Saladin's biographer, Baha ad-Din, wrote of him that 'The King of England was very powerful, very brave and full of resolution'.[1] This perhaps best epitomises the man as seen through

[1] Baha ad-Din: *Life of Saladin.*

Muslim eyes. When Richard, on his final departure from the country, said he would one day return to retake Jerusalem, Saladin made the well-known reply that he would rather lose Jerusalem to Richard than to any other man alive.

In a short reign, in which he scarcely ever set foot in England, this remarkable man was, at his zenith, one of the most powerful monarchs of his day. Surely the dominions over which he exercised real or nominal sway were more diversified than those of any other prince? He was King of England, Lord of Ireland, Scotland and Wales; he was Duke of Normandy, Aquitaine and Gascony; Count of Brittany, Auvergne and Toulouse; he was King of Arles and of Cyprus and, for a time, the ruler of Palestine.

William Stubbs refers to Richard as a bad man, a bad husband, a selfish and vicious ruler who none the less possessed great qualities that men of the time accepted. He was disliked by the Germans and considered perfidious by the French; yet it was these same French who at Ascalon deserted him and whose king left his troops in Palestine with no funds to pay them, a burden that Richard shouldered out of his own pocket. He loved war, not for the sake of glory so much as for the pure excitement of the struggle and the joy of victory; he was a loyal Crusader and dedicated to his task; he had a genius for military affairs, an unerring tactical sense, and the resolution and tenacity of purpose that are essential to a commander. Violent in his outbursts and at times cruel in his acts, he has been accused of some crimes that there is no evidence to support. If his dislikes were strong they were generally not without good reason; for instance, he had little respect for Philip of France whom he despised, and he had every reason to dislike the faithless Conrad of Montferrat. Yet he could rise above his personal failings. At the Council of the Knights he warned of his intending departure, asking that they should name their future king. When they selected Conrad, Richard without demur accepted their decision. He had the virtues of a brave man and he never employed artifices of falsehood and treachery. If hasty to offend, he was always ready to forgive. He never betrayed a friend, was open-handed and generous, loved the society of good men and he always chose good companions.

To a man with these characteristics Saladin was by nature drawn. Saladin, a Muslim, and Richard, a Christian, these two men had many similar qualities; both were liberal and honourable; both had cultivated minds and each was a great captain. The difference was that whereas Saladin would contrive to achieve his object, Richard would resort to force; the one was cautious, patient and prudent while the other was rude, haughty and impatient. Stubbs said that Saladin was a good heathen and Richard a bad Christian: a picturesque assessment but quite incorrect, as the former was not a heathen in any acceptable sense and Richard was certainly not all bad.

In regard to Richard's alleged cruelty much that has been said was based on the beheading of hostages at Acre. Of the massacre Baha ad-Din wrote of it merely as an historical fact. Finding no explanation and apparently baffled, he concluded, 'God knows what his reason really was.' There have, in fact, been many explanations: one was that Richard could not afford to leave so many prisoners behind; another that the act was in retribution for Saladin's massacre of the Templars after Hattin; yet another that it was to avenge those Christians whom the Muslims had slain during the siege; lastly, that it marked the expiration of the time Richard had granted for the surrender of the Holy Cross and those Christian prisoners Saladin still held. However, what is of interest is that he decided on this action only after deep consultation with his nobles, whose unanimous decision it was.

After the fall of Acre, Richard wished to meet Saladin and to come face to face with the man of whom he had heard so much. Saladin had not been willing to talk of a truce with Guy whom he felt he could no longer trust; but the coming of a king put a different complexion on matters, for to a king a king could talk. However, always cautious, he declined Richard's offer, probably because he wanted more time to think.

Acre having fallen, the eyes of the two commanders were now focused on one point, Jerusalem. Saladin was concerned with its defence and, if possible, the annihilation of the Christian army before it got there; for Richard the problem was to select the most profitable line of advance.

However, before he could do this he had to instil some sense of discipline and enthusiasm into the motley crowd that made up his army. He soon found that the Franks of Guy were more concerned with enjoying the fruits of victory than with the undertaking of what promised to be a hard campaign. The wine, the women and the soft living of Acre beckoned them and the King of England's call for action thus met with little more than sullen resistance. Many deserted him, and among these was Conrad, who took his followers off to Tyre. Nevertheless, in spite of all the difficulties, by 22nd August Richard was ready to march.

Of the roads that led to Jerusalem there were two principally from which he could choose; one by the Hills of Galilee, Mount Ephraim and the town of Bethel; the other by the coastal road and thence up one of the valleys of the Shephalah that led to the plain on which the Holy City lay. Richard chose the coastal route for a number of reasons. First he would have his fleet hard by for support, supply, and if necessary for re-embarkation; he would, when he took Jaffa, have a second port; finally, it would be a more well-worn and direct route to Jerusalem and avoid the risk of a head-on collision with Saladin in the difficult Galilean Hills. But all would not be easy along the coastal road, for his eastern flank would always be open to attack, there were many rivers to cross, though at that time of the year they would not be carrying much water, and there was the Carmel Ridge to negotiate.

Saladin had the advantages that go with operating on interior lines. He could stand back and meet Richard on ground of his own choice; should the Crusaders move along the coastal road he could attack them in flank and force Richard to fight at a disadvantage; and should Richard advance on Galilee he could oppose him in these hills or on the Heights of Ephraim. Saladin had, in point of fact, the initiative.

Richard conducted his march with every military circumspection. His infantry moved in mass, protecting his knights on horseback. His footmen all wore thick protective clothing on which Saracen arrows would have little effect. Those troops who marched nearest the shore, because they were not exposed to attack, were changed with the battalions on the more dangerous left flank. The knights were kept in strict discipline in the centre, protected by infantry and forbidden to charge unless ordered to do so. In this tight formation the column with all its baggage negotiated the dangerous Carmel Ridge and entered the Plain of Sharon.

In the meantime, Saladin, at first uncertain as to the route Richard would take, moved back to counter any attempt to cross the Hills of Galilee; but, by doing this, he missed a great oppor-

D

tunity in not attacking the Crusaders as they negotiated Carmel. He had, however, taken the precaution of sending his brother to shadow Richard's movements and he had reported that it was, in his view, useless to follow up the Crusaders as they were well closed up and there were no stragglers. He concluded that to attack now would merely result in a waste of valuable lives and with this opinion Saladin concurred. It was a mistake, and an opportunity to bring Richard to battle in unfavourable circumstances to the Crusaders had been missed.

Saladin now crossed the Carmel Ridge at Megiddo from whence he could overlook the Plain of Sharon. The Sultan himself rode down to the coastal road, which he struck some ten miles south of Haifa, to ascertain if the ground here would be suitable for a pitched battle. His mind was as yet not made up and, when asked by Baha ad-Din what his plan was, he replied that he had heard the Crusaders had not yet left Haifa and that he would wait till he got news and only then determine what it would be best to do.

Richard for his part, in order not to over-strain his foot soldiers, was making short marches, only reaching Caesarea on the 30th August. Saladin attacked the column on the following day but was unable to make any impression. Baha ad-Din, in commenting on the action, said that Richard's men showed wonderful self-control, going on their way without hurry, whilst their ships followed the line of march along the coast, adding that he could not help admiring the patience which Richard's troops displayed.

Some little distance to the south, between the marshes of Birket Ramadan and the village of Arsuf, lay an open stretch of ground ideally suited to the employment of the Arab horse, the approaches to which had the advantage of being covered by a line of low wooded hills. It was here that Saladin decided to force a battle. Richard, in no haste, had halted to await the reinforcements he expected from Acre. Realising that a battle was likely to be forced on him and wishing to avoid unnecessary casualties, he sent word to Saladin that he would like to parley with him or his representative. This the Sultan was willing to do, not so much because he, too, wished to avoid bloodshed, as because he also was expecting Turkoman forces to join him in a few days. His instructions to his brother, el-Adel, were that the negotiations should be protracted. However, when he heard that Richard's conditions were nothing short of a demand that all captured territories should be returned to the Crusaders and that Saracen troops should quit the country he broke off the talks. All was now set for the battle for which both men were prepared.

Richard's order of march was disciplined and militarily sound. The baggage train was concentrated along the coast and had a suitable guard of foot soldiers. The dangerous northern or rear flank was protected by the Hospitallers under the experienced Henry of Champagne. The remainder of the knights, moving in close formation, were led by the Templars, followed by the Angevins, the Poitevins and then the English and Normans who guarded the Standard. Strong flank and rear and advanced guards were provided by infantry.

It was on the morning of Saturday, 7th September, at about midday, that Saladin launched his attack. This was led by wave after wave of skirmishers whose attempts to break the Crusader ranks were only partially successful. The knights, keeping their tight formation, were unaffected. Breaking through such gaps as had been made the Muslim horsemen now poured in. Hoping to turn Richard's northern flank, Saladin concentrated on the Hospitallers, who, however, held their ground, re-forming with precision after each successive wave. Curbing the impatience of his knights, Richard would permit no counter-attack until he was convinced the moment was right. Eventually, calling on St George, they charged. Richard now entered the fray, putting order where there was disorder, spurring on the knights as they drove the Saracens before them. Nevertheless, he was able to restrain them at the right moment and Saladin's attempt to force the knights into a running fight failed. Never losing sight of his aim, which was to reach Jaffa, the King methodically and with no haste resumed his march. He knew that once within the protection of the city walls his tired men could have their well-earned rest. He had achieved much and the Crusaders had a great deal to thank their able general for.

Saladin was humiliated, he had been ineffectual at Acre and now had suffered a serious defeat in open battle in circumstances of his own choice. His task was to restore the confidence of his troops and, of equal importance, in himself as their leader. He withdrew to Ramleh where he set about sacking and dismantling Ascalon.

For his part, Richard was in no hurry to leave Jaffa. He had to fortify his base before leaving the sea and the fleet on which he so depended. The time he also spent in making fresh overtures for peace. He sent Humphrey of Toron, an old friend of Saladin. The Sultan on his part was not averse to negotiations. However, a new factor now complicated the proceedings. This was the opening of correspondence by Conrad of Montferrat with Saladin who offered to break with Richard and to become Saladin's ally. He suggested that he should capture Acre for the Saracens on condition that he was given Sidon and Beirut. When Richard heard of this he, too, put forward a series of propositions. Firstly he suggested that Saladin's brother should marry his, Richard's, sister Joana, who should live in Jerusalem and be dowered with the cities of Acre, Ascalon and Jaffa, while Saladin's brother was to rule the rest of Palestine. The Holy Cross was to be surrendered and the Hospitallers and Templars to be given establishments. Finally, Richard would return to England. Saladin, though professing interest, would not accept as he felt he could still play one bidder against the other. Moreover, winter was drawing on and time was on his side. He withdrew into Jerusalem and as was their custom many of his warriors returned to their homes.

Richard, unfamiliar with the country and its climate, marched on Jerusalem. As he lay in camp at Beit Nuba within ten miles of the Holy City the hardships of the winter were borne in on him. Day after day it rained and the fierce cold winds blew. The soldiers' armour and breast-plates became fouled with rust and their clothing was soaked. With all this their ardour waned and the only comfort that sustained them was the hope of visiting the Lord's Sepulchre. The older Crusaders strongly advised the King against any attempt to take Jerusalem, an operation which they doubted would succeed; but, if they did get in, they would soon be attacked by Saladin's army from Egypt and would then be besieged by superior forces. The wisdom of their counsel Richard saw, and so, reluctantly, he decided to withdraw. To sustain the morale of his men he said his object was to rebuild Ascalon which the Muslims had destroyed, and on this he got his men to work. It is strange how at this moment Ascalon played on Richard's mind and it was, later, this same Ascalon that proved the stumbling block to an otherwise possible peace.

For Richard things were not easy. From England he heard how sorely his presence was needed, while from Acre he heard that quarrels amounting to open conflict had broken out between the troops of Pisa and those from Genoa, with whom the French had joined forces. Moreover, the French, now without pay, were dissatisfied, as Richard could give them no further loans. Finally, the King's health was giving way under the strain. Nevertheless, he went to Acre and there by wise counsel he smoothed over most of the differences. But his heart was bent on returning to England and the latest news he had received concerning John's conduct gave him cause for anxiety. Calling the knights together, he warned them of his intention and it was on this occasion that they nominated Conrad to be their king. Conrad was, in fact, murdered and their choice then fell on the wise Henry of Champagne.

Saladin, too, had his difficulties and his health also was failing. As the spring advanced he called upon his followers to rejoin the colours, for the Holy War must be prosecuted. The reaction was disappointing, there was little enthusiasm and he received nothing like the numbers he required. This cooling off of support stemmed more from the inherent weakness of the tribal structure than from any disloyalty to the Sultan. Far removed from Palestine, Saladin was also faced with troubles between the Kurds and the Turks, while his young nephew was getting himself embroiled in alliances that could jeopardise his war effort. These diversions, though not lessening his resolve, affected his attitude to the peace feelers that Richard threw out.

Saladin's attitude to the Holy War is interesting. Though a devout Muslim beyond dispute, he never seemed to want to pursue the war to the point of annihilation; he had shown this after Hattin, at a moment when he had everything in his favour and his enemy lay prostrate. He had again and again displayed it in his conduct towards those Christian knights whose castles he had taken. Now that he, too, had his worries it is not surprising that he should be prepared to negotiate. By March 1192 he had worked out details for a peace which he sent to Richard and which for their reasonableness were quite extraordinary. He agreed to surrender the Cross, to the rights of pilgrimage to Jerusalem, to the permanent establishment of priests in the Church of the Resurrection, and to the partition of the country. When his emissary, Abu Bakr, returned he had apparently succeeded in reaching agreement on every point. This treaty was never ratified and it has never been made clear why. It is all the more baffling since at this time Richard bestowed a knighthood on one of Saladin's relatives, surely an indication of the English king's friendly attitude. In seeking to find some explanation for the non-ratification Baha ad-Din suggests that Richard was merely taking advantage of the temporary difficulties that he believed the Sultan was experiencing in far-off Mesopotamia, and this may well have been an accurate assessment. In the event, and in spite of an all but ratified treaty, Richard laid siege to and took Darum and in June once more advanced on Jerusalem.

Although more of Saladin's troops had by now rallied to his call, he was ill-at-ease; he still had trouble with the Kurds and Turks and he was by no means sure that he had sufficient troops to withstand an attack by the combined French and English Crusaders, who were for the time being now working well together. At the very moment when the fortunes of the Crusaders were or should have been most propitious for success there occurred one of those episodes that defy reason and which only go to show the frailty of alliances.

With Jerusalem almost within their grasp the Crusaders disagreed about their objective. The French were for assaulting the city at once, which they very properly pointed out was what they had come to Palestine for. The English and the Franks for some inexplicable reason, perhaps thinking of the old policy of Amalric, wanted to turn round and march on Cairo. Their argument prevailed and so it came about that the army wheeled around, now appearing to Saladin to be a force in full retreat.

Still intent on returning to England and with his health failing, Richard sent another letter to Saladin which he couched in the most conciliatory terms. The Sultan's council also wished for peace and so a friendly answer was returned. In fact all Richard asked for was granted, Saladin only stipulating that Ascalon should be handed over in return for which the Muslims would give up Lydda. To this Richard would not agree and thus once again an opportunity was lost. Peace was what so many yearned for, but it fell down on a matter of detail or so-called principle. This was Ascalon, which on principle, and on principle only, Richard would not give up. As so often the student of history might well ask whether prolonged fighting is preferable to adherence to a principle.

Richard still had trouble in the north and for this reason returned to Acre, where, if it was at all possible for him to do so, he could embark for England. In the meantime Saladin advanced on Jaffa, which he entered after some three days' fighting. This brought Richard back, who, sailing south with some eighty knights and a few hundred bowmen, relieved the city. For Saladin this was a bitter blow, for the King of England had routed a Muslim army, estimated to be of the order of sixty-two thousand, with a handful of men.

According to Baha ad-Din, at the King's request Saladin now sent his chamberlain, Abu Bakr, to visit. Saladin's biographer describes this interview in an entrancing way. When Abu Bakr arrived he found Richard railing in a good-humoured way at some of the Mamluks he had taken prisoner, telling them that he was dumbfounded at the ease with which he had, unarmed and wearing only the shoes he stood up in, retaken a city. Then, addressing the chamberlain he said, 'Greet the Sultan for me, and tell him that I beseech him, in God's name, to grant the peace I ask at his hands; this state of things must be put a stop to; my country beyond the seas is being ruined. There is no advantage either for you or me in suffering the present condition of things to continue.'[1] These were the words of a wise man for which in contemporary British history Richard seems to have had little credit.

The subsequent exchange of messages shows the characters of these two men. Always endeavouring to argue from strength, Saladin replied that Richard had originally asked for peace on certain terms when Jaffa and Ascalon in particular were the main points at issue. He now offered the King all the country from Tyre to Caesarea, which, of course, excluded Jaffa and Ascalon, and this he must have known Richard would not countenance. The King's answer was both courteous and wise. 'The King sends you his answer. Among the Franks it is customary for a man to whom a city has been granted to become the servant and ally of the giver. If, therefore, you give me these two cities, Jaffa and Ascalon, the troops I leave there will always be at your service, and, if you have any need of me, I will hasten to come to you, and be at your service, and you know that I can serve you.[2] But Saladin did not yield and so the negotiations once more foundered on the rock of Ascalon.

Another battle for Jaffa followed in which Saladin was again defeated. This account I take from Muslim sources. 'The Franks displayed such hardihood that our troops lost heart at their sturdy

---

[1] Baha ad-Din: *Life of Saladin.*
[2] Ibid.

resistance and were obliged to draw off.[1] All attempts by Saladin
to get his men to return to the charge failed and Richard, lance in
hand, rode along the whole length of the army from right to left,
and not one man left the ranks to attack him. What a picture this is.
It is not romance, it is the simple truth as told by a Muslim.

Two new factors now affected the situation. First, the Sultan
received reinforcements from both Mosul and Egypt; second,
Richard fell seriously ill. Thus reinforced Saladin marched on
Ramleh; yet, at the same time, he sent fruit and ice to the English
King; although some said it was in order to spy and find out his
strength it probably was sent in sympathy, which would be in keeping with Saladin's whole character. But the Sultan had his worries
and he now badly wanted peace. His troops had suffered a lot and his
funds were running low, he knew the tribesmen were anxious to return to their homes and, as a reminder, he could not forget their
reluctance to attack at Jaffa. Saladin's health, too, was failing and
with time running out he wanted to be free to undertake the re-
organisations he knew were wanted in his kingdom. These facts, all
weighty, must have lain behind terms that he now finally made to
Richard.

Jerusalem was to remain a Muslim city, but pilgrims were to be
free to visit the Holy Sepulchre. In the rest of the country the boundaries of the respective territories were to be those of the former
agreement. Jaffa and Caesarea with the dependencies of both cities
were to be made over to Richard, as also were Haifa and Acre, but
Nazareth and Suffurieh were to be Muslim. Finally Richard was to
give up Ascalon, which, however, was to be destroyed.

Richard accepted these terms and boarded his ship on 9th
October 1192. This was the occasion when he sent his message to
the Sultan containing his promise to come back and take the city of
Jerusalem, to which Saladin replied that if he had to lose the place
he would as soon leave it to the King of England as to any other
man. On the 4th March the following year Saladin died.

A great man judged on any showing, Saladin never sought
power but achieved it. He never abused or misused it. Stern when
sternness was required, he could always be merciful. Brave himself,
he admired true bravery in others. A good and devoutly religious
man, he was not a bigot; the world was the poorer when he died.

[1] Baha ad-Din: *Life of Saladin*.

6   Jenghiz Khan—The Making of a Leader

The centre of gravity now moves farther east. While Muhammad Ghuri was waging his holy wars dynamic forces were at play in Central Asia and beyond. The first to blaze this trail was Jenghiz Khan, or Temüjin, as he was originally named. Of the many great conquerors of history none is better known than Jenghiz Khan. His conquests are recorded and the width and depth of his empire are well known, but of the man himself, the forces that animated him and the influences that affected his outlook, much less has been written. In his war against the Chinese empire of the Chins how did he get forty-six Chinese divisions with their generals to fight on his side? Why did he grant privileges to the Buddhist monks and why did he ask the Taoist monk to visit him in far-off Samarkand? What were the real reasons for his wars and did he seek power for power's sake, or was it in the exercise of power that his genius lay? In the answers to these questions will be found the key to one of the greatest characters of history.

Jenghiz Khan was never able to read or write and his people were illiterate. The stories of his exploits were preserved only by tradition and handed down very largely by word of mouth, as were those conversations so often given verbatim by some historians. This putting of Western words into an Eastern mouth, this presumption of Western thought by an Eastern mind, can lead to erroneous conclusions. It was not until sixty or more years after his death that

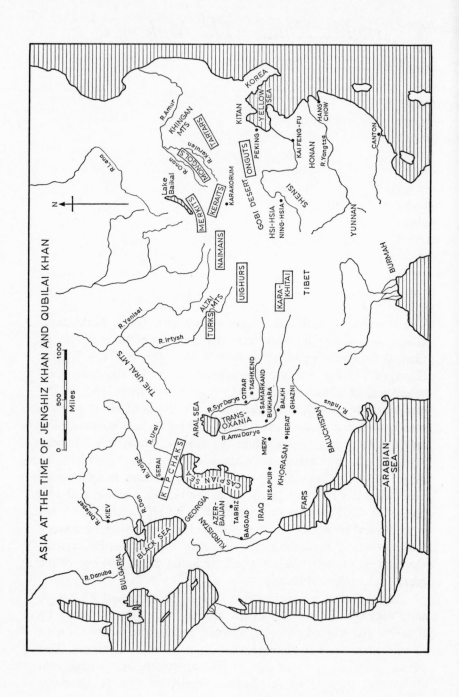

ASIA AT THE TIME OF JENGHIZ KHAN AND QUBILAI KHAN

any chronological written history of his times seems to have been attempted. Then, Fedlallah, the vizier of the Khan of Persia, composed a Mongol history which was based on stories in which truth inevitably vied with romance. There is also the *Secret History of the Mongols,*[1] compiled and kept by the Chinese, which has only recently been translated. The general lack of written record at the time has made it difficult to unravel fact from fiction. However, breaking like a ray of light we have the *Hai Yu Chi,* which was written by Li Ch'ih Ch'ang, the disciple and secretary of the Taoist Master who traversed Asia to visit the Great Khan.[2] This is a detailed record of an extraordinary journey, compiled at the time, recording descriptions of the country traversed, the people encountered and, finally, the verbatim conversations with the Khan himself.

Of the race from which Jenghiz Khan sprang, of his antecedents and place of birth, most that we read can be taken as fact. His home was in the wooded mountains separating the Onon and the Kerulen rivers. These fast-running cold streams, descending from the Karakorum Mountains, ran northwards to join the great Amur River, which after bending eastwards girdled the Khingan Mountains, the home of the Tartar and Mongol peoples. The general run of the mountain systems was north and south and this tended to divide the country into vertical tribal regions. To the east dwelt the Tartars, in the centre the Mongols, and westwards, astride the ore-producing Altai Mountains, lived the Turks. As time went on these distinctions became blurred, Tartars and Mongols mixing, the one carelessly adopting the name of the other. But at the time of Temüjin there was little unity, much jealousy and distrust which resulted in open conflict.

Whether tribally Mongol or Tartar they all had physical characteristics that marked them out from other races. They were thick-set, stocky people who were readily distinguished by their square-looking faces and prominent cheek-bones. They had sparse beards and olive complexions. Every man was a natural horseman, every man a hunter, every man an archer, and all were born soldiers. They did not cultivate the land; indeed in their wooded mountains this was not worth cultivating. These men and their women knew the meaning of poverty and they were proud. They had a traditional

[1] *The Secret History of the Mongols* — Wm. Hung.
[2] Li Ch'ih-Ch'ang — *The Travels of an Alchemist.*

aristocracy and they respected their unwritten laws. They would not tolerate dictatorship. They were tent-dwellers and lived not in villages but in camps. The tent represented the family and they were loyal to their tent and to their horde, the size of which was measured by the number of tents. In the winter months they were forced to move down into the plains in search of grazing; but, after this, they returned to their own territories, generally with some loot, wives and slaves.

It was among these hardy people and in this remote and romantic country that in 1162 Temüjin was born. His father, Yesügai, was a great soldier and the head of a horde with, so it was said, as many as forty thousand tents under his command. At his birth the child clenched in his little fist a clot of blood which, looking like a red jewel, led the local wise men to prophesy that he would grow to be a great warrior. Superstitious, these Mongols worshipped fire and river spirits, which they combined with a strong veneration for Heaven or Sky-Power, and this they called Tangri. Certain men were believed to be in communication with Heaven from which they derived magical powers. These men were known as baga or wizards. Jenghiz Khan placed great confidence in these wizards or visionaries until he was deceived by one, Kokchu, at that time his most trusted minister.

When his father was visiting one of the Tartar tribes the old warrior was murdered, dying of poison. Temüjin was then only thirteen years of age. Although Yesügai had succeeded in uniting many tribes under his banner, it was scarcely likely that these hardy independent men would willingly follow a mere boy. So one by one they broke away until eventually Temüjin with his mother, his brother Qachiun and his half-brothers Bektor and Belgutei found themselves deserted and alone. Quarrels broke out between the two brothers and their half-brothers in one of which Bektor was killed. All of them realised that in this kind of feud lay the seeds of trouble and so, for the future, they swore that they would always work together; from this beginning there grew up a strong and lasting friendship between Temüjin and Belgutei. In this incident one gets the first insight into Temüjin's character: once he made a friend he stuck to him and this is a trait that runs like a silver thread throughout his life. It dominated his relationship with his sons and his Orlok, his nine principal advisers or inner cabinet, and it was the cement that bound the empire he ultimately built. It was neither calculated nor was it a pose; it was natural and therein lay its strength.

Two instances, each occurring in his early life, bear out this idea. The first concerns an experience when he was hunted and taken prisoner by a tribe on whose grazing grounds he had trespassed. His life was saved by the intervention of an old man, Sorgan-Shira, with whose sons he had often played. Never did Temüjin forget this act and later when he was made khan he made Sorgan-Shira one of his nine Orlok. The second occurred one day when he was in pursuit of raiders who had driven off his horses. Temüjin was exhausted and his horse was stumbling with fatigue when he met Bogurchi, a youth of his own age. Enquiring of his lost horses, he gave his name, Temüjin the son of Yesügai. Bogurchi gave him food and drink and joined him in the pursuit of the horse thieves. From this moment these two men never separated. Years later it was this Bogurchi who became his chief of the Orlok and as such it was he whom Jenghiz Khan sent to conduct the Taoist Master on the last stages of his long journey from eastern China to the Hindu Kush.

By the time Temüjin was seventeen he had collected a considerable number of young followers and now felt himself strong enough to go to claim his bride, who had been promised him when, as a boy with his father, he had visited one of the Jungerat tribes far away to the south. Although his following was not great, Temüjin's reputation had spread far; he was known to be valiant and to be generally successful in his undertakings. He got his bride, Börte, and she, entitled to her own tent, brought with her her own train, thus further swelling Temüjin's horde.

His horde was growing. However, it was not success but disaster that turned the tide in his favour. Shortly after he had brought his bride back to his camp it was raided by the Merkits, a ferocious tribe dwelling in the northern Steppes, who, in addition to the goods they took, carried off his wife, Börte. Knowing that the Merkits were too strong for him unaided, he did what he had never done before, he begged for help. He appealed to the Khan of the Keraits, a powerful ruler whose rich lands lay on the caravan routes from east to west. Their Khan, Toghril, had been blood-brother to Temüjin's father and on this count he begged the privilege of becoming Toghril's adopted son. Remembering that Yesügai had come to his aid at a time of need, the Khan agreed and, in addition, he placed a considerable force at the young man's disposal. The news that Temüjin was the adopted son of the mighty Toghril quickly spread and many were now anxious to join his horde. Thus reinforced, he was strong enough to attack the Merkits and in a short campaign he was able to rescue his wife and recover his lost goods. What is of interest is that having gained his object he did not press the enemy any further, even though they were retreating in disorder before him. This was a foretaste of a policy that was to become constant; once he had achieved his aim he seemed more concerned with consolidating his position and making friends where this was possible than with increasing enmity.

As yet Temüjin had little of the material things of this world to offer, but there was one thing he could bestow and this was trust. To bind men to him he not only trusted them, he also gave, whenever this was appropriate, responsibility. Men thus treated became his friends for life. Typical of this was his treatment of Jirqo'adai, who, when captured, threw himself at Temüjin's feet, admitting that it was he who had shot the arrow that had wounded him. Raising Jirqo'adai to his feet he told him that henceforth he should be known as Jebai, the Arrow, and allowing him to choose nine men he then made him their leader. This young man eventually became Prince Arrow, was the first to enter China, to cross the Pamirs and to overrun Persia. As another example there was his dealing with the Taijiuts. This tribe had deserted him on his father's death and, though he showed no mercy to their leaders, when the tribesmen came in he gave them a friendly welcome taking them into his horde. In this way his following grew. Among these men was one Munlik, who with some trepidation came to make his peace. Completely won over to Temüjin, it was this warrior who, moving from clan to clan, successfully persuaded them to vote with one accord for Temüjin to be their khan.

Opportunities sometimes fall into the laps of the more fortunate, but generally opportunities have to be made. Sometimes a man will see the possibilities in a situation and will take advantage of them. Temüjin now saw such an opportunity. The Emperor at Peking had sent his emissaries to the Khan of the Keraits and Temüjin, on hearing of this, sent a messenger inviting the emissaries to visit his camp on their return. This the Chinese were only too willing to do, as they wished to see what sort of man this new khan might be. Always punctilious in their behaviour themselves, they were interested to find one who treated them with respect, yet who was untainted by any servility. They learned of his marriage with the daughter of a chieftain whose people resided close to their own frontier. They told Temüjin that the Emperor, Ch'ang-Tsung, had decided to eject from his territories the Tartars, whose raids he would no longer tolerate. This had been the purpose of their visit to the Khan of the Keraits whose co-operation in this venture they had sought.

Temüjin sent messengers to the Khan suggesting they should join forces; at the same time he instructed the Mongols on the frontier, under the guise of grazers, to spy into the Tartar territories. By these two acts he gained an ally and he obtained information. Pursued by the Chinese armies from the south and attacked in flank by the Keraits and Mongols, the Tartars were defeated. The loot, consisting mostly of the treasures the raiders had seized in China, was considerable and was divided among the horde. Temüjin had achieved much; he had avenged his father's death and he had established his position as Khan of the Mongols, while with the Chinese he had also made his mark, the Emperor bestowing on him the title of Chow-Churi or Warden. Thus the name Temüjin appears for the first time in the annals of the Chinese Empire. He was then thirty-two years old.

The following eight years, although they were eventually rewarding, were fraught with dangers that arose from the fears of those whom he took to be his friends and from desertions among his followers. Separate in themselves the two acted coincidentally. His old ally the Khan of the Keraits turned against him because his followers, jealous from and fearful of Temüjin's successes, poisoned his mind. It was in this new and unexpected predicament that his own clans began to desert him. Selfish and tribal in their outlook they asked themselves why they should fight his battles, asking what gain or what loot there was to be had. Morover, they argued, it was not within his right as khan to order them, as he had done, by messenger to fight his war, a conflict about which they had not been consulted. They had, they reminded him, only sworn fealty to him in a war engaged by common consent. Here was the writing on the wall and here, even among these elementary people, was democracy at work. We shall see how quick Temüjin was to appreciate this point. Weakened by lack of support he was forced more and more on the defensive, until ultimately he found himself on the shores of Lake Baikal, in which dreary waste he was comparatively secure.

Soon other factors began to move in his favour. Some of the clans joined him as they became aware of and alarmed at the rumours and stories that spread of the rapacity of the Keraits. Toghril also had his difficulties as among his men were many who, thinking Temüjin beaten, saw no gain in further fighting. Some even commenced to plot against Toghril. It was in these circumstances that Temüjin was at last able to contemplate the offensive. Hanging on to the outskirts of the Kerait camp, he waited an opportunity to strike. This came one night when, following their custom, the Keraits gave way to an orgy of drinking, and so, with scarcely an outpost on duty and the army drunk and incapable of action, he seized his chance. His force, now strong, well disciplined and carefully instructed, threw themselves on the unsuspecting enemy. The rout was complete, and Temüjin, a fugitive yesterday, was now a victor with the Kerait country at his mercy. At last also he was able to distribute loot to his followers. As with the Merkits, once he had achieved his end he made peace with the enemy. As a token of his wish to gain their friendship his son, Toli, was married to Toghril's niece, the Princess Sorqoqteni. This remarkable woman later played an important part in Mongol affairs as the mother of Hülegü and Qubilai, two successors of the Great Khan. It is interesting to note that the Princess was a Christian in the Nestorian Church.

But victory of itself was not enough. Temüjin had to assure himself that never again would he lose the confidence of his followers. He had learned the lesson that his leadership could only rest on mutual trust and for this consultation must be the normal practice. But he also realised that this must not be permitted to undermine his position as leader. If he had to seek the advice of his chieftains he had equally to be sure that he did this, not as a suppliant, but as a khan desiring to benefit from the wisdom of his advisers. He now evolved a method of constitutional leadership which was to form the basis of his future government. The corner-stones of the system were the Orlok or Council of Leaders and the Yasak or Code of Laws, both of which survived in the Quriltai and the Yasak for many centuries. Herein, even at this early stage, Temüjin was showing that his qualities as a general were matched with his abilities as an administrator.

His actions did not go unnoticed by his neighbours. The Onguts, a powerful people to his south, saw in him a khan with whom in case of need they could come to an understanding. It was not long after this that the Turkish Naimans from the Altai Mountains suggested that they and the Onguts should attack the Mongols, whose growing power they feared. Instead of complying, the Onguts sent warning of the plan to Temüjin, who promptly called a meeting of his chieftains. He told them of the Naiman plot and of the warning the Onguts had given him. The Naimans were powerful and it would be fatal to allow them to take the initiative, and for this reason he advocated taking the offensive himself. The council at first resisted him on the basis that he was being unnecessarily precipitate. Eventually his arguments prevailed and so, with a united horde, he was able to undertake this, his most important campaign.

His plan was not to rush into the attack, but rather to lure the Naimans into attacking him on his own terms. In this he was at first unsuccessful, but, undeterred, he next sent out a strong party to attack the enemy with instructions that when they were engaged they must withdraw. This ruse was successful, the Naimans following up what they thought to be Temüjin's main body were drawn on to the Mongol battle positions. Leaving the centre to take the main Naiman attack, Temüjin led a flanking counter-attack, which, achieving complete surprise, resulted in the confusion and defeat of what had been a superior enemy. The Mongols had won an outstanding victory.

Temüjin forbade his men to plunder the defeated enemy and not a single chieftain did he take prisoner. The arms of the soldiers were returned to them, in return for which they were asked only to serve him as faithfully as they had their last masters. So, as he had done before, Temüjin swelled the ranks of his army with further willing reinforcements. This time they were Turks, a hardy people who were both intelligent and valiant. Temüjin took to wife the Naiman chieftain's widow.

A saga, related as a poem, tells how an unarmed prisoner, a Uighur from the hills north-east of Sinkiang, when brought before the Khan, showed him his king's seal. On this were engraved char-

E

acters which attracted Temüjin's attention. His curiosity aroused on seeing letters for the first time he enquired after their significance. On being told the Khan appointed the Uighur as Keeper of the Seal and charged him to teach his sons and the sons of the Orlok the letters and their meaning. Illiterate himself, he was ensuring that those who followed should not be so.

He was in his forty-fifth year and had reached the turning point in his career. Calling a meeting of all his vast following in all the pomp and splendour associated with such gatherings, he sat in front of his tent, beyond which was the customary open space. The tent faced south and on either side of the great unoccupied area to the right and left the camps extended as far as the eye could see. Behind the Khan's tent were those of the chieftains, the army commanders and other dignitaries, all in order of precedence. The Shaman, or Mediator between Heaven and Earth, the High Priest, now declared Temüjin to be divinely appointed as Khakan or Khan of Khans, the Ruler of Rulers. It was from this moment that the title of Jenghiz Khan, used today as though it were a name, was adopted. The word in Mongolian implies the greatest of the great and has been spelt in many ways. I have chosen to use that adopted by contemporary English writers.

The Khakan might well have had his head turned, but he had not forgotten how too much presumption in the past had nearly cost him everything. If, therefore, he accepted this new title would he be able to exercise the authority implicit in it? He put the question point blank to the assembled chieftains: if they wished to have him as their ruler would they without exception be prepared to carry out all his orders, to come when he called and to go where sent? He was a khakan and as such was a ruler of rulers who must expect to issue instructions to subordinate khans. The assembly proclaimed their willingness to obey and all fell on their knees, each making obeisance four times. Never after this was Jenghiz Khan's authority challenged.

This closes the first or formative years of Jenghiz Khan's life. Left a boy when his father died, he had been a fugitive and he had had to struggle to regain and then to hold what he believed to be his right. The fight had lasted over a period of thirty-two years but in the end he had succeeded. If he had tasted the fruits of success he had also known the meaning of adversity. His preoccupation had frequently been to remain alive, to fight back for his heritage and then to hold what he had gained. His fortunes had flowed and they had ebbed and he had learned on the hard anvil of experience.

Men had come to his horde because in him they found a commander who was a man of courage and enthusiasm and, above all, one whom they could trust. He was cheerful in adversity, valiant in battle, loyal to his friends and frightening to his enemies. If he commanded respect he also commanded affection. His motive was understandable, to regain for himself the position that once his father had held. To read into his activities during this period grandiose schemes of invading China and of building a world empire is, it seems to me, to misread history and to misunderstand a character.

That he was far-seeing there is no doubt and that he developed a code of behaviour, a basic law for his people, a code of military discipline and of conduct in battle is clear. His organisational formula for fighting was simple and objective. It was based on the group of nine men, each group under its appointed leader. These groups were organised into squadrons and regiments. Men remained permanently in their units and in this way was established both a sense of discipline and a spirit of loyalty. Exercises, carried out as games, developed a habit of conduct, each man automatically knowing what he had to do and under whose command he was. Gone was the conception of a wild undisciplined horde, charging fearlessly on its enemy; in its place was controlled manœuvre, still composed of charging horsemen, but all working to a known plan and all constantly under effective command.

He has been called vicious, but there is nothing that shows him to have been any more so than his contemporaries. He punished leaders who attacked him and ruthlessly liquidated them—indeed, had he not done so he would scarcely have survived himself—but to the rank and file who fought against him he was always lenient. These men he enrolled among his followers and in this way won their loyalty. His commanders were always Mongols, for these alone he fully trusted. Men so won over soon discovered that his word was to be relied upon, that he could be trusted and that he would always stand by them. He laid down the rule that all must be prepared to face death rather than to abandon a comrade. He applied this on more than one occasion in his own conduct and made it clear in the law that any who forsook a comrade should be punished by death.

When, pocketing his pride, he sought the assistance of the Khan of the Keraits he had shown political wisdom and demonstrated his ability to see himself in perspective. He had seen the dangers of attempting to ride roughshod over his chieftains and had learned how to consult and take counsel while safeguarding his position as leader. He had established a system of loyal servitude not unlike the feudal system practised in England in which the barons owed their allegiance to the King as did the villeins too, but through their barons. He never forgot that he was an aristocrat by birth and he made a conscious effort to attract the aristocracy of the Steppes to his banner. He saw that in this way he could win prestige, for among his people custom and order of precedence were always observed. He had achieved much. Indeed it might be assumed that he had achieved all and even more than he had set out to do. Would he be content or would the lust for power drive him on to further conquests?

7 Jenghiz Khan—The Conqueror

What were the circumstances in which Jenghiz Khan and his followers now found themselves? The latter believed they had reached the goal of their desires and so, perhaps, could Jenghiz Khan. His realm stretched over a thousand miles from the Khingan Mountains to the Altais; and in depth it was nearly seven hundred miles from the Onon to the Tangut States of Hsi-Hsia. There were hundreds of thousands of souls ready to obey his every command and all in his tents were content to be his chosen followers. Great were the orgies and great the rejoicings in the Mongol camps. Yet the Khakan, with memories of the past still fresh in his mind, had sterner things to think on. What he had gained must be consolidated, not only on the basis of military preparedness but also on foundations of good administration and of law and order.

So it was to Tatatungo, the Uighur whom Jenghiz Khan had already made Keeper of the Seal, that he dictated a Code of Laws, thus committing them to writing for the first time. These Jenghiz Khan laid down, were to be binding on all who served him now as well as on those who, as yet unborn, were to follow. In marked contrast to Mahmud of Ghazni or Muhammad Ghuri who left no written constitution, he was handing down to posterity a code that lived for centuries after his passing. These laws have come down to us and it is a matter of historical fact that the Yasak, as they were called, formed the foundation on which nearly three hundred years later Babur, the Great Moghul, established his rule in India.

To Shigi Qutuku, a disciple of Tatatungo, he assigned the role of Chief Justice of the Realm with authority to handle all cases of fraud, theft or any other breach of the law, that law that was to become the pillar of all subsequent Mongolian legal procedures.

To Bogurchi, who, when a boy nearly thirty years earlier, had helped him recover his lost horses, he assigned the supreme command of his army with the title which went with the office of Kuluk, the highest in the kingdom. Always anxious to maintain control over the landed aristocracy, he decided to form a *corps d'élite* from the sons of his chieftains and other dignitaries. These he formed into a large personal bodyguard, a household brigade from which he could draw to fill important posts as they fell vacant. In this way he intended to bind to himself the youth of the aristocracy while, at the same time, these sons of the nobility serving in his horde would be hostages for good behaviour among their parents.

He established an officers' corps in which his Mongols held the commanding posts. This was a practice he always adhered to, however large and diversified his forces became. He set up a school or academy for the training of leaders which all who were called upon were, on pain of death, forced to attend. He introduced a system of 'arrow' messengers who had complete priority wherever they rode; even the highest princes in the land had to make way for them when the sound of their horses' bells were heard. They were trained to ride by day and night and to cross areas in a few days which normally would take weeks to traverse. This system not only enabled him to make his wishes known throughout his realm, but it ensured that he always received immediate warning of happenings far afield. In war it made it possible to communicate with widely dispersed elements of his army, to concentrate when required and gave a flexibility that later surprised and astounded his enemies. His army consisted entirely of horsemen who could always outmanœuvre the slower-moving hostile infantry.

Jenghiz Khan was one of the first monarchs to emancipate women. He gave to the wives of his soldiers responsibilities which went with privileges. They were to be responsible for their husbands' accoutrements and service clothing, for preparing the salted meat which formed the basis of their service rations and for looking after their homes and the land when the army was fighting. Denuded of men in war, it was the women who ran the country; for when Jenghiz Khan went to war he took all his fighting men with him, where they would be less of a liability than they might be if plotting behind his back while he was away. In relationship to their women he insisted on the highest standards of moral conduct, failure to observe which was punishable by death; but with these primitive people moral standards were generally high.

Experience leaves its mark on most men and often the stronger the character the deeper rooted are these effects. What were the results of past experience on Jenghiz Khan's military thinking? Sufficient has been said to show that he had learned how to organise the military and administrative framework of his new kingdom. When a man has behind him a record of military successes it is only reasonable to suppose that his outlook will be influenced by these, and so one asks whether, in the past campaigns, there were any discernible patterns that could lead to a forecast for the future. He had always appeared to take the offensive with a view to gaining the initiative; yet, though tactically offensive, his battles were in fact fought for defensive reasons. They were fought in order to regain or to hold a position and the gains that had resulted were incidental. For example, his campaign against the Merkits had been to rescue his wife; he had been forced to attack the Keraits only after he was convinced they intended to attack him; and his war against the Naimans was fought for the same reason. Hard experience had taught him that powerful neighbours could become powerful enemies. In an age when might was right it paid to be mighty. If, therefore, a neighbour posed a threat to his security, as in the case of the Naimans, he attacked in a pre-emptive bid to save himself. If there is any conclusion to be drawn from these wars it is that, foreseeing a danger, he was always prepared to take the initiative. In fact he believed in the policy of pre-emptive war and experience had proved this paid. Though he did not seem to seek power for power's sake, he certainly realised that it was in the proper exercise of power that security lay. So, always alert to the possibility of hostility by those surrounding him, Jenghiz Khan now gave thought to his position relative to his new neighbours. Who were these and to what extent would or could any of them be considered a risk to his security?

Their historic background is important as from this, to no small extent, their subsequent attitude to Jenghiz Khan becomes intelligible. The old Chinese Empire of the T'ang Dynasty which, so it was picturesquely said, extended from the regions of perpetual ice to the regions of perpetual sun, had disintegrated. The first break occurred in the tenth century when the Khitais formed their own kingdom on the borders of the Yellow Sea. It is from them that the term Cathay was derived and applied by Europeans generally as referring to northern China. About a hundred and twenty years prior to Jenghiz Khan's time the Chin Tartars, coming down from the north, overran the Khitai country as far south as the Yangtze. The Chins adopted Chinese customs and Chinese culture, but they were never liked and were always regarded as usurpers. When they invaded northern China some of the Khitais remained, forming the province of Khitai (Kitan); the others, refusing to submit, migrated westwards.

Lying between the Gobi Desert and Tibet were the Hsi-Hsia people who had been ruled on behalf of the Chinese emperors by Tangut princes acting as viceroys. These princes eventually revolted and formed their own independent kingdom. Their civilisation was based more closely on Tibet than on China, though their administration and their army were founded on Chinese systems. They regarded the Mongols as rough and uncouth and certainly inferior to themselves.

Though this disintegration of the old Chinese Empire left the Sung emperors with a sadly depleted realm bound by the Yangtze, it was the only genuine Chinese Kingdom. The Chin empire with its capital at Peking, though nominally Chinese, was not truly so.

Those Khitais who had moved westwards sought the protection of the Uighurs in whose country, under their prince, Ta-shih, they organised an army. Ta-shih embarked on a career of conquest that ultimately established a kingdom stretching from the Hsi-Hsia and Uighur lands to the borders of Afghanistan. To the Muslims these people were known as the Kara-Khitai or Black Cathayans.

These, then, were Jenghiz Khan's neighbours. Had he anything to fear, any grounds for misgivings? Two factors affected judgement on this issue. One was the justifiable or imagined fears of Jenghiz Khan, and the other was the matter of the personality of the Chin emperor. It would be surprising indeed if the convulsions in Mongolia had gone unnoticed in the Emperor's court, but Mongolia was far beyond the Great Wall of China and between the Chin Empire and the Mongols were the peaceful and friendly Ongut people. Nevertheless, the old emperor at Peking, Ch'ang Tsung, had been wondering what was happing to his Chow-Churi or Warden, who, incidentally, was getting behind with his tribute. Therefore he sent his nephew, Prince Yuen-Chi, into the distant lands to discover what the situation was. The erstwhile Khan, Temüjin, was now the great Jenghiz Khan and so, arriving at the time when the Mongols were still celebrating, the Prince received a somewhat discourteous reception. He made a poor impression on the Khakan, who, nevertheless, presented him with all the appropriate gifts. When subsequently this prince succeeded the Emperor, both he and Jenghiz Khan had reason to recall this meeting.

The Peking government, though accustomed to periodic raids from the Tartars of the northern regions, had never been worried by the Mongols as a people. The Peking policy had been designed primarily to perpetuate the inter-tribal jealousies among the Tartar and Mongol clans. Thus the Chinese purpose was not to divide and rule but to divide and rest secure. Peking regarded these wild northern races as tributary people whom it was prepared to leave alone only so long as they behaved themselves. The Mongols on their part had always had the greatest respect for their southern neighbours whose military strength they recognised as far superior to their own.

Much trade by Muslim merchants between the Mongols and the Chins had taken place, and relations, anyhow on the surface, could be said to have been good. Through these Muslim traders Jenghiz Khan learned much of the Chin Chinese, of their country and their customs. His curiosity in this, as in all matters, was insatiable. He learned of the great size of the cities—a type of human habitation entirely strange to him and his tent-dwelling followers—he heard of the armies they possessed and of the almost inexhaustible resources of manpower they had. In spite of this he did not consider that militarily they were a threat; rather did he fear their cunning. They could, and he thought would, try to sow discontent among his newly won following, to stimulate rebellion and, although he felt that in the immediate future he might be able to handle this, would his children be so capable? Perhaps the greatest danger would lie in their setting one son against the other. The conclusion that he reached was that in Peking a real source of danger lay, a danger that at some time and in some way he must combat.

Of his other neighbours the Onguts he knew were friendly and he had nothing to fear from the Uighurs. The Hsi-Hsia state he held in much the same contempt that they held him. In no circumstances would they be likely to constitute a threat to Mongol security. Yet it was these people whom Jenghiz Khan decided to attack. It has been suggested that he did this to test his ability to deal with a Chinese trained and possibly led army. Although there is no evidence to indicate his true object, there is no doubt that from this campaign he learned much that would help him in the attack on the Chins which he now contemplated. His invasion met with initial success, but when he reached the walled city of Volohai he came across something that his tactics were powerless against. Against bricks and mortar his wild horsemen were useless; manœuvre in the open was one thing, but to his cost he learned that siege warfare was another. He was quick to appreciate that the hazards of a direct assault would cost him dear and even then would be no guarantee of success. Eventually he took the place by a ruse and there followed a patched-up peace which did not last. He invaded the wretched country a second time and this time was able to obtain a lasting treaty, the terms of which included tribute and a pledge of military assistance if required. As an earnest, the Tangut prince gave his daughter to Jenghiz Khan as wife.

News now arrived of the death of the old emperor at Peking and that he had been succeeded by his nephew, Yuen-Chi. While on his way back to the Onon, Jenghiz Khan stopped to receive a delegation from the new emperor. By his peremptory treatment of the delegation he showed his contempt for Yuen-Chi and he refused the customary obeisances to his representative. In spite of this provocation Yuen-Chi's reaction was so negative that Jenghiz Khan had plenty of time to consider his action and to perfect such plans as he had by then developed.

If it was to be war what form should this take? To make deep and punishing raids into Chin territory would not be beyond his means and the loot that would result could be considerable, but he was not concerned with loot for his goal was the seat of government, the capital at Peking, as only by overrunning this could he ensure against the threat which he was now sure existed. The task was a frightening and a formidable one.

Whereas his army was entirely mounted, that of the Chins consisted almost exclusively of infantry; he thus possessed the advantages of superior mobility. His troops were trained to operate on extremely wide frontages, and, when required to do so, could concentrate with great rapidity; this would give him the advantages of surprise, an all-important factor in his tactics. Although mobility would give him great advantages on the plains and in the open country, his lack of infantry would mean that walled cities and fortifications could present him with problems to which as yet he had no answer. Numerically he was much the weaker; he could muster some two hundred thousand riders behind whom there were no reserves, whereas the armies of the Chins were supported by a population of the order of fifty million. In a war of attrition he was almost bound to lose. Though he had the utmost contempt for the young emperor as a man and as a leader, yet he knew that the Chins were good administrators and that their generals were men of ability. The Great Wall of China was an obstacle of considerable dimensions, but it was not impassable. It was the Chins' inexhaustible strength in manpower that gave him most cause for anxiety. Such were the factors, they were daunting and scarcely reassuring.

Whatever forebodings he had, in the spring of 1211 he launched his campaign, one that, although eventually successful, lasted many years. Moving his armies on an enormously wide front, a policy to no small extent dictated by the necessity of living on the country, he exploited his mobility to the full and unquestionably achieved surprise. His main army was directed on Peking, while three others crossed the Great Wall over a hundred miles further west. Caught unawares by this move, the Chin infantry, which had been positioned for the defence of the capital, was now directed towards the new threat, thus placing itself between Jenghiz Khan's main body and the outflanking armies to the west. In the action which ensued the Chin army was defeated for the first time.

However, Peking was the objective and so the Mongol armies now converged on the capital. The Chins prayed that the enemy would assault the city, confident in their ability to withstand attack. But Jenghiz Khan would not be drawn; for he, too, could see that the task would be beyond his power, having neither the equipment nor the technique for siege warfare. He contented himself with riding round the walls out of range of the Chin weapons. A campaign that had started so successfully was now dragging on with the goal, Peking, standing defiant like the Rock of Gibraltar. Jenghiz Khan

was disillusioned and now thought seriously of returning to the
Onon.

It was at this point that quite unexpectedly he received a visit
from a Chin general, a Chinese, who whether by design or inepti-
tude gave him invaluable information. In the first instance he
learned that his victories had caused greater consternation in the
capital than he had realised. He also became aware for the first time
of the true weakness of the Chin regime and that many Chinese
were lukewarm, if not actively disloyal, to the Emperor. Of equal
significance was the fact that the Prince of Liao in the province of
Khitai, whose people for historic reasons had every reason to hate
the Chins, was prepared to join forces with him. Greatly heartened,
the Mongol went into winter quarters near the Great Wall where
he would be safe from surprise attack, yet well placed for the following year's campaign.

That was the turning point. From then on he had the Khitai
people as allies and he had ever-growing Chinese co-operation. He
mastered the technique of siege warfare, which enabled him to take
city after city. Within three years he overran the provinces of Chili,
Shansi and Shantung and his hordes invaded Korea and Khitai,
where they were received as liberators. As the cities fell to him, he
spared them and their garrisons if they came over to him, otherwise
they were razed to the ground. Peking, however, continued to fight
on, even though one of the Chin generals revolted and murdered the
Emperor. Later the rebel was unseated and a new emperor, Hsuan-
tsung, was placed on the throne; but the kingdom was toppling and
the end, it seemed, could not be postponed for long.

Jenghiz Khan, too, was wearying of the war. It was true that
his main objective, Peking, had not been taken, but his armies had
roamed the country at will, burning, destroying and pillaging each
city that attempted to hold out against him. He had lost many men
and now pestilence had commenced further to reduce his numbers.
Believing the moment propitious, he sent an envoy to the Emperor
with a message that clearly showed how tired he was of the war.
Recalling that all the provinces north of the Hoang-ho or Yellow
River were in his hands and that little was left save his capital, he
did not wish to push the Emperor yet further for fear of what
heaven might say of him. Fearing the wrath of heaven, he would
prefer to withdraw his army, and, this being so, could the Emperor

not make some gift to the Mongol generals to content them with this decision? At a Crown Council held at Peking the Emperor obtained agreement on the terms which were to be offered. These included a general amnesty, a promise that the Khitai prince was to be recognised as the independent ruler of Liao-tung and, finally, the Emperor was to give one of his daughters to Jenghiz Khan as wife. All this was agreed and by the end of the spring of 1214 a peace was signed.

Jenghiz Khan yearned to return to his beloved streams in the Khingan Mountains, but as it was now late and too hot to cross the Gobi Desert he went into camp at an oasis at Dolon-nor. This, as events turned out, was fortunate for the Mongol had misjudged the resilience of his adversaries. Soon rumours reached him indicating that Hsuan-tsung was proposing to move his capital from Peking to Kai-feng fu, on the southern bank of the Hoang-ho River; while, in order to ensure stability in the northern provinces, the Crown Prince and the general, Prince Wan-yen, were to remain in Peking. Unless he had warlike intentions, why, thought Jenghiz Khan, should he take these steps? At about the same time an envoy arrived at Dolon-nor from the Sung emperor, expressing the latter's concern about the move of the Chin capital, only to be told that Jenghiz Khan now considered himself at peace with Hsuan-tsung. A little after this some Khitai troops, who formed part of the Chin emperor's bodyguard, revolted and, in complete violation of their recently signed treaty, the Chins attacked Liao-tung. The Khitais sent delegates to the Khakan reminding him that they were his vassals and asking for his help. Many Chinese troops, who wished neither to side with the Chins nor the Khitais but only with the Mongols, now placed themselves under Jenghiz Khan's orders.

All these incidents made it inevitable that Jenghiz Khan should reopen the war. With characteristic vigour he despatched one army under Mukuli to the aid of the Prince of Liao, another under Sabutai to Korea and a third southwards to assist the revolting Khitai guards.

Mukuli's Army found Liao-tung already in the hands of the Emperor's troops, but the viceroy whom he had sent from Kai-feng fu had as yet not arrived. Blocking all the roads to the capital, Mukuli apprehended the viceroy and, as town after town came over to his banner, the whole of Khitai was soon purged of Chin troops.

Hsuan-tsung at this juncture decided to bring the Crown Prince down from Peking to join him on the Hoang-ho, which, as his general Prince Wan-yen predicted, resulted in the northern provinces laying down their arms, save for Peking, which continued to hold out. Jenghiz Khan by now had some forty-six divisions of Chinese soldiers fighting with him, but wisely he distributed these throughout his army where they would be under Mongol command. The army he had despatched to the south joined up with the revolting Khitai guards and with them marched on Peking. This brave city held out throughout the winter, but eventually had to give in. With five thousand Mongol soldiers, and the Chinese who had joined him, Mukuli took the city. This marked the end of the struggle and, defeated on every front, the once proud Chin Empire was no more than a shadow.

Laden with booty beyond their wildest dreams, the hordes withdrew to the Onon. Before he departed, Jenghiz Khan left Mukuli in control of the country as his viceroy with twenty-three thousand Mongols and twenty thousand Khitais under his command. The object had been achieved and the fear was gone which he had nursed; the southern flank seemed to be secure.

However one looks at this campaign one cannot help but be impressed by its scale. Here was a comparatively small and newly formed nation going to war with one of the greatest kingdoms of the period; a war in which ultimately it was victorious. Not only had Jenghiz Khan shown that he possessed all the elements of great generalship, he had shown that he had a keen political vision. He had been quick to see the weaknesses in the Chin imperialism and he had exploited these weaknesses, driving wedges between the Chins and the Khitais and exploiting the Sung fear of their northern neighbours. Though at first feeling his ground cautiously, he made friends with the Sung emperor and, from that time onwards the Chinese in the lands north of the Yangtze were his allies, which was a great political achievement. Militarily he had achieved strategical surprise and by his exploitation of his inherent mobility had thrown his opponent off balance. He overcame the difficulties of dealing with large walled cities and fortified places. The breadth of his operations showed a master-mind able to direct while not personally commanding his widely dispersed forces. When his short-lived peace broke down he directed his operations from his camp at

Dolon-nor, never himself even putting foot on Chinese soil. Like Nelson before the Battle of the Nile, he had, with his arrow messengers, perfected a system of communications that gave him a control as beneficial to himself as it was baffling to his opponents.

This war was undertaken for self-preservation and not with a view to conquest. None the less, like so many of his other campaigns, this is precisely what is achieved. That his fears of and mistrust in Chinese policy were justified history bore witness. When later the Mongols, through internal dissensions, grew weak and the Ming Dynasty was strong, the latter incited Mongol against Mongol, sowing mistrust among the proud nomadic tribes, but this time there was no Jenghiz Khan to save them.

Finally one cannot leave Jenghiz Khan's Chinese War without referring to his attitude towards Buddhism and religion generally. In his campaign against the Tangut prince of Hsi-Hsia he had met many Tibetan Buddhists, but there is no record of any effect these had on him and whether this was due to preoccupation or sheer lack of interest cannot be told. That he was, however, deeply interested in religious philosophies this story, as well as his later association with the Taoist Master Ch'ang-Ch'un, leaves in no doubt. The incident I am about to recount originated when a Zin priest, living in the city of Lan Ch'ang, recorded with pleasure his having met the great Khan. This, however, was an obvious mistake, as Jenghiz Khan was not on this front and it must be assumed that it was one of his sons to whom the priest referred. This incident of itself might not mean much, but read with the later experiences of the same monk it takes on a more meaningful light. Three years after, when the city was again occupied, Mukuli with two Chinese generals met the same priest with his young disciple, Hai Yun, with whom they had many talks. Interested in the philosophy dividing the two opposing Buddhist schools, the Zins and the Doctrines, they asked Hai Yun which he followed. His reply was that, like the two wings of a bird, both, though quite different, were equally important; an argument which he aptly pointed out applied with equal force to soldiers and scholars, both being indispensable to the state. Mukuli, fascinated by this and with their talks generally, sent a detailed report to Jenghiz Khan, whose reply, sent through his chamberlains, Toisabuka and Ma-lai, is reported as follows: 'From what your messengers have told me it appears that the old reverend one and the young reverend one are both true speakers to Heaven. Feed and clothe them well, and if you find any others of the same sort gather them all in and let them speak to Heaven as much as they will. They are not to be treated with disrespect by any one and are to rank as Mongol freemen.'[1]

It is remarkable that in the midst of a great campaign, and when his mind was concentrated on what history calls a ruthless war, his interest should have been so keenly aroused in a theological philosophy. His attitude was certainly not that of a crude barbarian, but rather of a discerning mind. He was in his fifty-third year.

[1] Li Ch'ih-Ch'ang: *The Travels of an Alchemist.*

8 *Jenghiz Khan—The Emperor*

It is from this stage that Jenghiz Khan's sons played an increasingly important part in his military achievements. These sons were Jöchi, Chaghatai, Ögetei and Toli. So many oriental monarchs mistrusted their heirs on the basis that they or those supporting them would promote revolt. Jenghiz Khan, on the other hand, placed great trust in his sons, giving them high command, directing but not interfering with their execution of it. If he felt there was need for advice he attached one of his elder Orlok as a chief of staff or adviser.

During the campaigns in China the Merkits had raided the Mongol borderlands; so, when he returned to the Onon, one of his first acts was to despatch his eldest son Jöchi to settle once and for all the account with the Merkits. To Jöchi as adviser he attached the wise Orlok, Subetei. Jöchi's campaign was short and successful, after which he moved on to the Steppe country of the Kipchaks, where he consolidated his hold on the territory which his father had previously made over to him. It was Jöchi who founded the dynasty of the Khans of the Golden Horde, whose kingdom stretched ultimately from Poland across Russia to the Urals, and by whose grace for years the Princes of Russia ruled.

Jenghiz Khan, through a tangled set of circumstances, found himself involved with the Kara-Khitai with whom he had never had any real contact and certainly no quarrel. These people were now

F

ruled by a Naiman, Kuchluk, an old enemy of the Mongol who had
fled before him when the latter defeated the Naiman army. Kuchluk,
having sought the protection of the King of Kara-Khitai, turned with
characteristic treachery on his benefactor and usurped the throne.
A Nestorian Christian, originally, he had, through the influence of
his wife, turned Lamaist. His reign was harsh. The majority of his
population outside the urban districts were Muslim, whom he treated
badly, confiscating their property and destroying and closing their
mosques. Jenghiz Khan mistrusted Kuchluk, and sent Jebei the
Arrow with twenty thousand men to help the Muslims. He had instructions to reopen the mosques and was otherwise left to do as he
thought fit. With the Muslims fighting on his side Jebei easily defeated Kuchluk, who, hounded by his pursuers, fled to the Pamirs
where he was ultimately killed.

Though Jenghiz Khan, now styling himself emperor, controlled
an immense domain stretching as far as the borders of Transoxania,
he did not seem to have any desire to extend his kingdom. In fact
he embarked on a plan of peaceful co-existence with his neighbour,
Ala-ad-din Muhammad, Shah of Khwarazm, whose vast kingdom
extended from Transoxania to the Arabian Sea. Although these two
men had never met an understanding grew up between them and a
treaty of mutual trade was drawn up. Jenghiz Khan's message in
this connection gives an indication of his peaceful intent. In sending
his greetings he paid the usual polite tribute to the Shah's power
and, whilst referring to his own strong position, made it clear that
he had no territorial ambitions and he took it, he said, that they
each had a mutual interest in encouraging trade between their two
peoples. The message was well received, trade did commence and,
save for the foolishness of one man, all might have been well.

A party of Mongol traders who were passing through Transoxania were detained by the governor of Otrar, who, without any justification and believing them to be spies, had them put to death. When
Jenghiz Khan heard this he was very justifiably enraged. He sent
a mission to the Shah demanding that the governor responsible
should be punished. Muhammad, far from agreeing, beheaded the
leader of the mission and sent the remainder back without their
beards. This combination of foolishness and misunderstanding
marked the end of a period that had seemed to portend nothing but
good. As a result, war was inevitable; a war which was destined to

last for four years and result in the collapse and disappearance of the great Khwarazm Empire; a war that ended with Jenghiz Khan's possessions extending from the River Indus and the Arabian Sea to the lower water of the Dnieper.

To Jenghiz Khan this was a campaign of vengeance, and it would call for every man that he could muster. He despatched his famous arrow messengers to all his peoples with instructions to muster for a campaign the objects of which he made plain. All from the age of sixteen to sixty were to take up arms, including those from Kara-Khitai and the Kipchak Steppes.

Jenghiz Khan's army was still predominantly cavalry, but in addition he now had yaks and camels for the carriage of his heavier equipment, while for siege work he had Chinese artillery. For the erection of siege towers and for bridging there were engineers with all the necessary paraphernalia. In all these matters he had learned and profited from his experiences in the Chin War. For the long marches, with each of his armies he had quartermasters for the selection of and preparation for camps. His riders had three spare horses, a bow, two quivers, and a javelin on which was a hook for unseating riders. Jenghiz Khan had a well-balanced army, equipped and prepared for any task, whether the crossing of great rivers or the capturing of walled cities.

By the spring of 1219 this great force assembled near the upper waters of the Irtysh in the Uighur country. Here they awaited the melting of the worst of the snows. This was a war of hate, for no man had murdered a Mongol without paying the price and the Islamic kingdom of the Shah was to pay that price. In his object the Khakan had the whole-hearted support of his Orlok whom he consulted in all details of the plan. In this atmosphere a campaign started that was destined to be as startling in its immediate results as it was far-reaching in its consequences.

The initial plan had been to advance across the well-worn route used by the nomad tribesmen from Central Asia to the Syr-Darya, which involved the crossing of about four hundred miles of waterless waste. Jebei the Arrow, however, discovered another road which, crossing the mountains by a pass between the Great Pamirs and the Tian Shans, led into the Fergana Valley and the headwaters of the Syr-Darya and thence into Khwarazm. With the agreement of the Orlok, Jenghiz Khan despatched Jöchi with Jebei to explore this route while he with the main force went by the road to the north. His armies here were led by Chaghatai and Ogetei and his youngest son, Toli, remained with him. Hearing that Toli had suffered a set-back, he instructed Jebei with a small force to move farther to the south and make for the upper waters of the Amu-Darya, while in the meantime his main armies continued their advance.

As in the case of his invasion of China, Jenghiz Khan was operating on a broad front, with his widely deployed armies, like the arms of an octopus, seeking out the enemy and attacking him where he was least expecting it. In the north the armies of Chaghatai and Ögetei crossed the Syr-Darya above Otrar, which they besieged and took; in the centre Jenghiz Khan with his youngest son Toli advanced on Bukhara, which fell; in the Fergana Valley Jöchi, taking Khojend, pushed on; and in the south Jebei invaded Khwarazm via the Amu-Darya. Assaulted on all fronts, his principal cities fallen and with the initiative lost, the Shah faced utter defeat.

It was at the fall of Bukhara that Jenghiz Khan was reported to have stood on the steps of the principal mosque shouting to his followers: 'The hay is cut, give your horses fodder.' The ravenous men needed no second invitation to plunder, the city was sacked and the inhabitants either escaped beyond the walls or were compelled to submit to infamies worse than death itself.

The Shah's armies defeated in battle and his people all seized with terror, his will to fight evaporated. He fled to Merv where he received no support. Jenghiz Khan sent Jebei with the experienced Sübetei in pursuit and for weeks they followed the wretched man. They searched Merv, Herat and a number of smaller places which for the most part they left undisturbed. Their quarry, in constant fear of death, lacked both the courage or will to fight, and each night, dreading an attempt on his life, was forced to sleep in a different place. Now a sovereign in no more than name, he fled unashamedly across what had been his realm. His mother and harem were captured, as were his crown jewels and treasures, all of which were sent to Samarkand where Jenghiz Khan had established his headquarters. Beyond Qazvin the pursuers lost the trail and so they split into several small parties. One encountered him, but, though wounded, he managed to escape. Reaching the Caspian, he took to a boat and landed on a small island. Here, a broken man, he died. This once great emperor was so poor that those who were with him could not even provide him with a shroud and he was buried in the clothes he wore. His escape had been reported to Jenghiz Khan, who in the meantime had sent Jöchi on a fruitless search in the area between the Caspian and Aral seas.

Many of the sheikhs, the emirs and imams with their retainers now went over to Jenghiz Khan, who pursued the policy he had so often adopted in the past, of dividing and ruling. From the sheikhs and emirs he appointed governors or viceroys acting in his name; but he had not reckoned on two elements. The first was the unreliability of the people with whom he was dealing—so different from the Chinese, on whose word he could rely. The second was the strength of character of Jalal-ad-din, the Shah's son, who by his leadership was able to rally the hitherto wavering peoples. Feeling that they had one in whom they could place their trust, they switched their loyalties to join what for them was to be a Holy War.

There had been signs of discontent among some of the Mongols' allies and so Jenghiz Khan deemed it avisable to let the Uighurs and others return to their homes. Of his own trusted Mongol army he had thirty thousand men detached with Jebei and Sübetai, and a further fifty thousand were with Jöchi heading north. Without withdrawing these forces he could not muster much more than a hundred thousand on his own front. This was the position when he began to receive reports of small risings, even of murders of his appointed native officials, of attacks on isolated posts and of revolts in other outlying places. His peaceful plan was not working out and vigorous action would be essential if his position was not to become untenable.

What followed has been referred to as a 'war of annihilation'. First he despatched Toli with half his army to Khorasan with orders not just to maintain order but to exterminate. Toli reached Merv early in 1221 and the city surrendered, the inhabitants passively obeying the orders to assemble beyond the walls of the city, where, according to reports, all were butchered. Toli then moved on to Nisapur, whose famous buildings, colleges and libraries were razed to the ground. Herat was taken, but Toli's heart softened, and this city, for the time at least, escaped the terrible fate of the others.

After the fall of Herat, Toli was instructed to join his father at Badakhshan in northern Afghanistan, where he was making preparations for a campaign against Jalal-ad-din, who, in the meantime, had established himself at Ghazni where he received a tumultuous welcome. Jenghiz Khan, advancing southwards, first attacked Bamian on the road to Ghazni. It was shortly after this that Jalal-ad-din fought his first and only successful engagement with the Mongols. Jenghiz Khan, to cover his move to Ghazni, had placed a strong flank guard to protect him during his march through the Hindu Kush. It was against this flank guard and from the direction of Pervan that the young shah put in his attack which was of sufficient strength to call for the personal intervention of the Great Khan himself. An interesting sidelight is thrown on this incident which underlines its importance. In the Chinese account of the visit of the Taoist Master to Jenghiz Khan there is a description of how, just as the time was arriving for the meeting to take place, news came in of the Persian attack. In the words of the narrator: 'The Emperor was determined to deal with them himself and put off the meeting till the first of the tenth month.'[1]

In spite of his tactical success at Pervan, the Shah was forced to withdraw through the Khyber Pass, hard-pressed by the Mongols. Following an heroic stand on the banks of the Indus in the vicinity of Peshawar, the Muslim army was able to get away. Jalal-ad-din, fighting to the last, plunged into the dangerous river on his horse and under the eyes of Jenghiz Khan succeeded in reaching the far bank. It was then that the Mongol leader remarked that it seemed difficult to understand that such a father as Muhammad should have produced such a son. He held up Jalal-ad-din's courage and resolution as an example to his own sons. The Shah escaped to Delhi and was never caught, but the Mongols ravaged the country as far as Lahore before they eventually returned to Ghazni.

In the meantime Jebei and Sübetei had advanced through Azerbaijan into Georgia, where they overran the Circassians and defeated a Kipchak army which they pursued to Astrakhan. They then pressed on to the River Don, and the Russians, hearing of the extraordinary victories of a mysterious and unknown people, whose name they did not even know, at the instigation of the Prince of Galicia assembled an army on the banks of the Dnieper. Here they received envoys from the Mongol camp whom they barbarously killed. The Mongol reply was typical. The Russians had killed Mongol envoys who had meant no harm; but, since they wished it, they should have

[1] Li Ch'ih-Ch'ang: *The Travels of an Alchemist.*

war and the impartial god must decide the issue. At a battle on the River Kaleza the Russians were defeated, and the Mongols, after ravaging Bulgaria, retired with their booty through Siskin to Mongolia, which they reached in 1224.

The following year Jenghiz Khan returned to the Onon after an absence of six years. And so this great campaign came to its close. Undertaken in a fit of rage to avenge a wrong, it ended in the annexation of Transoxania, Persia, Afghanistan, Baluchistan and India up to the line of the Indus, of all the territories to the shores of the Black Sea, of Bulgaria and the Volga Basin, six hundred miles north of the Caspian, as well as the whole of the Kipchak Steppes.

The interesting part of this campaign is not so much the extent of the conquests, important as these were, as the light that it throws on Jenghiz Khan's generalship. It was the breadth and extent of his vision that was so remarkable. While his general, Jebei, was conducting a war that took him across Georgia into Bulgaria, his eldest son was operating between the Caspian and the Sea of Aral, and another son, Toli, was invading India. To give an idea of the distances involved and the size of this canvas, it was two thousand five hundred miles from Lahore to the Dnieper and over two thousand miles from the Onon to Jenghiz Khan's headquarters at Samarkand. Unlike either Alexander or Napoleon, he did not conduct these campaigns himself, marching with his army concentrated from great battlefield to great battlefield. His sons, working under his broad direction, conducted their campaigns individually. This trait of his of placing confidence in his subordinates had run like a shaft of light throughout his career. Of all the great monarchs of these ages, he alone seemed to have no fear of his sons or subordinates, and rarely was there any evidence of their jealousy or rivalry. How was this? Such a degree of loyalty could never, surely, have been based on fear; rather did it spring from a confidence that was mutual and trust that was shared.

The Shah of Khwarazm had been fighting on his own territory, ground that he knew, and he had the advantage of being on interior lines. Jenghiz Khan, on the other hand, was far away from his own land at the end of an immensely long line of communication. He had deserts and snow-covered mountains to traverse and though he had a large army it was numerically no greater than his opponent's. Why, then, did the Shah fail? In war many a campaign has been lost by the incompetence of a commander, and, although this does not necessarily detract from the achievements of the victor, its importance as a contribution should not be overlooked. Three things are essential to success: a just appreciation of the ability and likely plan of action of the enemy; a well-thought-out plan of action that should force the enemy opponent to dance to one's tune; and, perhaps most important of all, the ability to retain the confidence of one's troops even in the hour of adversity. On all these counts the Shah failed. From the outset he underestimated the military skill of the Mongols, neither did he correctly assess their likely plan. He had, for example, distributed a large part of his army in the defence of cities under the impression that Jenghiz Khan would confine his operations to the open country, hitting the air, as it were, and doing no particular harm. He does not appear to have known of the Mongol campaign in China, nor did he realise that in their army were Chinese gunners and engineers with all the skill and equipment for assaulting fortresses and walled cities. His own plan seemed to possess no overall strategy, but rather to consist of piecemeal unco-ordinated operations. There was no effort to draw his opponent on to ground of his own choosing and there to fight a battle as he had designed it. In stark contrast the Mongol plan was diversified yet designed to a specific end. Finally, through lack of personal courage and military skill, the Shah had forfeited the confidence of his followers, who fell from him as rapidly as they later rallied to his son.

Finally, although this campaign resulted in a gigantic extension to the Mongol Empire, Jenghiz Khan had not set out with this goal in view. His avowed intention had been to punish the Shah and when he had done this he was only too anxious, by putting his trust in the Muslim sheikhs and other leaders, to achieve a peaceful settlement. He had done this with the Merkits, the Keraits and the Chinese; it was, therefore, nothing new. While at war this remarkable man had conversed with imams and other religious leaders on the basis of their beliefs, seeking to find out for himself the secret of eternal life. Finally near Samarkand he summoned the Taoist Master to talk to him, from two thousand miles away.

9 Jenghiz Khan and the Alchemist

Perhaps one of the most remarkable characteristics of Jenghiz Khan was his ability to detach himself from the detail of battle and to think on deeper things, and nothing exemplified this more than his action in sending for the Taoist Master to discuss with him the issues and secrets of perpetual life, whatever this might mean. How could a man do this who, above everything else, was a protagonist of the absolute, whether in war or political intent? Concentration on the objective of the moment is normally considered essential to success and such concentration has generally characterised the great captains of history.

One of the sayings attributed to Jenghiz Khan would seem to indicate that lust and the desire to conquer alone motivated him, 'The greatest joy,' he was reported to have said, 'a man can know is to conquer his enemies and drive them before him. To ride their horses and take away their possessions. To see the faces of those who were dear to them bedewed with tears and to clasp their wives and daughters in his arms.'[1] Yet, when he had fought the Kara-Khitai, the Khitais and the Chinese he had shown that, so far from wishing to do all these things, once his object had been achieved, he only wanted to make friends and bury enmity. His treatment of and instructions to his generals concerning the Buddhist monks was understanding and humanitarian. There was, in fact, another side

[1] Michael Prawdin: *The Mongol Empire.*

to this apparently remorseless man, and this is borne out by the
story told in the *Travels of an Alchemist*[1] The *Hsi Yu Chi*, to give
this work its Chinese name, was the day-to-day diary of the secretary to the Taoist Master, Ch'ang Ch'un. It is unique in its importance as a source of early Mongol history and it has an especial
interest for the light that it throws on the cultural and geographical
detail of the Mongolia of this period. Starting from the crowded
Chinese plains, it takes one through the lands of the Mongol nomads
with their wagons and flocks, their quaint fur-trimmed coats and
weird head-dress, to the turbaned Muslim farmers, and, finally, to
the jostling cosmopolitan people of Samarkand and the fierce tribesmen of Afghanistan.

It was in the spring of 1219, when Jenghiz Khan was assembling
his vast army before he set out for Khwarazm on a campaign the
full significance of which he could not have known, that he sent his
personal minister, Liu Wen, for the Taoist Heavenly Master or
Adept, Ch'ang Ch'un, with implicit instructions to bring the holy
man back with him. Ch'ang Ch'un was then in eastern China, somewhere between Peking and the Yellow Sea, some two thousand miles
away. That the journey would take a long time Jenghiz Khan knew,
for in his instructions to Liu Wen he said that, though the journey
might take years, he was not to return empty-handed.

This Liu Wen, sometimes called Liu Chung Lu, had entered
the Khakan's service much earlier as a herbalist, but he had become
so highly regarded that he had attained the position of a personal
minister. To ensure the Taoist Master's safety on the journey,
Jenghiz Khan gave Liu Wen a golden tablet on which was written
words to the effect that the bearer was empowered to act as the
Khakan might act if he were there in person. No greater authority
could be given to a man and it indicated both Jenghiz Khan's trust
in his emissary and the importance he attached to meeting the
Taoist Master. It was a remarkable act on the part of a general on
the eve of a great campaign. Why did he do it?

A simple explanation might be that as a great monarch he felt
he should be supported by an equally great sage. But this is not born
out by the conversations that did take place nor by the fact that the
Taoist Master was allowed to return to his own country, though
Jenghiz Khan did not want him to. We know that the Khakan had

[1] Li Ch'ih-Ch'ang: *The Travels of an Alchemist.*

shown a keen interest in the philosophy of the Buddhists and later of the Muslims. What aspects of Taoism attracted him?

The strength of the cult was said to consist in the fact that, as opposed to Buddhism, it had a definite ecclesiastical organisation controlled by a head who was called the Heavenly Master or Adept and who, by some Europeans, has been called the Taoist Pope. Over a long period of time they had produced a mass of scriptural writings and had assembled texts and doctrines both philosophic and pseudo-scientific on such matters as alchemy, astrology and divination. It is the Taoists' deep study of alchemy that is our particular interest. In the remote past the alchemists held the belief that certain substances, if absorbed into the body, could produce, if not perpetual life, certainly longevity. To the Taoist of the period with which we are concerned, and particularly to Ch'ang Ch'un, alchemy had come to mean not so much an experiment with chemicals as a system of mental re-education. That Ch'ung Ch'un was called an alchemist can, therefore, be misleading. To some it might infer that through chemicals or other means he had the key to eternal life. It was in all probability this misbelief that prompted Jenghiz Khan to send for him, as his first question was: 'Adept, what medicine of long life have you brought me from afar?'[1] Also Liu Wen, according to a Chinese report, had told Jenghiz Khan that the alchemist Ch'ang Ch'un was three hundred years old and had the power to teach others how to live to a similar age. It is, therefore, small wonder that when the Khakan wished to see Ch'ang Ch'un he should send as his emissary this same Liu Wen.

Ch'ang Ch'un was born in 1148, which made him fourteen years older than Jenghiz Khan. At the age of eighteen he had become a Taoist monk and had studied in the K'un-lun Mountains in Shantung. In the following year he became a pupil of Wang Cha, the founder of the 'Completely Subliminated Sect' of the Taoists. When, in 1170, Wang Cha died he was succeeded by Ch'ang Ch'un, whose reputation had by now spread across all northern China. At this time he lived in the T'ai-hsu Kuan temple where, in 1207, he was presented by the Chin Princess Yuan Fu with a complete copy of the Taoist canon. At the period when his voyage was undertaken he was the Heavenly Master or Adept.

He was seventy-two when, in 1220, he commenced his epic

[1] Ibid.

journey to the Mongol Emperor and on his arrival back at Shantung he was seventy-six. His travels, which in all took him across
seven thousand miles of country, over desert, mountains and
great rivers, through sand and through snow, were an undertaking
that would have thwarted many a younger man. Physically he was
impressive. Sun Hai, the Recluse, who wrote the preface to the
Travels of an Alchemist, gave his impressions on meeting him for the
first time and just before he set out. 'He sat with the rigidity of a
corpse, stood with the stiffness of a tree, moved swift as lightning
and walked like a whirlwind.'[1] He was, furthermore, struck by the
depth of his knowledge and the extent of his reading. He was impressed by Ch'ang Ch'un's accurate forecast of the time his
journey would take which, considering it was to be a matter of years
and not of months, was remarkable.

If one is impressed by one characteristic of Ch'ang Ch'un more
than another it is of his calmness under all circumstances, a calmness which often called for great moral courage. When, for instance,
on Jenghiz Khan's instructions he found that he would be travelling
with a number of girls who had been collected for the Khakan's
harem, he refused, saying, 'I do not think it right to expect me to
travel with harem girls.'[2] He, in fact, did not. On another occasion
when out hunting Jenghiz Khan's horse stumbled and he fell in front
of a wild boar. The Heavenly Master, instead of sympathising, re-
proached the Emperor, telling him that in the eyes of heaven life,
even of an animal, was a precious thing. To a Mongol hunting was
natural and indeed essential for food, but this did not deter Ch'ang
Ch'un. At the same time he had political sagacity. When, on his
return to his own country, he was told that unless the people of
Shantung unreservedly surrendered to the Mongols there might be
carnage and that a word from him might save much suffering he
conceded, saying that it was better to risk failure in an effort to
save life than to sit by and watch slaughter.

The emissary, Liu Wen, on reaching Peking learned that the
Heavenly Master was some four hundred miles further away than
he had expected, on the most southern point of the Yellow Sea at
Lai Ch'ou. He wanted to send a large body of soldiers for the safe
conduct of the Adept, but the local officials said this would be most

[1] Ibid.
[2] Ibid.

unwise, as at the time the Mongols and Chins were negotiating details of the peace treaty. They also considered it might alarm the local inhabitants just when they were beginning to settle down. Instead of a body of five thousand, Liu Wen, therefore, took merely twenty volunteers. He reached the Adept in December, nearly nine months after he had set out from the imperial camp.

Liu Wen's anxieties for the safety of the Adept were not without good foundation. The process of establishing complete control over northern China was long drawn out and, in fact, the Chin kingdom did not end until 1223 when the Emperor Sua Tsung died. It was only after that date that Jenghiz Khan's lands became conterminous with those of the Sung emperor. There were at this time large bands of brigands still roaming the countryside. Indeed, while the Adept was on the first part of his journey Liu Wen was forced to retrace his steps to deal with some four hundred horsemen who were harrying local people.

When the Adept received the invitation to visit the Emperor he knew that refusal was out of the question. He did, however, stipulate that he was not prepared to go until after the Feast of the Lanterns in the last week of February. His most direct route would have been across the Gobi Desert to Chinkai, the way by which he returned; but he was persuaded by Jenghiz Khan's youngest brother, the Prince Temüge Otchigiu, to visit his camp some six hundred miles to the north in the Khingan Mountains. It was while on this march that he received a message of goodwill and welcome from the Khakan, addressed: 'From the Emperor Jenghiz Khan to the Adept, Master Ch'iu'—a misspelling of the Adept's name. This letter is interesting in that in praising the 'Tao' of the Adept, Jenghiz Khan was displaying a knowledge of Taoism one would scarcely have expected. He declared that the Master's Tao was superior to that of Lao Tzu, Lieh Tzu and Chuang Tzu, the three ancient philosophers on whose work the canons of Taoism were based. He referred to the early voyages of Lao Tzu and of his conversations with and conversion of many Central Asian peoples; peoples whom later the Adept met. He regretted that the way was long; but he trusted that the comforts he provided would not make it seem too much so. He also gave personal instructions to Liu Wen that the Adept was not to over-exert himself.

The journey across the waste country between China and the

Khingans to the Prince's camp took fifty-three days. By now the ice was beginning to melt and there was a faint touch of colour in the grass. From hundreds of miles around the headsmen of the tribes had come in, bringing with them presents of mares' milk. Their black wagons and felt tents stood in rows. After a fortnight's stay the Adept made his departure, travelling along the south bank of the Kerulen River where he picked and ate wild garlic. On both banks of the river grew tall willows from which the Mongols constructed the framework of their tents. The peaks of the great mountains were now becoming visible and from here onwards the country was hilly and well populated. The men were all herdsmen and hunters, wearing clothes made of hides and fur, living on meat and curdled milk. The males wore their hair in two plaits that they hung behind their ears: the married women wore a head-dress of birch bark about two feet high which was covered with a black material and seemed to be in constant fear of knocking it, going backwards and crouching through the doorways of their tents. Having no writing, their contracts were either verbal or recorded by wooden tokens, but their word was their bond. The Adept and his mission found much that was pleasing among these primitive people, the simplicity of whose life they admired.

Their long trek now took them across the mountains south of Lake Baikal, their path leading in a general south-westerly direction. The road was rough, always twisting and turning, but the scenery was enchanting, and the mountains, stretching as far as the eye could see, were thickly wooded, clothed in huge pines while on the lower slopes grew birches and other trees. It was here near the River Tola that they came to the Ordo or temporary palace of the Emperor's wives, the Empresses Börte, Qulan, Yusui and Yasugan. Here they were received with luxuriant hospitality; the Ordo, with its palanquins, pavilions and other splendours, astonishing the Adept and his retinue.

It was farther on, at the city of Chinkai, that they met their first Muslims, the Hui-ho, as they called them, while in the same area they discovered many Chinese craftsmen who came out to acclaim the Adept. The party then crossed the Altai Mountains along a road that had been constructed by Jenghiz Khan's third son, Ögetei, who in addition to being a general was an engineer. The cavalry escort had to help with the wagons, dragging them up the extremely steep slopes and on the downward gradients using ropes to lock the wheels. Then the caravans passed the battlefield called the Domain of Bones where the Mongols had defeated the Naiman army. At Beshbaligh in the territory of the Uighurs they found many Buddhists and Taoists, no doubt the descendants of those whom Lao Tzu was reported to have converted. Marching on, they reached a lake which the Adept called the Heavenly Lake, from the shores of which they descended into a deep ravine, whose precipitous sides were covered with a profusion of pines and birches. Stream after stream rushed down into this beautiful defile and they crossed them on bridges that they noted had been constructed by Ögetei. They were massive timber affairs wide enough for two carts to drive abreast. In the country of the Kara-Khitai at Almaligh on the Ili River they were met by the Muslim ruler and the Mongol governor or darughachi as he was called. For the first time in their lives the Chinese saw cotton which they could only describe as sheep's wool planted in the ground. In texture they likened it to Chinese willow-down.

The land was becoming flat, the fields irrigated by canals, and they noticed many huge mulberry trees for the breeding of silk-worms. Away to the north-east and north-west, stretching as far as the eye could see, were the peaks of the great mountain ranges, looking forbidding and reminding them of their past labours. When in a small village on this road they met an old man driving a bullock which was turning a water-wheel. Jenghiz Khan, they were told, had noticed this man and after talking to him had ordered that he should in future be exempt from all forms of taxation. It was nearing the end of November 1221 and, after passing through Tashkent, they approached Samarkand which they entered in December. Jenghiz Khan at this time was away pusuing Jalal-ad-din.

Within Samarkand they found that only about a quarter of the original population now remained. There were too few to manage the land and look after the orchards and Chinese, Khitai and Tungut labour was being used to help them out. Chinese craftsmen, they noted, were in evidence everywhere. The administration of the city was carried on by an international body and, in order not to ferment trouble, the Mongol governor lived in a camp outside the walls. However, the Adept was installed in the Shah's old palace and he

and his retinue were sumptuously entertained. With Jenghiz Khan
away and the passes under snow the Adept found he was to spend
the winter in the city which, tired after his long journey, he was
not loath to do.

There is a vivid description of the scenery around Samarkand
and of the impressions this made on the Adept and his disciples.
They were fascinated by the almond trees in bloom at the end of
February. With not a cloud in the sky and the air crystal clear they
looked over the terraces, lakes, pagodas and towers, at the orchards
and the flower and vegetable gardens. The grass on which they lay
was thick and green, greener than they had ever seen before. Indeed, they thought, there was no garden in China to surpass these.
but they remarked on the silence in the woods, for here the birds
did not seem to sing.

In April A-li-hsein, a Tangut who for many years the Emperor
had employed on missions to the Chins, arrived with a message from
Jenghiz Khan. 'Adept,' the missive ran, 'you have spared yourself
no pains in coming to me across hill and stream, all the way from
the lands of sunrise. Now I am on my way home and am impatient
to hear your teaching. I hope you are not too tired to come and meet
me.'[1] But the snow was still about and A-li-hsein said that with his
long whip he could not reach the bottom and even on the trodden
road it lay five feet deep. The Emperor's camp was at Kabul and the
road they had to traverse crossed the great Hindu Kush. On 28th
April the party which consisted of the Adept and six disciples set
out. They were met by one of the Khakan's commanders with
an escort of a thousand Mongol and native troops. After crossing
the Amu Darya, on 15th May they reached Jenghiz Khan's
camp.

The Adept was at once presented to the Emperor, who said that
he took it as a great compliment that he had come ten thousand li
to see him. Other rulers, he said, had summoned him but he had
not gone to them. In reply the Adept merely remarked that the fact
that he had come was the will of heaven. It was then that Jenghiz
Khan asked what medicine of long life he had brought. The reply
was significant. 'I have means of protecting life, but no elixir that
will prolong it.'[2] If, indeed, it had only been the desire to find the

[1] Ibid.
[2] Ibid.

Above *Saladin:*
portrait painted
Persia about
D. 1180

Right *Jenghiz*
han

3 *A Mongol Warrior,
from a drawing by
Pisanello*

4 *Qubilai Khan*

5 Opposite *A Moghul
view of Jenghiz Khan's
troops, capturing a
Chinese town*

6   Top *A Japanese view of Mongol soldiers*

7   Above *A French view of Jenghiz Khan, going hunting*

8   *Tamerlane as seen by European eyes*

9   *Tamerlane: a reconstruction from his skull by Professor Gerassimov*

10 *Babur*

11 *Akbar*

12 Opposite
*Akbar and his for-
bears.*
*Top right: Babur,
top left: Humayun,
bottom left:
Jahanjin, bottom
right: Akbar*

13   *A procession led by Akbar*

secret of eternal worldly life that had actuated the Emperor this reply, chilling in its simplicity, might have soured the despot; but it did not. Quietly Jenghiz Khan now asked the Adept how he came by the name Tangri Mungka Kun, meaning the Heavenly Eternal Man, to which the reply was, 'I, the hermit of the mountains, did not give myself this name. Others gave it to me.' Jenghiz Khan seemed to have some doubts as to what he should call Ch'ang Ch'un. He was told by Chinkai who had accompanied the Master on his journey from the city which bore his name—Chinkai—that some called him Father and Master, others Holy Hsein and others the Adept. From now onwards the Emperor said he would always call him by this last name.

By now the weather was beginning to get hotter and so Jenghiz Khan moved up into the higher ground, but before doing so he appointed a date for the continuance of their conversations. It was at this point that Jalal-ad din's attack from Pervan developed which the Emperor decided to deal with personally and the meeting had, therefore, to be postponed. The Adept then asked that he might be permitted to return to Samarkand, to which Jenghiz Khan replied that if he did this it would only face him with all the fatigue of travelling back again. The Adept argued and eventually he got his way, the Emperor giving him an escort of native horsemen under a native commander. This use of native soldiery and commanders showed that Jenghiz Khan was not fighting all the inhabitants all the time and that he had not lost the art of winning people over to him. At this time of the year the heat of the sun was becoming oppressive and there was neither grass nor vegetation, so in order to take advantage of the cool they decided to move by night.

Back in Samarkand they had time to observe the people more closely, their customs and their dress. They reported on the fast of Ramadan and the fact that food was only taken after sundown. They noticed that the mullahs called the people to prayer, that all bowed to the west and that they prayed to their god but not to either Buddha or the Taoist divinities. From the disciple's writings we also learn much about the dress and customs. All holders of official positions, from notables downwards, wore hats that were trimmed with many-coloured stuffs from which hung tasselled penants. Women always wore their hair hanging down, some carrying it in bags of floss-silk, either plain or coloured. Their vessels and cooking

G

pots were of brass and copper and they had a delicate kind of porcelain, usually white, which reminded them of Ting ware. Their coins
were of gold and their weapons made of steel. Physically the people
of both sexes were tall and the men were strongly built. They carried great loads on their heads, in contrast to the Chinese, who
used a carrying beam. There were official writers called dashman,
who were in charge of the city records and documents.

Time passed very pleasantly in Samarkand, but the Adept felt
the moment for further conversations must be drawing near, so he
sent A-li-hsein to the Emperor to ascertain his wishes. The Khakan
concurred and the governor provided a large military escort. The
Adept remarked that there had been disturbances in the Muslim
part of the city and that night after night the sky was lit by flames;
furthermore, among the people there was much anxiety. It would
be better, he said, if the troops he had been offered as an escort
remained behind, but the governor was worried lest something
should happen to the Adept on the road. 'That,' said the Adept, 'is
none of your business! '[1] and persuaded him to return.

On the road they passed through Balkh which Jenghiz Khan had
recently destroyed; this once-crowded city now was deserted and all
they could hear was the barking of the hungry dogs. Eventually they
reached the imperial camp where on meeting the Emperor they did
not bow down, merely inclining their bodies and pressing their hands
together. The talks commenced at once and only a select few were
permitted to be present. At the Emperor's request the Adept expounded the tenets of the Tao philosophy.

Tao, he said, was the producer of heaven and the nurturer of
earth; everything, the sun and moon, the stars, men, objects,
demons and spirits all grew from Tao. First heaven and earth
were made and they then produced man. The earth, continued the
Adept, bore fungoids which man ate, attracted by their scent and
relishing their taste. But man must not desire the licentious things,
neither must he want the things that other men have nor the places
where other men live. If the eye sees pleasant things or the ear hears
pleasant sounds, if the mouth enjoys pleasant tastes or if the natural
state is disturbed by emotions, the original spirit is scattered and
lost.

The element of the male is fire and like a flame is always stretch-

[1] Ibid.

ing upwards, the element of the woman is water and water conquers fire. For this reason the true Taoist must abstain from lust. The sky is male and belongs to the element of fire and the earth is female and belongs to the element of water.

Continuing, he said the common people possessed only one wife and if they can ruin themselves by excessive indulgence, what must happen to monarchs whose palaces are filled with concubines? He then said that he knew Liu Wen had been commissioned to search Peking for women to fill Jenghiz Khan's harem. He warned the Emperor to abstain from things that arouse desire as this keeps the mind free from disorders, but once such things have been seen it is hard to exercise self-restraint. He suggested sleeping alone for a month, and said he would be surprised what an improvement there would be in his vigour, spirit and energy. To take medicine for a thousand days did less good than to lie alone for a single night. He had a numerous progeny and could afford to husband his strength. If anything demonstrates both the courage of the Adept and the restraint of Jenghiz Khan this lecture certainly does.

Reference has already been made to the political sagacity of the Adept. He now displayed this in good measure. Speaking of China, he strongly advocated large remissions in taxation, for the people had been harassed by a long war and were weary and impoverished. At the same time he recognised that there must be means provided to support the Mongol troops of occupation and to provide for government officials. He advocated the employment of Chinese in the capacity of go-betweens or agents, citing the case of the Chin invasion, when the relations were strained between the people and their invaders, as an example of what could happen. It was the Chinese Liu Yu who smoothed over the difficulties that arose and in eight years he succeeded in getting the people thoroughly accustomed to the foreign rule.

All this was faithfully translated into Mongol by the governor, A-hai. Jenghiz Khan appeared to be delighted with the doctrine that had been expounded and ordered that the Adept's words be written in Chinese characters that they might be recorded for posterity. To those who were present he reminded them that they had on three occasions listened to the discourse of the Adept upon the art of nurturing the vital spirit; his words, Jenghiz Khan said, had sunk deeply into his heart.

The campaign in India now finished, the journey back to Samarkand was commenced and during this further discussions took place. When they reached the city the Emperor made his camp some few miles outside the walls. It was then that the Adept asked the governor to approach Jenghiz Khan with a view to his being permitted to reside in the city and when travelling, to rest some way from the imperial camp, explaining that as a recluse he found the hustle and bustle of army routine too distracting. The privilege was granted.

The rainy season now set in; the grass once more became green. When they reached the Syr Darya they found that in a severe thunderstorm the bridge of boats had been swept away. The halt here gave the Adept an opportunity to comment on Mongol superstitions. In the summer months—the season of God's wrath—bathing in a river was not permitted and the washing of clothes was not allowed at this time or, indeed, at any other time, lest the water spirits should be offended. This was why the Mongols wore their clothes until they fell off in rags. Remarking on this, the Adept asked why to avoid the wrath of heaven these prohibitions were made, for this, he added, was not the way to heaven and there surely were greater sins. It was said, he continued, that of the three thousand sins the worst was ill-treatment of one's parents. If the Emperor's subjects were at fault in this it would be as well if he used his influence to reform them. He even went on to ask that what he had said might be made known to the Emperor's subjects and this Jenghiz Khan agreed to do, saying, 'Holy Immortal, your words are exceedingly true; such is indeed my own belief.' He then gave instructions that the Adept's words be recorded in Uighur characters, and he recommended their study to his sons.

The journey continued at a leisurely pace and by March the Adept had grown impatient to return to China. Jenghiz Khan was unwilling to part with his company, but the Adept, pointing out that he had made promises to return by a certain date, said he felt bound to go. Jenghiz Khan apparently had his way, for it was shortly after this that the following incident took place. The Emperor while hunting a wild boar fell and was fortunate to escape being gored by the boar. Commenting on this, the Adept reminded him that he was no longer a young man and that he should take this as a warning. The failure of the boar to gore him was nothing less than an act of God. Jenghiz Khan, in admitting that the advice might be sound, added that Mongols were brought up from childhood to hunt; nevertheless, he turned to a faithful Kerait retainer and said that in future he would do exactly as the Holy Immortal had advised, and for two months it is said he kept his word.

Before these two men parted they had another conversation, largely consisting of farewells. However, there was one interesting consequence. To an enquiry as to how many disciples the Master had in China, A-li-hsein, who was interpreting, said there were a very great many as he had seen the tax-collector's list of assessment. Jenghiz Khan then issued an edict of which there is a record. It was dated 3rd March 1223 and exempted all who were the Master's pupils from taxation. The edict was sealed with the imperial seal.

Ch'ang Ch'un now arranged for his departure. A-li-hsein was to accompany him as special envoy and was to be supported by the Mongols Ho-la and Pa-hai. The return journey did not take so long as the outward one, for they went by the shorter route across the Gobi Desert. On arriving back at his home the Master found a message from the Emperor which showed something of the deep impression this man had made on the Mongolian. It ran as follows: 'Holy Adept, between the spring and the summer you have performed no easy journey. I wish to know whether you were properly supplied with provisions and remounts. At Hsuan-te and other places you have lately stayed, did the officials make satisfactory provision for your board and lodging? Have your appeals to the common people resulted in their coming over to you? I am always thinking of you and I hope you do not forget me.'[1]

Neither Jenghiz Khan nor Ch'ang Ch'un lived long after their return, both dying in the same year and, in point of fact, they never met again, but had they done so one wonders what the consequences of this friendship would have been. Each in his own way had made an impact on history and the world was the poorer for their passing.

Jenghiz Khan's return to his native land on the Onon was leisurely. Whilst on the way he was saddened to hear of the death of his faithful Mukuli, whose loyalty had never wavered and who, with Sübetei and Jebei, had been one of his trusted band of leaders. He shortly afterwards heard of the passing of his eldest son Jöchi,

[1] Ibid.

which cut him deeply; particularly because, under the false impression that his son had wilfully defied him, he had issed orders for a punitive operation against him. The thought of this was a cross that he found hard to bear.

It was no less than six years after embarking on his campaign against the Shah that he arrived back home and within two years of this he died. There were many sides to this great character, but it is probably by his campaigns that he is best known. He was a great general and has been referred to as 'great as any commander and leader in history'.[1] What were the principal characteristics of this man? Perhaps that most commonly associated with him was his ruthlessness. This narrative has shown that there were other sides to his character, but before enlarging on these let us for a moment assess his qualities as a general. That he was ruthless, utterly ruthless, there is no doubt. The point is whether this was merely the beast in the man or whether it had a military justification. In the first instance he had to consider the material that constituted his army. What will make men fight? The most successful generals always seem to have found the answer to this. Saladin knew that the Muslims would fight for the Holy Cause of Islam; Prithivi Raj knew that the Rajputs would fight for their way of life and all that the Hindu held most dear. A poor and half-starved people with little or no religious background, the Mongols fought for loot, food, the material things and women; this Jenghiz Khan knew and on this he was bound to play. His skill lay not so much in his exploitation of this factor as in his ability to check it when he deemed this necessary. It is a remarkable fact that his wild and savage hordes were so disciplined that orders he issued were never disobeyed; when he said there was to be no destruction or looting none took place.

Ruthlessness was also part of his general plan. Only by this could he ensure success; but, of even greater importance, he knew that his reputation for ruthlessness spelt fear and, in consequence, obedience to his will. In reviewing his campaigns against the Islamic peoples of Khorasan and Afghanistan one sees this almost vicious ruthlessness pushed to the extreme. Yet, himself always true to his word, it was the abuse of the trust he had placed in the emirs and other leaders that he found impossible to forgive. Treachery was unknown to the Mongols and treachery in others demanded the

[1] Montgomery of Alamein: *A History of Warfare.*

ultimate penalty, death. His brutality was designed to teach a lesson, rather than being the outcome of a lust for ruin. Much has been written of Mongol looting and robbery in northern China. When an army lives on the country and loot is the only pay the soldier gets there is bound to be suffering. Nevertheless division after division of Chinese troops fought for him. His word could be relied upon, as the Khitais found when he sent Mukuli to their assistance. When he said Chinese cities were to be neither looted nor destroyed they were safe. Reliability is one of the hallmarks of great leadership and Jenghiz Khan could always be relied upon.

To turn now to other aspects of generalship. First the commander must have an aim and this must be understood by all who fight for him. Having achieved his aim he must be prepared to halt and this is one of the hardest of decisions to make. Jenghiz Khan could do this, as his campaigns against the Merkits, the Keraits and the Naimans had demonstrated.

Surprise in battle can be of vital importance, for generally only by surprise can the enemy be caught off balance. This will, however, only give an initial advantage and must be followed by a relentless and ruthless pressure, where it hurts most and where it is least expected. It was the relentlessness of the Mongol pressure that wore down the Chins and spelt the ruin of the Shah of Khwarazm.

When one looks at the size of the canvas on which Jenghiz Khan's strategy was based one is immediately struck not so much by the breadth of his vision as by his courage in acting as he did. Concentration at the vital point has been a time-honoured principle of war, but Jenghiz Khan believed that concentration could bring an equally concentrated force to oppose him. Wide dispersion, on the other hand, apart from exploiting his inherent mobility, would divide the enemy, add to the latter's uncertainty, and result in his being defeated in detail. Though widely deployed, Jenghiz Khan's armies were always of adequate size for their task. It is interesting to note his reaction to the repulse of his army in the vicinity of Kashgar. On hearing of this set-back, instead of withdrawing this exposed force, he ordered Sübetei to go even further south to the upper reaches of the Syr Darya, a plan that caught the Shah off balance, forcing him further to disperse his forces. Seeming parallels, because they are not always truly parallel, may be dangerous, but the protagonists of the Western Front in the First World War perhaps could have learned something to their advantage had they studied the thinking of the Mongol emperor.

Wide dispersion, among other things, postulates confidence in one's subordinates. Confidence comes from two sources, one the clarity of the commander's orders and the other from training. The former ensures the correct action and the latter the ability to react when the unexpected happens. Good communications are vital and this Jenghiz Khan's arrow messengers provided. As an example of careful planning we have the record of the Khakan's instructions to Toli, given by the Emperor shortly before his death. These were concerned with his reopening the war with the Chins, whom he now had reason to mistrust. The Chins' best soldiers, he said, were in the west, where they were protected by the mountain ranges on the south and by the Hoang-ho River on the west and the north. The Sung emperor, being hostile to the Chins, would permit the Mongols to pass through his dominions and into the lowlands, from where they could with best advantage assault the capital at Kai-feng fu. This would draw the Chin army in from the west which, after a march of several hundred miles, would be at a disadvantage and should be easily dealt with. Toli thus not only knew his father's intentions but his reasons for them.

Jenghiz Khan's strategy was always based on an understanding of his enemy. He exploited his own assets and always refrained from the temptation of going beyond his limits. He did not, for instance, allow himself to be drawn into a head-on fight for Peking, because he knew this was beyond his power. It was this coupling of restraint with a ruthless aggressive policy that was most remarkable.

Finally, though the ranks of his army were swelled by the soldiery of those whom he had conquered or by those who for other reasons threw in their lot with him, he never allowed his command structure to be watered down. This the Persians permitted to happen and it was a contributory factor in their defeat at Plataea. From the beginning the Mongol had always insisted that the command must rest with men of his own race, men whom he had not only trained but men whom he could trust. The ability to select the right men for command is a vital factor in generalship. Napoleon understood this and so did Jenghiz Khan.

Jenghiz Khan from his earliest days showed that he possessed a political wisdom that was far more than native cunning. When he heard that the Chinese emperor had sent a mission to the Khan of the Keraits he seized the opportunity of making contact with his powerful neighbour. Earlier, in appealing to the Khan on the grounds of his father's blood brothership, he displayed a sense of political reality that gave him advantages far beyond his immediate goal. With consummate skill he played the Sung Chinese off against the Chins in the north and, in supporting the Khitais, he drove a wedge into the Chin hegemony in northern China. His handling of the Onguts and the Uighurs was skilful and far-seeing. All these people he eventually had fighting on his side, loyal to him, and none were doing it from fear. Although it was true that he was loved by his Mongols and feared by his enemies, his allies all respected him, for they knew his word was his bond.

Was Jenghiz Khan a mere aggressor, seeking only new lands to conquer, always greedy and never satisfied? The more one studies the way he went about things, the less surely is this seen to be the case. Though he frequently struck first, he did this as a means of defence. He was an artist at the pre-emptive bid. He was always prepared to make peace, as he showed with the Persians. He trusted the Khan of the Keraits and only when he found this trust misplaced did he resort to war. He had the gravest misgivings about the Chin Chinese, which history showed were justified. The wild rush of Sübetei into and across south-eastern Europe was, however, in contrast. Here it would appear Jenghiz Khan lost control. Whether or not this was the case, there is no evidence to show that Sübetei was conducting a prearranged campaign.

That Jenghiz Khan was a man given to deep thought is borne out by his association with the Taoist Master. It had been evidenced earlier by his attitude to the Buddhist monks in northern China. The Mongols were an elementary and superstitious people, but their leader tried to get beyond this. He discussed the tenets of the Muslim faith with imams and, seeing the weaknesses of their argument, he turned to Ch'ang Ch'un. His sympathy with the Taoist doctrine was borne out when he enquired of the Master whether his appeals to the common people were meeting with any success.

That he had thoughts for the future is clear. He had the Yasak translated and committed to writing. In this way the principles of government and the laws were laid down, as was the system for election of khans in the future. He established a High Court and a system of administering justice that lasted for generations after his passing.

Last, but not least, he emancipated women.

Great as his military achievements were, he should also be remembered for his administrative genius and political sagacity.

Often when an oriental king died, besides leaving much wealth and a vastly enlarged kingdom, he also bequeathed the elements of instability. An autocrat and a successful general, in all probability he had had no statesmen to advise him and to watch over the larger political issues, and if such a man had existed he would have been a mere cipher in the court; moreover, the king being fearful of his sons, often antagonised them. Standing alone and isolated, when the king died he left a vacuum. This pattern was common among the monarchs of the medieval period, but what, if any, of this can be said to be true of Jenghiz Khan?

Let us for a moment look at what actually happened and then examine some of the reasons. In the long term the empire he left lasted for many years, though not in the form he built it. But was it an empire in terms of exact territory he set out to establish, or was it Mongol supremacy and the Mongol way of life? If the latter, it continued in varying forms for centuries. Under Qubilai Khan it is true that it was ruled from Peking but Qubilai, as we shall see, though accepting much of Chinese culture, always remained at heart a Mongol. Under Tamerlane the regime was once again typically Mongol and his military skill, his early life, his vast wide-ranging campaigns as well as the expansion of his kingdom were all reminiscent of Jenghiz Khan. And although a certain decay set in after Tamerlane it was Babur, a direct descendant of his, who, with an

army organised in accordance with the Yasak, laid the foundations
of an empire in India, and a Mogul dynasty was founded which
lasted for centuries.

The position that Qubilai Khan ultimately held and his attitude
to the old Mongolian kingdom were influenced by a number of
important factors. First Jenghiz Khan's division of his kingdom
among his sons; second, the political skill of his principal minister,
Yeh-lu-Ch'u-Tsai, and, third, the wisdom of one of Jenghiz Khan's
daughters-in-law, the Princess Sorqoqtani, the widow of his eldest
son and the mother of Qubilai.

Jenghiz Khan's treatment of his sons was far-sighted. During
his lifetime, as we have seen, he gave them independent commands
and did not interfere; thus was built up a mutual trust and affection.
On his death he gave to Jöchi's successors the lands of the Kipchak Steppes and the realms beyond; to Chaghatai he assigned the
lands of the Uighurs, Kara-Khitai and all to the west of it; to Ögetei
went Hsi-Hsia and Chin China; while to Toli, the youngest, he
left, as was the tradition, the homeland of Mongolia. This division
did not imply, as it might seem to do, the dismemberment of the
realm.

There was to be a national leader, a khakan, and, as stated
in the Yasak, the quriltai must elect this man. Such was the
machinery by which he had hoped to ensure unity, to avoid civil war
and the risks of disintegration through the machinations of opposing
factions. Although it was well understood that only the most
worthy and most capable should be elected, all knew that the
Emperor had hoped the choice might fall on Ögetei. The part that
Yeh-lu-Ch'u-Tsai played in this will emerge later.

At the time when Jenghiz Khan invaded Chin China the Chinese
governor of Peking was a respected member of the Lao royal
family. Yeh-lu-Ch'u-Tsai was a scholar and a writer of some repute.
He became the Khakan's Chinese secretary and for fourteen years
after Jenghiz Khan's death was the principal link between the Mongols and the Chinese. He was thirty-two at the time of the Taoist
Master's visit to Samarkand and it was he who recorded for the
Emperor the conversations that then took place. He was one of the
most notable statesmen of his day and one who was fully compet-
ent to handle the political problems of his master. When Jenghiz
Khan died he had, therefore, left one who at least should be able

to provide continuity. For years past all knew that matters other than those that were purely military had been referred to Yeh-lu-Ch'u-Tsai, consequently everyone was accustomed to going to him on political issues. In regard to the machinery of government, we have seen that Jenghiz Khan respected the quriltai of chieftains, a body somewhat analogous to a court of barons in medieval England; that he always made use of his orlok or cabinet; and that, while generally getting his way, he did not embark on any enterprise without proper prior consultation with these bodies. Thus, he not only left a statesman, he handed over a system which, provided it was respected by his successors, should ensure continuity.

The matter of Jenghiz Khan's immediate successor was not as simple as it might have been. Ögetei was neither the eldest nor was he the strongest of the sons; but he had wisdom, would take advice and had the knack of turning other people's capacities to best account. He understood human nature and was by nature kindhearted. Yeh-lu-Ch'u-Tsai, knowing full well his late master's ideas, did not try to force the issue but allowed the quriltai ample time to consider the problem. In the meantime he worked on the sons, particularly the eldest, Chaghatai, who eventually came forward to say that he was willing and would be happy to serve under his younger brother. At the end of two years a unanimous vote gave the succession to Ögetei. The unity of the kingdom was assured and the prestige of the quriltai had been upheld.

When the Khakan gave the Kerait Princess Sorqoqtani, the widow of Toli, to his son he set in motion a sequence of events he could never have foreseen. There were many by-products of the Mongol habit of taking the princesses of vanquished royalty as their wives, the most important of which was the intellectual improvement of the stock. Something of Qubilai Khan's genius can be attributed to this cause. His mother, Sorqoqtani, had four sons of which he was the third. This woman lived for her sons and on them and their education she lavished all her care. Nevertheless, she did not neglect the wider political issues which, if mishandled, could so easily have undermined all Jenghiz Khan's good work. She was trusted by the quriltai who constantly sought her advice. She played her part in keeping the hordes fit to go to war and it was to no small extent due to her that Mongol fighting power remained at a high level. Always looking to her sons' future, she made it her business

to maintain order and ensure prosperity in their fiefs. In her own
domain, which was Mongolia proper, an admirable law and order
prevailed, taxes being paid and rivalry stamped out. She was broad-
minded and, although brought up as a Christian, she built a mosque
and founded a Muslim library which was named after her. Of her
four sons, Möngke, the eldest, she sent to the West to broaden his
education; Hülegü was taught by a Nestorian and Qubilai was in
the charge of a Chinese sage, Yao-Shi; the youngest, Arigh-Böke, she
kept at home.

To return to the activities of Ögetei. Soon after his accession
and knowing of his father's misgivings about the resurgent Chin
kingdom, he commenced activities against the Chins. His object was
to destroy and indeed to exterminate Chin China, to devastate the
whole land which he proposed should be turned over entirely to
pasture.

The issue was terrifying. The whole future of Eastern civilisation was at stake, and any idea of a realm in which conqueror and
conquered could live together was to be cast aside. It was only the
wisdom of Yeh-lu-Ch'u-Tsai that saved Ögetei from embarking on
an enterprise the success of which, even were this feasible, could have
been devastating. He pointed out that from a ruined country no taxes
could be expected, and the vast payments which the Chinese could at
present make in silver, silks and grain would all be lost. Kingdoms
might be won from horseback, but they could not be ruled from the
saddle, he argued. Earlier in Samarkand he had reminded Jenghiz
Khan that one who set out to conquer could not afford to dispense
with the politicians who were trained to understand the art of
government and, he reminded Ögetei, the same argument held good
today. Though still determined to deliver a finishing blow to the
Chin monarchy, Ögetei did in fact leave the task of government to his
wise minister. The work Yeh-lu-Ch'u-Tsai then did to cement good
feeling between the two races and their civilisations bore fruit when,
in 1259, after his death, Qubilai Khan was crowned Son of Heaven
in Peking by the Chinese mandarins and princes.

Before he died Ögetei's horsemen had ridden across eastern
Europe. Passing over the Volga, through Vladimir and Kiev on
towards Moscow and thence to Poland and Hungary, like an irresist-
ible tide they swept all before them. When, on Christmas Day
1241, while his armies were crossing the frozen danube, Ogetei died,

the western boundaries of the Mongol Empire stretched from the Baltic to the Black Sea. Ögetei was succeeded by his son Güyük who reigned only for two years. The quriltai now chose Möngke the eldest son of the Princess Sorqoqtani as khakan.

Möngke made his younger brother, Qubilai, viceroy of Chin China. For some time there had been unrest on the borders between Chin China and the Sung kingdom to the south. Möngke, fearing Chinese intentions, instructed his brother to prepare plans for the invasion of that country, Qubilai's plan was based on an ambitious wide turning movement which had the advantage of avoiding the more obvious and well-defended direct route. In this campaign Qubilai showed he possessed all the qualities of a great general. Commencing in 1252, he marched from Ning-Hsia, the old capital of Hsi-Hsia, southwards across the regions of the ice-covered mountains that formed the eastern extensions of the Himalayas and Kwen-Luns which separated the plains of China from the plateau of Tibet. Then he crossed the Kin-Shah-Kian or upper reaches of the Yangtze, entering Yunnan near the city of Tali, within a few miles of the frontier of Burma. His great achievement in overcoming enormous difficulties paled even that of Hannibal's crossing of the Alps. Neither snow, ice, cold, lack of roads nor any of the other hazards of this march seemed to have either frightened or deterred him. It was not until he reached the Chinese plain that he met serious resistance; and then he realised that he might face hard and bloody fighting, for which, however, he was prepared.

As Jenghiz Khan had listened to the advice of Yeh-lu-Ch'u-Tsai, so now did Qubilai pay attention to the sage Yao-Shi, who suggested to him that he would achieve his object without bloodshed simply by assuring the population that his soldiers would not kill. To the bewilderment of his men Qubilai sent them into Yunnan with banners declaring there would be no killing and in spite of some provocation there was none. As Yao-Shi had predicted, the policy was successful. With Yunnan in his hands, he returned to Peking, leaving his army under the command of one of his generals, to whom he gave implicit instructions to establish a firm base for further operations when and if this became necessary.

In Chin China Qubilai confined his activities to the preparation of his army for the next phase of the war, leaving the administration of the country largely to his Chinese officials. The policy he laid down was to be conciliatory and to be based on giving all the help possible to re-establish the economy of the country, so essential after the devastation of a long war. To this end he even went so far as to remit all taxation for a certain period. While this won the hearts of the Chinese, it filled his own people with resentment and mistrust; and so strong was the feeling that Möngke had to order his return to Mongolia. There under the new regime he saw most of the work he had accomplished being destroyed. Eventually he became so disgusted that he contemplated going to war with his brother, a course which could only have ended in tragedy.

This was the cross-roads for Qubilai. Fortunately, he still had Yao-Shi to advise him, advice which he wisely took. Pocketing his pride, he humbly pleaded with his brother, assuring him of his loyalty, even offering him all his possessions, his wife, his family and his own life. Fortunately between these two, in spite of the temporary differences, there had always been a natural understanding, and so Möngke, believing in his brother's integrity, reinstated him. He had, in fact, stern work for Qubilai.

In 1258, four years after the capture of Yunnan, Möngke was ready once and for all to finish off the Chinese War. Two armies, one under himself and the other under Qubilai, were to advance south; Möngke's army on the west flank directed on Ho Chow and Qubilai's on the east on Hang-chow. At the same time Qubilai's old army was to sweep south from the direction of Yunnan and then north on to the line of the Yangtze where, had it not been for two unexpected happenings, it would have had to fight a decisive battle. But, just at the time when the campaign reached its climax Möngke was struck down by dysentery from which he died; and the Chinese, instead of joining battle, considered it more prudent to open negotiations for peace. They offered an annual tribute, agreed a new frontier and accepted Mongol suzerainty. Qubilai agreed to these terms.

In the meantime in Mongolia the immediate issue was to select a successor to Möngke. For this, according to the Yasak, all the princes wherever they might be were to join the quriltai. This proved difficult because Batu, the Ruler of the Golden Horde, was busy founding a new capital on the mouth of the Volga; Hülegü was involved in war with Egypt; as was understandable, Qubilai was delayed with arrangements with the Chinese; and of them all only the youngest brother, Arigh-Böke, was in Mongolia and available. The situation was aggravated by the fact that among many of the older chieftains on the Onon there was little love for Qubilai. These men were, therefore, unlikely to support his claim if he were not present to argue his case. Furthermore those chieftains on whom Qubilai could rely would naturally be with him in China. With three of the princes absent and many of the Mongol leaders away with them a full quriltai could not be assembled. Neverthless, those in Mongolia, assembling in haste and not properly constituted, decided to elect Arigh-Böke as Khakan. Their excuse was that by implication this had been Möngke's wish, as when he went on his campaign in China he had made Arigh-Böke his viceroy. The excuse was flimsy and Arigh-Böke was certainly not of the stature for the post. When Qubilai became aware of this he was incensed and, calling on the generals loyal to him as well as those Mongol chieftains who were in China, he assembled his own quriltai and had himself declared Khakan. Not entirely satisfied that his election would be legally upheld he safeguarded his position by having himself crowned in Peking, which the Chinese were happy to do, styling him as their emperor and 'Son of Heaven'. Thus, quite independently of the Mongol quriltai, he became the lawful heir of the Chinese throne and Empire. It is hard to overemphasise the significance of this act by which he, in effect, relegated Mongolia to provincial status in a new kingdom.

Qubilai was Khakan and also Emperor of China. The Golden Horde owed allegiance to him; Hülegü acknowledged him and when he died his son, Abaka, did not ascend the throne until the Khakan had confirmed the choice. Coins of Tabriz bore his name and among his bodyguard were fair-skinned Christian Caucasians, and he had soldiers serving him from the banks of the Dnieper and the Volga. Although the Chinese described all these peoples as Chinese citizens, in reality they owed their allegiance to Qubilai as khakan and not as the Emperor of China. So long as Qubilai lived this duality mattered little, but in it were the seeds of ultimate dissension. The important implication, of course, was that the old Mongolian Empire based on the Onon with its capital at Karakorum had ceased to exist. This act therefore not only affected the Mongol people, it altered the history of Asia; and one must ask whether this implied the break-up of the very thing Jenghiz Khan had striven to create. But, in many

H

ways, it was nothing more than natural evolution. It was not so much that the Chinese had managed to disrupt Mongolian life, as that a great Mongol leader had moved with the times. The influences of Yeh-lu-Ch'u-Tsai and of Yao-Shi, coupled with the wisdom of the Kerait princess who was his mother, had had their effects. None the less, Qubilai Khan was always a Mongol; it is true he had moved his capital, but he had not changed heart. The backbone of his armies was his Mongol soldiery and his generals were Mongols also.

Arigh-Böke, whose election as Khakan Qubilai would not recognise, attempted for some time to resist him. At Karakorum, where he was forced to withdraw, he was starved out and eventually he had to quit the province. He feigned submission and Qubilai Khan believed him. However, soon realising that his brother's word could not be relied upon, the Khakan was forced to take action. Eventually, abandoned by his supporters, Arigh-Böke was forced into unconditional surrender.

The rest of this story concerns Qubilai Khan as Emperor of China and Khakan of the Mongols.

Qubilai Khan was now in his forty-third year. The picture we have of him at this time is one of a robust man, vigorous in action when his interests were crossed, yet tolerant to those he governed. He was probably kind because he knew when it paid to be kind. In matters of religion, like most Mongols, he was not bigoted and he was always willing to learn and to make friends. However, in the early days his position was precarious.

In the south the Chinese, once he had withdrawn his army, abrogated the treaty they had solemnly undertaken with him on the Yangtze. In the north many of the Mongols rejected him and even prepared for war against him. He overcame both by a combination of political acumen and military skill. Though he could not be considered as great a general as Jenghiz Khan, he, nevertheless, had an ability that enabled him to build up a kingdom that in size was greater than any other the world had previously known, the extent of which has already been described.

Let us first consider some of the main problems with which he had to contend. In Mongolia there was the resistance of Arigh-Böke whom, following on the surrender of Karakorum, he forced back into the desert where, short of food and fodder, he was compelled to submit. Kaidu, Qubilai Khan's nephew, was the next to raise the standard of resistance, raiding his uncle's lands in direct defiance of his authority. Qubilai at first endeavoured to deal with him by cordoning off his forces, but later when the incursions came too deep was forced to join battle with him. At the same time he did not permit these troubles to interfere with his main problem of dealing with China. To his general, Bayan, who could rate as high as any of Jenghiz Khan's commanders, he entrusted this campaign.

Bayan not only displayed military skill, he also showed that he had a political wisdom, as his conduct in this campaign will bear witness. He first marched on the Sung capital at Hang-chow. This was a beautiful city, not unlike Venice. It was served by innumerable canals both large and small; it was an *entrepôt* for trade and, with its population of over a million and a half, it vied with the greatest cities of the day. Well ordered, it had a police and a fire-fighting service, and on the door of every house was a list of those who dwelt there, while the inns had to report all arrivals and departures. Parks, pleasure grounds, temples and monasteries abounded. Here in this, the 'Celestial City', dwelt the Empress-Mother. When the city surrendered, Bayan's conduct and the behaviour of his men were both exemplary. The army marched in with dignity and there was neither bloodshed nor pillaging. Only the official seals, art treasures, books and records were seized; but all were properly listed and sent under careful guard to Qubilai Khan. The Empress-Mother was treated with every respect. The impression all this made on the Chinese was deep, and from this and the general conduct of the Mongol armies a spirit of co-operation rather than one of antagonism sprang up. How different, many thought, was this to the attitude of the Chins of whose rule they had heard in northern China and always resented.

Nevertheless, in the far south the fighting continued for a long time; but eventually the citadel of resistance at Canton fell. The Emperor fled to sea and there took his life by jumping overboard, clasping his son and heir in his arms. In this pathetic way came an end to the Sung Dynasty.

Now Qubilai Khan was Khakan of the Mongols and Tien-tse or Emperor of all China. As khakan his word was law from the Baltic to the Yellow Sea and as emperor all China was his. That this all tended to draw him away from his own people and to orient himself more and more towards the Chinese was perhaps inevitable. But let us, before passing judgement, see how he behaved and discover where, in fact, his heart lay.

Although he had Chinese advisers and in spite of the fact that he listened to and acted on their counsel, he never put Chinese in the top positions; these went to Mongols on whom he knew he could rely. He never really trusted the Chinese, perhaps because he was influenced by their abrogation of the treaty he had so solemnly made with them on the Yangtze; but more likely because, a Mongol himself, he felt in the end he could only trust a Mongol. He maintained order in China by means of garrisons which he placed in camps some four or five miles outside the principal cities, the latter not being permitted to build walls or to take any other steps that might impede the entry of his troops. A foreign garrison in a community would be bound to be unpopular with the civilians, while a camp was better and healthier for his soldiers than city life. He knew, also, that troops get stale if left in one place too long and that officers can become too influenced by local politics unless they are moved from time to time; therefore every two years garrisons were changed and moved not locally but right across the breadth of the country. He maintained the system of arrow messengers and this resulted in his intelligence always being up to date. As an administrator he was both wise and cautious.

While in his palaces and gardens and in the fabulous beauty of his parks, in which trees were planted that he had obtained from all parts of the world, he seemed outwardly to be absorbing much that was foreign to his ancestral background, yet in his heart he tried to remain Mongol. He loved hunting and yet as he grew older his participation was more as an observer than a performer. Reminiscent of the Mongol's affection for his tent, Qubilai's pleasure was to sit in his garden in one, but this had gilded bamboos and the tent ropes were made of silken thread. He still preferred his koumiss to the wine of the country; the former was, however, made from the milk of specially selected white mares. If the man was not in danger of becoming decadent his trappings were frighteningly near so. The grandeur of his court and the extravagance of his spending are more reminiscent of Solomon than of his Mongol predecessors; but this, like all other apparent similarities, must not be stretched too far. What Solomon did or attempted to do by business acumen, Qubilai Khan attempted by military action, sometimes with success and sometimes only at great cost: his attack on Japan, for which he paid dear and from which he gained nothing, springs to mind. His mother's upbringing had developed his intellectual qualities of which he took full advantage. The gap between Jenghiz Khan's death and Qubilai Khan's accession was only a matter of thirty-one years, but the gulf between these two men, though short in terms of time, was in all other respects immense.

It is interesting to see how these two reacted to power. Jenghiz Khan gained it as it were incidentally and having got it utilised it, not to further personal ambition so much as to keep hold of what he had gained. Qubilai Khan was ambitious and his greed insatiable. A review of his military campaigns will show that he sought power, undertaking military exploits not for the security of his realm but from sheer greed.

When, for instance, the King of Cochin-China refused to appear in person at his court it is said that the great khan was so enraged that he despatched an army to destroy the capital. Beyond this it achieved little else, as the people disappeared into the thickly wooded mountains where their pursuers were easily evaded. Annam refused the passage of Mongol troops through her territory and, even though she was prepared to pay tribute, an army was sent which, fighting in tropical conditions, suffered losses from illness far in excess of those from actual fighting. No less than three wars were fought in the inhospitable highlands of Mien, the Burma of today, merely because the King could not send his son to pay homage to Qubilai. This campaign was, however, ultimately successful, the Mongol armies penetrating as far as the Irrawaddy Delta, which gave Qubilai Khan egress to the Bay of Bengal and the Indian Ocean beyond. A somewhat florid description of the Mongol battle with the King of Burma and Bengal is given in Marco Polo's *Travels*, which is to some extent corroborated by Chinese writers. Qubilai Khan's armies sailed the southern seas, invading the Philippines and passed through the Sunda Straits. Siam and Java fell, southern India was invaded and his men reached East Africa and occupied Madagascar.

Earlier, when Qubilai Khan heard reports of the reputed wealth of Japan, he sent envoys to the Imperial Family demanding that they should acknowledge Mongol suzerainty, a request that was politely ignored. Mustering an army of forty-five thousand Mongols and some hundred thousand Chinese, an expedition was embarked on what turned out to be a disastrous enterprise. Although initially successful in making landings over open beaches, no fortress or place of importance was captured. A terrifying typhoon, for which the area is so famed, struck the Mongol fleet, driving their ships ashore. In the havoc that ensued those who were not drowned were taken prisoner and put to work as slaves. Dreams of revenge never left the Emperor's mind, but he died before these could be put into effect.

All these military adventures build up the picture of a man suffering from an acute lust for power. His successes, and there were many, resulted in an extension of his already vast kingdom. Beyond mere conquest did this really mean anything? Did he bene-fit from it in trade and commerce and were his word and his law respected? The answers to much of this can be found in the *Travels* of Niccolo Polo and later of his son Marco. Whatever minor inac-curacies may be in these records their general truth is not in much doubt and is sustained in history. The Great Khan, as Marco refers to him, was respected in Rome, was obeyed and feared throughout Asia, and all who travelled over these vast areas with his blessing did so in utter safety. That this is true is borne out by the ease with which the Venetians could cross Asia on their way to Peking; by the accounts of travels from this capital to India; by their sea voyages across the China seas and the Indian Ocean to Arabia. The only passport that was necessary was the Great Khan's sanction and the golden tablets he gave to the travellers. It was not long after Qubilai Khan's death that the *Merchant's Handbook* described the road from the Black Sea to Cathay as 'perfectly safe whether by day or by night.'[1] That the opening up of these new trade routes, and particularly those by sea, meant increased wealth is without doubt quite true. Water-borne trade from China and up the great waterways included items such as grain, salt, iron, wood and hemp. Marco Polo gives spirited descriptions of the trade between Aden, Madagascar, Arabia and India and from all this the Emperor bene-fited. It was in his ships that Marco Polo sailed over the intervening seas.

Apart from the clear description of the lives and customs of the peoples of Central Asia, the Venetians' narrative is particularly interesting on two counts. First were the impressions they had of Jenghiz Khan, for their assessment of him was made on the spot and before they had come under the influence of Qubilai Khan. They

[1] R. E. Latham: *The Travels of Marco Polo.*

remarked that the Khakan had exercised his power both well and honourably, furthermore they added that he had not harmed or robbed the inhabitants of the provinces he overran. Those whom he had conquered when they saw his good government '. . . asked nothing better than to join his following'.[1] The Mongols had been tolerant in matters of religion and native custom and the travellers found that wherever they went people were going on in their own accustomed way; Muslims, Buddhists and Christians living harmoniously, each respecting the other and none suffering interference from their Mongol masters.

The second point was the credibility they gave to the stories that surrounded the mythical 'Prester John'. The cause is not difficult to find and lay in the foothold the Nestorian Church had obtained in Eastern and Central Asia. Their missionaries, who had landed at Canton as early as the seventh century, had spread through China and penetrated as far north as the land of the Keraits and to the east into the territory of the Naimans. Kuchluk, the Naiman, had been a Nestorian Christian and so was the Princess Sorqoqtani, the niece of Toghril Khan, the Wang-Khan of the Keraits. The story of the Venetians was that this Wang-Khan was none other than 'Prester John'. That Marco Polo was muddled in his interpretation of all this is borne out by his statement that Wang-Khan lived in the Tangut territory of Hsi-Hsia, which he certainly did not. Marco Polo's location was certainly erroneous and the stories he reported as facts were based on romance.

Marco Polo and his two companions stayed with Qubilai Khan for over seventeen years, during which time they made many journeys on special missions ordered by the Emperor. Their impressions of this great man were, therefore, based on knowledge gained over a considerable period of time. What did they make of him? In Qubilai they saw a king who, for all his ambitions and love of pomp, placed the well-being of his people first in all his priorities. He consistently made it his business to see that the peasants were supplied with cattle and seed, to which end officials traversed the country, studying and reporting on the economic condition of the masses. The poor were given clothing and food while the elderly, the orphans and the sick received public aid. Surplus from harvests was stored in great granaries to provide reserves against disaster.

[1] Ibid.

It is worth recalling that within a hundred years of Qubilai Khan's death England witnessed the peasant revolt under Wat Tyler. In spite of this, the pomp and ceremony the Great Khan surrounded himself with almost beggars description. In his palaces, chamberlains and courtiers strutted about whose duty it was to move among and to look after the needs of the many guests. When holding court or at a banquet the Emperor sat on a higher seat than any other, even including his own family. The setting was regal and the conduct of affairs dignified. He was courteous to all visitors, whose comfort was always his first thought. He was surrounded by intelligent people and intellectuals from all over Asia and the capitals of Europe, among whom were priests, poets, mathematicians, astrologers and artists.

His palace lay in grounds covering some six hundred and fifty acres. It was surrounded by two walls between which was a large area of tree-covered lawns in which were deer and other animals. There were artificial lakes of artistic beauty. The paths, which were raised above the level of the grass, were swept and kept free of mud. There were in all eight gates, one being reserved for the Great Khan, and in the walls were magazines for the storage of military equipment. The main hall or audience chamber was as impressive as it was beautiful, the exceptionally high ceiling being covered with paintings in every hue and colour depicting exotic birds and animals. The walls were similarly decorated. Around the great hall were chambers and offices. The outside of the palace was surrounded by a wide terrace giving to the whole place an air of spaciousness and quiet dignity. Beyond the great palace were similar but smaller ones for his sons Jenghiz and Timur.

Was this grandeur just a façade to cover the squalor of an untidy and poor city—not so unusual in the East? According to Marco Polo the answer was, no. The city he described as being full of fine mansions, inns and dwelling houses, all bordering broad open thoroughfares that ran as far as the eye could see. Each had a large courtyard and a garden and all were allotted to families according to rank. Beyond the city stretched a vast suburban area in which the houses were as well built as those in the city itself. Here there were hostels specially set aside for merchants from foreign lands, each nation having its own lodgings. Such was the administration of the kingdom and the capital city of Qubilai Khan. Hang-chow, Canton, Ho Chow and other Chinese cities were no less elegant.

We know something about and have already mentioned the curiosity of Jenghiz Khan on religion; what of Qubilai Khan? When Marco Polo's father, Niccolo, visited Cathay in 1265 he had lengthy conversations with the Emperor, who questioned him closely on the basis of the Christian faith. Sincere in his desire to know more of the philosophy as well as the beliefs of the Christians, he wrote to Pope Clement IV, entrusting the letter to Niccolo and sending one of his barons with him. In this letter he asked that one hundred religious men versed in the arts and capable of arguing the tenets of their faith should be sent to him. He particularly wanted men who would be able to show him convincingly that the Christian religion was preferable to his own. He further asked that when the Venetians returned they should bring with them some oil from the lamp in the Holy Sepulchre. Before Niccolo got back to China Pope Clement had died and there were considerable delays before his successor was chosen. When eventually Niccolo's son, Marco, set out on his now famous travels he was only able to take two monks with him, and neither lasted out the journey. Perhaps a great opportunity had been lost.

While Marco was at Peking, Qubilai Khan, on learning that Easter was one of the principal Christian feasts, asked for the book containing the four gospels. Being questioned as to the reasons for his interest he said, 'There are four prophets who are worshipped and to whom all the world does reverence. The Christians say that their god was Jesus Christ, the Saracens Muhammad, the Jews Moses, and the idolaters Sakyaminu Burjhan, who was the first to be represented as God in the form of an idol?' He added that he did honour and reverence to all four. In Marco's opinion he regarded the Christian faith as best. He showed that his imagination was caught by the crucifixion when he forbade Christians to carry the Cross before them because on it Christ had suffered and died. In spite of this he never embraced the Christian religion, which, bearing in mind that his mother was reputed to be a Nestorian, is perhaps surprising. There were, however, compelling reasons of a political nature. If, he said, he embraced Christianity he would become estranged from his barons and from the common people. This further emphasises our assessment of his character; he was, above all, an astute politician.

It was not until 1292, almost twenty years after leaving Europe, that the Polos returned to their homeland. They went back by sea, circumnavigating Ceylon and India, and finally disembarking in the Gulf of Oman. At Qubilai Khan's request they escorted a Mongol bride for Hülegü's grandson, Argun, now reigning as Ilkhan. While they were on this journey Qubilai Khan died at the age of seventy-eight, having reigned for thirty-four years. True to his Mongol heritage and at his express wish, he was interred near the source of the Onon and Kerulen rivers where rested his grandfather, Jenghiz Khan, his father and his mother, Princess Sorqoqtani.

If one can epitomise Qubilai Khan's achievements it might be said that what Jenghiz Khan had commenced he perfected. In welding the Mongolian and ancient Chinese empires into one homogeneous whole he achieved a piece of statecraft almost second to none: and he overcame difficulties that, at first sight, would have seemed insuperable. Great as were the Greek and Roman empires, they did not encompass such space or such a variety of different nations. He was quite justifiably renowned for his justice and the wisdom of his decisions. A Chinese writer in later times recorded that he must be regarded as one of the greatest rulers that ever lived, for his successes were lasting. Power he certainly strove for, and, although there were examples of his striving for power for power's sake, ultimately it can be said that he exercised it with courage and great sagacity.

It is interesting to note that his reign coincided with that of King Edward I of England, than whom perhaps there was no greater administrator. In the fields of jurisprudence the Statutes of Westminster are unique; but, whereas Edward ruled a small realm with consummate skill, Qubilai Khan controlled an empire of vast dimensions with no less ability. While the Mongol emperor was building his magnificent palace at Peking, on the marshy banks of the River Thames Westminster Abbey was nearing completion; the one a monument to man, the other a place of worship in which kings were crowned and great men buried. The Christian Church, and indeed the Statutes of Westminster, have outlived the religion of the Mongols and the Laws of the Yasak. The roots of the difference may well rest in the strength of the Christian Church, but it would be wrong to let this detract from the stature of the Great Khan.

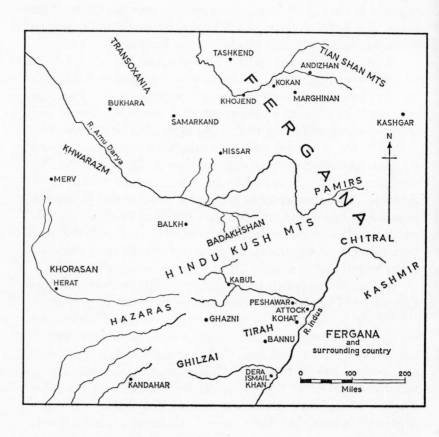

The conceit that drives some men to build great capitals is one of the by-products of power, for in the cities that they erect they see, perhaps, a reflection of themselves. The monument of stone will live and be a lasting reminder of the great man who erected it. Sometimes these cities last as capitals but, more frequently, with the sovereign's death they wither. Tamerlane built such a capital at Samarkand, a beautiful city of many palaces and gardens; yet, as a capital, it did not live. Alexander never built a capital; but he established something that far outlived his short life: Greek civilisation and the Hellenistic way of life. Though Jenghiz Khan had his capital at Karakorum, the edifices to which he devoted his life were the Mongol heritage and the Laws of the Yasak, which epitomised all he held most dear and, though truncated, lasted for centuries after his passing. But what did Tamerlane bequeath to posterity? If the empire that he created did not last for long, what of his philosophies, his thoughts and his ideals? Some of the answers to these questions will be found as we examine his achievements and study those forces which motivated him when he undertook his great campaigns. First, however, let us look at the political background into which he was born.

When Qubilai Khan came under the influence of Chinese culture, making his capital at Peking and not at Karakorum, he set in motion a train of circumstances he surely could never have foreseen. While

it is true that, as khakan, he ruled over all Mongol peoples and
their domains, the sheer fact of geography, separating Peking from
his kinsmen in far-away lands led inevitably to a feeling of independence on their part. As he had succumbed to the desire for
wealth, so the descendants of Hülegü gave way to similar tempta-
tions. The rigours of the old Mongol way of life were slowly discarded and, because it paid them to do so, many Mongols adopted
the Islamic faith. Viceroys and emirs gradually grew more powerful
until eventually khans, though still selected by the quriltai, were
little more than figureheads. By the middle of the fourteenth century
the only truly Mongol area was Chaghatai, that stretch of country
lying between the Altais and Transoxania. At this time, seventy-two
years after Qubilai's death, the Yuan Dynasty he had founded came
to an end. Overcome by the Mings, the Mongols were pushed north
and Chinese dominance, which Jenghiz Khan had striven so hard to
avoid, came about. Kings were on the move, dynasties changing,
empires breaking up and little kings were basking in the sunshine of
short success. It was into this maelstrom that Tamerlane was born
in 1336, and it was these circumstances that gave him those opportunities that he proved so capable of grasping.

Tamerlane was not in the strict sense a Mongol. His father was
a chieftain named Taragai, of Turkic extraction, and head of the
tribe called Barlas. Tamerlane seemed, however, always to be
jealous of his connection with Jenghiz Khan, which was on the female side of his family. He never became nor did he call himself a
khan; for, by the Law of the Yasak, only a direct descendant of
Jenghiz Khan could become a khan. When Tamerlane was later
ruler of all Transoxania he held this position as Emir el Kadir, and
he had to appoint as khan a descendant of Jenghiz, Syurharmish,
whose name was engraved on the coinage minted by Tamerlane.
At the height of his career he was known as Timur Beg. Timur was
the name given him at birth, a Turkish name meaning iron. It was
said that, as a result of an arrow wound he received when a boy,
from which he limped for the rest of his life, his companions nick-
named him Timur-i-Lang or Timur the Lame and from this the
name Tamerlane is derived.

His parents were Muslims and he himself a devout follower of
the Prophet. His home was in Transoxania, that prosperous stretch
of country lying between the Syr-Darya and Amu-Darya rivers. It

was a land of big cities, having a well-developed civilisation. Rich in vineyards and orchards, it also had an abundance of mulberry trees. The pastureland was rich and across it ran some of the most import-ant trade routes from far-off China. It was ruled by a one-eyed and ruthless emir named Kurzan. Though neighbours looked with envy at Transoxania, as long as Kurzan lived it was secure, but when he died divisions reared their ugly heads. Tamerlane was caught up in these intrigues, and though at one time he succeeded beyond his expectations, eventually the tide of fortune turned and he found himself a fugitive. Unlike Qubilai, who was born to greatness, he and Jenghiz Khan had to fight for what they ultimately achieved and this had as much to do with the moulding of their later characters as anything else. The vicissitudes of Tamerlane's early fortunes are only of passing interest; what are of concern are the methods he employed to gain his ends, for in these we shall see some of the fundamental differences between him and the great Jenghiz Khan. Both were outstanding generals and both were ruthless, but there the parallel ends.

The confusion that existed after Kurzan's death gave to Toghluk, Khan of Kashgar, the ruler of Turkestan and Lord of Chaghatai, the opportunity he had for so long been waiting, to in-vade Transoxania. Some of the local chieftains resisted and others fled, but Tamerlane, realising that resistance would be foolish, went as a suppliant to meet the great khan. Whenever he met any of the numerous generals on his progress to Toghluk, he presented lavish gifts to each of them and when eventually he met the Khan he apologised for the poorness of his offerings, explaining that so much of what he had brought for him he had been forced to give to the Khan's subordinates on the way. Toghluk's reaction was as Tamer-lane had expected: the generals were compelled to disgorge supposed bribes they had wrung from him, bribes which in point of fact had been gifts freely given. Even at this early age Tamerlane was as astute a politician as he was a capable soldier. Good policy, he wrote, could do more than heroic courage and a clever idea might be worth more than an army, for, he went on, an arrow which was feathered by policy would find its mark in the heart of a foe.[1] He had judged Toghluk accurately and found favour in the eyes of his new

---

[1] *Malfuzat Timuri* or *Institutes*. Though the authorship is in some doubt, most authorities have accepted it as reliable.

master, who later even went so far as to make him his viceroy. Never-theless, in a mood of overconfidence, he mistook both Toghluk and the support he thought he had from his own people when, in the Khan's absence, he was foolish enough to lead a revolt. This he did initially against the Khan's subordinates, who were generally hated for their rapacity, and later against Toghluk himself, whose ven-geance was swift. Tamerlane was forced to flee the country, but, un-like Jenghiz Khan, whose exile was no fault of his own, Tamerlane had brought his misfortune on himself.

Eventually, however, he regained all he had lost and by the time he was thirty-five had so improved his standing that he was formally elected emir. This success was attributable to his personal bravery, his political acumen and his undoubted qualities as a leader. He was a striking figure, and his limp, rather than diminishing his stature, gave character to his appearance. His olive-coloured complexion was set off by a thick pointed black beard and his hair was prematurely white. He always wore a pointed Tartar helmet which was heavily encrusted with jewels. Although he never wore a turban, and never shaved his head, he always professed himself a devout Muslim. His Tartar head-dress, either from policy or because at heart he was a Mongol, was in strange contrast with his professed zeal for the faith. He was, in point of fact, forced on the one hand to carry the Mongols with him, for it was from them that he largely drew his best soldiery, and, on the other, the more educated Muslims on whom he relied for the filling of higher political appoint-ments. Thus he deliberately established a position on two elements which were mutually antagonistic, each owing allegiance to its own book; the one to the Yasak and the other to the Koran. He showed in this political aptitude as well as courage.

In military affairs, as one might suppose, he was thorough and painstaking. In his *Institutions*, the document that he is alleged to have drawn up for posterity, he laid down the organisation for the army, its system of command, the principles that should govern its tactics, its weapon employment and details of its accoutrements. We find here that the multiple of ten, nine men and a leader, as insti-tuted by Jenghiz Khan was the basis of command structure. Onbashis commanded his tens, yüzbashis hundreds and ming-bashis thousands. Each soldier was equipped with two horses, a bow, a quiver of arrows, sword and axe. Each had thread and ten needles and a leather knapsack and thus the care of clothing and equipment was assured. The scale of tents was laid down as one per eighteen men. Instructions to govern the siting of camps were given in great detail: they were to be near water, on open rising ground, with flanks and rear amply protected. This care for minute detail in military matters was also manifested in the realm of administration. There was a council of ministers presided over by the diranbegi and there were four viziers, each with his particular responsibility. The administration of land revenue, the major source of regular income, was laid down and a tax of a third of the produce of irrigated land was demanded. There were in addition appropriate water dues, and Tamerlane also had a public works department for the care and maintenance of roads and bridges.

Having firmly established his government and organised his army, he now felt he could give rein to some of his ambition. His attention was not unnaturally directed to the neighbouring area of Khorasan. After the death of Abusaid in 1355, The last of the descendants of Hülegü, the Mongol kingdom of the West had fallen to pieces. Jealous of their neighbours, the various emirs became involved in local conflicts, and in these circumstances it is scarcely surprising that Tamerlane saw an opportunity to gain both prestige and wealth. Although, had they united, these people might have collectively been capable of defending their country, they chose to stand separately, and separately they fell. Giving as his reason for invasion his desire to save the people from petty oppression he felt justified in doing as he did. In his memoirs he wrote: 'It is the duty of a victorious king to bring under his authority every kingdom where the people are oppressed by their rulers; and thus I delivered Khorasan and purified the Kingdom of Fars and Iraq.'[1] These lines, if indeed penned by him, were committed to paper after the event and, in the light of all he actually did, the sceptic might well say *'Qui s'excuse, s'accuse'*.

Before he set out he called the customary meeting of the chieftains to tell them of his proposed plans with which they heartily agreed, for the country was rich and full of treasure for the taking. Thus, he embarked on his first campaign of conquest. Was there any justification other than sheer greed? He was not threatened, though, of course, he might claim that an unruly and turbulent state

[1] Ibid.

I

on his immediate border was a source of danger; but this campaign took him to Afghanistan, Azerbaijan and even far-off Georgia, for which countries this excuse could scarcely hold good.

Let us for a moment look at the campaign, his actions and the methods by which he saved the 'oppressed' people from their harsh rulers. In April 1381 he attacked Herat, a city that had been peacefully governed by the princes of the House of the Karts for a hundred and thirty years. A short-lived resistance was put down with the utmost brutality, the heads of the victims being erected into towers. In the following year he marched south to the city of Zaranj where everyone was killed from men of great age to babes at the breast. From here he proceeded to Kandahar, and then, turning north, he passed through the State of Mazandaran on the southern shores of the Caspian, where he had the entire population of the capital put to the sword. Pursuing his march northwards he entered Georgia on what he claimed was a Holy War against the idolatrous Christians. There, those who would not accept Islam were thrown from the battlements to their death.

While in Georgia he heard of the death of the old shah of South Khorasan. He promptly sent instructions to the Shah's heirs to appear before him and, as these orders were not immediately obeyed, he sent an army to obtain by force what he deemed to be his due. The capital, Isfahan, which the old shah had by skill managed to preserve, offered no resistance and surrendered. But the inhabitants were horror-stricken when they were told of the indemnity they would have to pay, for that which was demanded was far in excess of their overall means. The city successfully revolted and it was reported that some three thousand of Tamerlane's men lost their lives. Tamerlane came down to Khorasan himself; he soon recaptured Isfahan and before his men were permitted to pillage he gave instructions that the dwellings of all scholars and priests should be spared. So far and no further did his magnanimity go, for the next order was as terrible as it was bloody. He demanded that the heads of seventy thousand of the inhabitants, one for every man in his army, should be brought to him. So ghastly was the implication of this that even among his own men many preferred to buy heads rather than to take part themselves in the horrible deed. When the gory trophies arrived, Tamerlane, following the usual custom, had them piled in pyramids along the walls of the city.

From here he went to Shiraz and it was not until 1388 that he finally got back to Samarkand after an absence of seven years. He was now master of Khorasan, Fars, Iraq, Azerbaijan and Georgia, rich in loot and treasure, but hated by all whom he had ruthlessly subjugated. If his aim had been to terrify, he had succeeded.

How much further afield his ambitions would have taken him at this stage is a matter for conjecture. While Anatolia and the wealth of Constantinople might have tempted him, there is nothing to show that at this time he considered campaigns in this quarter. It also seems most unlikely that his greedy eyes would have looked with envy at the barren and unknown lands of the Kipchak, occupied by the descendants of Jöchi, now called the Golden Horde. Though his raid on and capture of Urganj, about a hundred miles to the south of the Sea of Aral, had involved him in a skirmish with the famous horde, there was a gulf separating such a minor affair from any thought of all-out war.

His fight for existence looked as though it was now over, when an event occurred the consequences of which were to threaten his hard-won kingdom and bring him close to annihilation. Tokhtamish, a prince of the Crimea, had as a result of a quarrel fled from his kinsmen of the Golden Horde and sought refuge in the camp of Tamerlane. Urus Khan, Lord of the Horde, demanded his release and this Tamerlane refused, saying that as Tokhtamish had placed himself under his protection he would defend him no matter what the cost.

He grew fond of the fugitive, calling him his son, and placing at his disposal troops of his own. Thus equipped, Tokhtamish attacked the Horde, but was defeated and once again forced to seek shelter. At this point Urus Khan died, and Tokhtamish, as the lawful descendant of Jenghiz Khan, was elected to the throne of the Golden Horde. Power went to his head. He turned on the hand that had fed him and making the excuse that Tamerlane had earlier taken Urganj which properly belonged to the Golden Horde, he treacherously attacked his old friend. Sweeping down the Amu-Darya, he got as far as Samarkand and Bukhara, whilst Tamerlane was engaged near the Caspian. Tokhtamish, on hearing that Tamerlane was hastening south, departed as swiftly as he had come, but not before burning the palace and suburbs of Bukhara.

A real struggle for mastery was now inevitable, with the apparent odds very much against Tamerlane. On the one hand there was Tokhtamish, born of the seed of Jenghiz Khan, the king of a vast realm that lay deep in well-nigh impenetrable country, with the immense strength of the Golden Horde and the mass of the Mongols as a people behind him; on the other was Tamerlane, son of a chieftain of a local clan, with by comparison a small but loyal following, whose success up to date, though impressive, had been against men possessing neither the will nor the ability to offer serious resistance. In this situation Tamerlane's position was similar to that which had faced Jenghiz Khan so often. If he was to survive he was forced to go to war and like Jenghiz Khan he chose to take the offensive, deeming that this was preferable to inaction and waiting to be attacked by a man having superiority in numbers and the advantages of the initiative. However, Tokhtamish was cautious and in no sense anxious to force a direct conflict and so, typical of the people of the Steppes, he slipped back like a fox into his own country, ready to attack, but only when and where the opportunity was propitious. In the following winter, when the snow lay thick and the weather was at its worst, he returned. Tamerlane, having determined to fight, was faced with three possible courses of action: to defend Samarkand, which would leave the Golden Horde free to ravage his country; to withdraw to the south and there to concentrate, which would leave Samarkand open and an easy prey to the enemy; or, finally, to attack the Golden Horde now with those forces that were immediately available. It was a mark of his genius and of his courage that he adopted this last course. In this decision he was influenced by three principles from which he never deviated. These were: never to fight in his own country; never to permit himself to be thrown on to the defensive; and always to attack swiftly, holding to the idea that it was better to be at the right place with ten men than to be absent with a thousand. If he was to follow these principles he must attack at once; so, riding through the rain and snow, he made contact with Tokhtamish's outposts, infiltrating where he could and attacking where opportunity presented itself. Tokhtamish was deceived and, believing that Tamerlane's army was far larger than it was and fearing for his own lines of communication and line of retreat, he withdrew. Tamerlane pursued, never releasing his pressure until he had reached Urganj, which he re-took. Only then did he return to Samarkand, where he did not rest but set about collecting an army, not for its defence but for the purpose of pursuit and to bring the Khan of the Golden Horde to battle.

This plan to pursue had inherent dangers. If he advanced into the Steppes of Russia what would Tokhtamish do? He could stand and fight, which would suit Tamerlane; he could ignore Tamerlane and return to Transoxania and attack his capital at Samarkand, but this would leave Tokhtamish's own territories unguarded and was, therefore, unlikely; or, finally, he could withdraw deep into the heart of Russia. If Tamerlane pressed him how far should the pursuit go? The farther it went, the greater would be the strain on his men and his horses, and would he then find himself committed to a decisive battle weakened and tired and on ground of Tokhtamish's choosing? Tamerlane's only alternative was to withdraw, but this would bring his enemy on him like a pack of wolves; some would harry his retreating army, while others could circle round him and attack Samarkand before he could arrive. For Tamerlane there was no turning back.

He marched on, therefore, into the Land of the Shadows, where for days and weeks his men wearily trod their way. Though they moved on a wide front in order that the horses might get what grazing there was to be had, these individual divisions kept in tight formation. They invariably camped in the same order so that in emergency each man would know where he was and who was his neighbour. At noon each day Tamerlane called a halt to rest the animals and before they made camp in the evening scouts who had been sent on in advance cleared the way. These scouts habitually moved before and on the wings of the army and every night brought in their reports for the day. In this manner Tamerlane covered literally hundreds of miles without coming into contact with a living soul, but he knew that although he saw no one unseen eyes were watching him. Nevertheless, Tokhtamish, although having the advantage of manœuvring in his own country with which he was familiar and in spite of an ever-decreasing line of communication with his base, was being forced to conform to Tamerlane's strategy, for the Horde must at all costs keep themselves between their homes and the ever-advancing enemy.

The first contacts came when Tamerlane reached the Ural River, which here ran east and west. He captured a few prisoners from whom he learned that there were three fords. However, he decided not to cross by any of these but to swim the turgid river. Leading

his men himself, he met no opposition and, penetrating the woods
on the far side, he was able to take some prisoners. From these he
learned that Tokhtamish had been holding the very fords he had
disdained to use. From now onwards he knew he must expect to meet
his enemy and so he issued the strictest orders concerning security.
No lights or fires were permitted after dark and all were to remain
in their regimental lines. The scouts each day kept contact with
Tokhtamish's rearguards as the pursuit continued.

Eventually, after a march of over seventeen hundred miles which
had lasted four and a half weary months, on the banks of the Volga
River he came up with the Golden Horde. Now for the first time he
saw the famous horned standards and the domed tents of the Horde.
This was the heart of the enemy, this his objective; but it was a terrifying sight. Tokhtamish had the advantage of superior numbers, of
fighting on his own ground and his men and his horses were comparatively fresh. He had every reason to be satisfied, for he had carried out a great and well-executed withdrawal and was now poised
for a defensive battle with superiority in numbers.

The great battle that ensued was fought and won in a few hours.
Tokhtamish, recklessly throwing away all the advantages his defensive position had, opened by attacking. Had he, like the Duke of
Wellington at the lines of Torres Vedras, held his ground and forced
Tamerlane to attack him things might have been very different. As it
was he charged headlong on to Tamerlane's right flank where the
latter had placed the pick of his cavalry and some of his best commanders. Holding the centre himself, where he had placed his
reserve, Tamerlane refused his other flank. This was Tamerlane's
general practice. The hard and persistent training he had given his
men had the advantage that every division knew what was expected
of it. The Golden Horde pressed their attack and as Tamerlane's
men withdrew, Tokhtamish personally entered the fray. At the head
of his horsemen he penetrated the rear of Tamerlane's centre; but
Tokhtamish had fallen into a trap and Tamerlane, who had waited
for this moment, advanced with his reserve, effectively cutting
Tokhtamish off from the rest of his army. In the hand-to-hand
fighting that followed, the Horde, without a leader, became disorganised. Tokhtamish fled and the standard of the Golden Horde fell; it
was the end.

It had been an unparalleled campaign. Tamerlane was not the

only one to pursue a retreating enemy into the heart of Russia; but he is the only one who has done so and succeeded. Napoleon was forced to retreat from Moscow and Hitler from Stalingrad. Tamerlane's achievement was a classic of relentless pursuit and of inspired leadership and depended on an army not only magnificently trained but possessing a superb discipline. There have been many arguments about the pros and cons of defensive and offensive stategy, but his campaign is certainly an example of the rewards that the latter can bring; and is exemplified again in European military history by Marlborough both at Blenheim and in his conduct of the war against Louis XIV in the Low Countries.

Tamerlane returned to Samarkand, leaving the remnants of the Golden Horde to the mercy of providence. Tokhtamish, however, made one last attempt to regain his lost position. This proved abortive and defeated once more he was forced to flee to the northern forests; his host was scattered, some going into the Crimea, some to Adrianople and some to Hungary. The kingdom founded by Jöchi was now no more.

Tamerlane spared no one. As he retraced his steps he sacked and burned Sarai on the Volga, he stormed Astrakhan whose whole population he put to the sword in payment, he said, for the burning of the palace at Bukhara. He marched to Moscow but spared it, a town of only fifty thousand inhabitants and which had in fact recently been ravaged by Tokhtamish. Later, Witfeld, Duke of Lithuania, led a mad crusade against the Tartars. Terrible in his anger, Tamerlane stormed across the country burning and pillaging wherever he went, his men going as far as the Dnieper and penetrating as far north as the borders of Poland.

In contrast with his previous campaign, Tamerlane's war against the Golden Horde and his invasion of Russia, although agressive, were brought about not by ambition or greed but from sheer necessity. His immediate reaction to success had not been vindictive, for he allowed Tokhtamish to go and had shown that he was prepared to forget the past. It was in self-defence that he again fought Tokhtamish, the Lithuanians and the Poles, and his cruelties after these campaigns were, even though regrettable, at least understandable.

At this stage he might be said to have reached the pinnacle of his ambition. Lord of Samarkand and Transoxania, of Khorasan,

Fars and Iraq, of the Caucasus and the Steppes of Russia, of Mongolia and of Afghanistan as well as the territories of Chaghatai, he was a mighty ruler. Surely with this he could and should have been contented? Later events will, however, show that he was not. There were to be more wars with greater military glory if, sadly, this was combined with shame. But before considering these let us for a moment examine his position as a ruler, his methods, in broad outline, of administration and his code of discipline in the army.

His empire had no name and he was simply known as 'Lord of beyond the River'. His title was Emir Timur. His nominal sovereign was still the Khan, who had his own palace in Samarkand and whose name was used on Mongolian ceremonial occasions such as the Sacrifice of the White Horse. The kingdoms Tamerlane had overrun were not organised into an administrative whole, however tight his personal grip in fact was. A conquered realm he gave to one of his sons or to some outstanding emir. He had a well-organised service of information not dissimilar to that of Qubilai Khan. His writ ran throughout all his lands and punishment was meted out to those who failed in any detail. When Clavijo passed through these territories he remarked how the lord had relays of horses waiting at the end of each stage of the journey. If anyone failed to do the lord's bidding it 'cost him his head'.[1] If the local people did not provide for travellers all that was required 'they immediately received such a number of blows with sticks and whips that it was wonderful'.[2]

Throughout his territories there was an established system for the collection of taxes and all merchandise entering the country was subject to entry duties. The main trade routes were kept in good repair; these were the great[3] North Road passing across the Gobi Desert to Samarkand and onwards to Tabriz and the Black Sea; another through Urganj to Georgia and on to Russia; and one that ran south to Ormuz and the Arabian Sea. He also opened trade with Hindustan via the Khyber Pass and across the Hindu Kush, and Samarkand was the great emporium to which all roads led.

The army, as this story has already shown, was well disciplined and the soldiers received regular pay from the treasury. No soldier was permitted to enter a civilian house without permission nor

---

[1] Narrative of the Embassy of Ruy Gonzalez de Clavijo.
[2] Ibid.
[3] Ibid.

was he allowed to take a bribe. The élite was the Guard, chosen from the bravest of his men. Promotion was by merit, the leader from the platoon becoming the captain of the company. There were awards for bravery and actions of distinction were recorded by secretaries. Tamerlane expected and obtained a high standard of intelligence among his commanders and he could not stand stupidity, saying that a wise enemy was less harmful than a foolish friend. The shrewdness of his observations were indicative of his clarity of thought.

Gibbon, in his chapter on Tamerlane, wrote: 'For every war a motive of safety or revenge, of honour or zeal, of right or convenience, may readily be found in the jurisprudence of the conqueror'.[1] Tamerlane, now resplendent in all his glory, decided to invade India. There was no reason for revenge and could be no threat to his sovereignty from there. In the *Institutes,* written after the event, he gave an excuse that it was essential to wage a Holy War against an idolatorous race of infidels, apparently ignoring the fact that India was ruled by Muslims to whom the Hindus were subservient. The real truth was that merchants and his spies had told him of both India's wealth and weakness of government. This was enough and, in spite of the misgivings of his emirs, he went ahead with plans for invasion. That the country was in a state of disunity there is no doubt, for since the death of Feroz Shah, a wise if not a strong ruler, a period of misrule bordering on anarchy had been the country's lot.

Petty Hindu chieftains vied with renegade courtiers; in Delhi there were two kings, one with his capital set up in Kanauj and the other with his at Ferozabad. The renegade courtiers were mostly Hindus who having been converted to Islam had been assigned important fiefs. 'Such was the chaotic state of the kingdom of Delhi when Timur descended upon it with his ninety-two regiments of a thousand horse each.'[2]

The invasion commenced in 1397 when an advance force under his grandson, Pir Muhammad, moved on Multan. In the following March Tamerlane himself set out from Samarkand and, after crossing the snow-covered mountains, reached the Indus at Attock without encountering opposition. From thence he pressed on across the Panjab to the River Chenab where he was joined by Pir Muham-

[1] E. Gibbon: *Decline and Fall of the Roman Empire.*
[2] Stanley Lane-Poole: *Medieval India.*

mad. In vain the Rajput fortress at Bhatinda stood out against him
and in the fight that ensued ten thousand Hindus were reported to
have been slain. By December the invaders were encamped on
the Plains of Panipat.

At Delhi the Indians, under the command of Iqbal Khan and
the Sultan Mahmud, were drawn up for battle. They were a formidable host, numbering over fifty thousand, of which ten thousand
were horse. The fighting qualities of these soldiers were of a high
order. There were also a hundred and twenty-five war elephants,
dressed in mail with polished blades fastened to their tusks, while in
the howdahs sat men with grenades and fireworks, whose purpose
was to frighten the enemy horses. Whatever Tamerlane thought of
these elephants he must have been impressed, for, later in his war
against the Ottoman, Bayazid, his army included elephants from
India.

As was his custom Tamerlane took every precaution against any
form of surprise attack, protecting his camp with abatis of thick
brushwood and trees. Stores, cattle and women were placed in the
centre with the professors and other learned men who had
accompanied him. At the time he had several thousand Hindu
prisoners whom he felt he could not with safety leave in the camp when
he went to battle, and these he inhumanly ordered to be killed in
cold blood. No stone was left unturned to ensure his security, no act
was too brutal to achieve this end.

The fight opened on 17th December with the customary roll of
drums, the signal for Tamerlane's attack to commence. This, delivered on one flank, gained an initial success. While this was hap-
pening a steady discharge of arrows by Pir Muhammad's men on
the other flank heralded a charge by cavalry with drawn swords.
Under Iqbal the Indians in the centre held firm, the soldiers showing no lack of courage; but, being greatly outnumbered, they were
gradually forced to give ground. Tamerlane had instructed his men
to pick out the mahouts on the elephants and then to wound the
riderless beasts. The fight was bitter while it lasted but by the evening it was over. The victorious Tamerlane that night pitched his
tent by the tomb of Feroz where he gave thanks to Allah.

In spite of his assertion that he forbade looting, for three or more
days the unhappy city was ransacked. In his own words: 'All my
army, no longer under control, rushed to the city and thought of

nothing but killing, plundering and making prisoners.'[1] Many men obtained a hundred captives and these Tamerlane sent to Samarkand to teach the handicrafts of India to his own people. There was also, of course, an immense amount of treasure in precious stones, gold and silver, silks and brocades. Only the quarters occupied by the heads of the Muslim Church were saved.

From here his path ran south to Meerut and the Ganges, then up through the Siwaliks along the foothills of the Himalayas, through Nagarkot, Jummu and Lahore, finally disappearing up the valleys of the Hindu Kush to Samarkand. Laden with loot, the Scourge of India had departed, his whole ghastly campaign having been completed within a year. No good did he do and nothing but misery did he leave in his train. Although the Hindus had suffered, they remained, able to rebuild as they had previously after Mahmud of Ghazni and Muhammad Ghuri.

Historically, Tamerlane's invasion of India had achieved nothing. If it were power that he had been seeking, why did he not leave a governor? After his departure Mahmud was restored to the throne at Delhi and on Mahmud's death the government of the land fell into the hands of the Lodi emir, Daulat Khan. If Tamerlane had wanted to stamp out Hindiusm as Hitler tried to stamp out the Jews in Germany he could only have done so by remaining, and even then the task would have been impossibly difficult. Surely his judgement was not so much at fault that he really believed he could do this? One is left with the conviction that his objective had been to plunder, rob and destroy and that his vain boast of a Holy War was a mere excuse. Is it, for instance, reasonable to think that this man, who had such complete control over his soldiers, could so far have lost his grip that for days he was incapable of preventing the sack of Delhi? Whatever glory may be attributed to his previous campaign, his invasion of India did little other than tarnish a great reputation.

---

[1] *Malfuzat Timuri* or *Institutes.*

13 *Tamerlane—Ultimate Power*

It was while Tamerlane was in India that news reached him of disturbances in Georgia as well as in the Tigris and Euphrates valleys. Baghdad, which he had taken in 1393, had been reoccupied by the Sultan Ahmad, with apparently the support of the Mamluks of Egypt. It was these reports that in all probability were the main cause of his rapid return to Samarkand. In addition to this, whilst he had no quarrel with the fast-growing Ottoman Empire, he was none the less becoming apprehensive of the attitude of their leader, Bayazid, an ambitious and headstrong man. His expeditions of 1399 were thus undertaken against a background which justified action. There was another factor that it has been said influenced him in his decision: he was now seriously contemplating war against China. He was in fact under some form of tribute to Peking and, although it is not clear why this was so, the most probable explanation is that it was a legacy of the old Yuan Dynasty. Be that as it may, for some years this tribute had not been paid and Peking was wanting to know why. If Tamerlane did seriously contemplate this war, and later events showed that he certainly did, it would obviously involve his being away from Samarkand for years and so naturally his first thought would be to ensure a stable situation on his western flank.

To deal with the unrest in Georgia was a simple matter, but to eradicate the subversive influences of the Mamluks in Syria might turn out to be a more difficult affair, and it is in the light of this that one should perhaps look at his brutal attacks on Damascus, Aleppo and Baghdad. Finally the problems raised by Bayazid did not seem to be of a serious nature. A punitive expedition that might have lasted a few months in the event turned out to be a campaign which dragged on for three years; this Tamerlane could neither have expected nor wanted.

When he returned from India he paid off those soldiers who had accompanied him and who now wanted rest. After he had mustered a new army, which he recruited largely from Khorasan, he marched north and, passing through Azerbaijan, reached Georgia one month later, in November 1399. He took Tiflis with ease and sacked it, and the King and those Christians who were not killed were forced to embrace Islam. Immediately following this he had some acrimonious correspondence with Bayazid. There was much in the character of these two men that was similar; but, as Gibbon put it 'Timur was impatient of an equal, while the other was ignorant of a superior'.[1] Tamerlane, endeavouring to avoid an open breach, spoke of their unity of purpose pointing out that they were both at war with the infidels. Let Bayazid confine his attention to the Christians in Europe and he would deal with the others. Tamerlane had objected to Bayazid's seizure of Sivas, a city lying between Erzurum and Ankara, and to show his displeasure he laid siege to it. The place fell within twenty days and although the lives of the Muslim population were spared, four thousand Armenian Christians were buried alive. He hoped thus to force Bayazid to see reason.

Tamerlane now turned his attention to Syria where the local emirs, confident in the power of the Mamluks, were prepared to fight. Tamerlane's army, which now included elephants from India, advanced on Aleppo. Here disunity among the Syrians and Tamerlane's superior strength quickly decided the issue and the wretched city fell. While he carried on peaceful discourses with the doctors of religion, outside in the streets his men pillaged and murdered. The customary heads were demanded which, when they were brought in, were piled in pyramids.

Moving on to Damascus he found the citizens were prepared to accept his suzerainty. Having agreed to pay a certain tribute they opened their gates to his soldiers. No sooner was Tamerlane in than

[1] E. Gibbon: *Decline and Fall of the Roman Empire.*

he violated all the agreements, imposing a fine of ten million pieces of gold, which, even had they been willing to pay, the people could not possibly find. Once again the soldiers were let loose and after an orgy of blood the proud city of Damascus was reduced to ashes.

He next advanced on Baghdad, which in September 1401 he besieged. Although the Sultan, Ahmad, fled to join the Ottomans in Asia Minor, the people remained undeterred and decided to resist. For six long weeks the defenders held out, repairing breaches as they occurred and, in the summer heat, suffering every hardship. Eventually the place was carried by assault and then occurred a bloodbath in which as many as ninety thousand were butchered. To satisfy Tamerlane's lust one hundred and twenty towers were erected with the skulls of those who were slain. He had achieved his object; he had retaken Baghdad and re-established his position in Syria; the Mamluks were discredited; and fear had entered the hearts of all who had attempted to oppose him. Tamerlane went into winter quarters in Azerbaijan, leaving several divisions in the country to ensure there would be no further trouble.

In the meantime there had been no reconciliation with Bayazid. At this point it is well to consider the Ottoman power, its origins and present position, for no appreciation of the trial of strength that was about to take place is possible without this. The founder, Osman, was an Anatolian Turk who died in 1326. Two years before his death, he occupied the Christian city of Bursa, which lay some twenty miles inland from the Sea of Marmora. The city surrendered to him, there was no bloodshed and many of the Christians adopted Islam. He was succeeded by Orkhan, who, by cautious and non-belligerent methods, extended his boundaries westwards to the Dardanelles and across on to the mainland of Thrace to a distance of some sixty miles along the eastern bank of the Maritza River. The Osmanlis did not apparently persecute the Christians, possibly because this might have brought retaliation and revivified the decaying Orthodox Church. On his death in 1359 he was succeeded by his son, Murad. A great statesman and a great soldier, Murad set about extending his kingdom, not in Asia, but in Europe. Under him the Ottomans, as they were now called, became a European power. In 1366 Murad moved his capital across the water to Adrianople, thus clearly indicating the pole or axis of his new kingdom. In a series of actions against the Bulgarians and Serbs he pushed his boundaries up to the line of the Danube and in the west almost to the borders of Albania. As he advanced his kingdom, he systematically consolidated his position by planting settlers. He established a well-organised administration under which many of those he had conquered voluntarily adopted the Islamic faith and enlisted in his army. This policy was in marked contrast with the negative one Tamerlane seemed to follow.

When, in 1389, at the Battle of Kossovo Murad died he was succeeded by his son, Bayazid Yilderim, the Lightning, a restless, able, extremely ambitious man and it is with him that this story will deal. He harried the Hungarians and Serbs, penetrating into the heart of Moldavia, and, not content with his European successes, his armies ravaged Asia Minor from Ankara to Erzurum. In the words of Gibbon: 'Whatever yet adhered to the Greek Empire in Thrace, Macedonia and Thessaly acknowledged a Turkish Master; an obsequious bishop led him [Bayazid] through the gates of Thermopylae.'[1]

It is against this background of aggressive Ottoman power that the sadly declining Christian kingdom founded by Constantine must be viewed. Not only were there schisms between the Churches of Rome and of Greece but the very House of Constantine was divided. His great kingdom had by now shrunk to a small enclave around the walled city of Constantinople, which Bayazid now laid siege to, calling on its emperor, Manuel, to surrender. This Manuel courageously refused to do and, making his escape in a Venetian galley, he set out on a last appeal for help. Although the title of emperor still carried the glamour of past centuries of glory, he received no help from Venice, Paris or London, all of which he visited. The irony was that Constantinople was to be saved not by any Christian act but as we shall see by the intervention on the scene of Tamerlane.

While engaged in the siege of Baghdad Tamerlane had been corresponding with Bayazid, whose capture of Erzincan on the upper Euphrates had angered him. Constantinople, still under siege, had solicited Tamerlane's aid, offering assistance with troops and galleys that they claimed could be used to prevent Bayazid's army from crossing the Bosphorus and entering Anatolia. Tamerlane did

[1] Ibid.

not take this offer up, and Bayazid, crossing by the Dardanelles, encamped his main army at Ankara. There could be only
one interpretation of his move: Bayazid meant war and the challenge
would have to be accepted.

On the fall of Baghdad, Tamerlane moved to Tabriz, there to
concentrate an army for the now inevitable conflict. It was during
this period that he wrote to Charles VI of France, probably at the
instigation of Bishop John of Sultaniah, by whom his letter was
carried. In this he informed the King that he was marching against
their common enemy, Bayazid, and among other things said he hoped
that their two countries could trade with one another. There were
two letters and contrary to some beliefs there is no evidence to
indicate that in these he suggested the sharing of the world by himself and France. However, he did say that Bishop John would speak
for him on all matters except those of religion. This was Tamerlane
the politician, as astute as he was cautious, as curious as he
was adventurous. This was the side of his character that he also showed to the Spanish Ambassador, Ruy Gonzalez de Clavijo, who undoubtedly fell under his spell. For all his brutality, Tamerlane was
a man of fine feelings, of intellect and discernment. However, this
narrative is at the moment concerned with him as a general.

In terms of numbers Bayazid was superior to Tamerlane whose
total force has been put at between eighty and a hundred and twenty
thousand men. The Ottoman's army included all those veteran
regiments that had fought with him so successfully at Kossova and
Nicopolis, where the Crusaders were so hopelessly beaten. At Bursa
he received welcome reinforcements from his well-tried troops
in Anatolia as well as a force of over twenty thousand cavalry under
Peter Lazarus, the King of Serbia. New contingents also arrived
from Greece with whom were Wallachian infantry. His army included the Sipahis and the Janissaries, *corps d'élite*, and well-
disciplined regular soldiers who were always under arms. In all, his
force well exceeded one hundred and twenty thousand. It was predominantly composed of infantry, which in defence should give him
an advantage, if he could only tempt Tamerlane to attack him. It
was on this that he based his strategy.

There were two areas that would suit this strategy and both
were suitable for defence; they were Ankara where he now was and
the area around Tokat, about forty miles to the north of Sivas. It

was now late summer and the crops were ready for reaping. If he took up a position at Ankara the harvest which he was anxious to gather would fall into the enemy's hands and certainly be destroyed by him. If he moved to Tokat he knew that Tamerlane, sensitive about Sivas, would be tempted to attack him for here he would pose a threat which his enemy he felt would not ignore. So, leaving his baggage and stores at Ankara, he marched to Tokat. Militarily his arguments were sound; the only weakness was that they did not allow for the unexpected, for Tamerlane not reacting as Bayazid was convinced he would.

Tamerlane's strategy was masterful. He was not going to be drawn into action on ground unsuited to his horsemen, of which his army almost entirely consisted. If Bayazid thought that a threat to Sivas would tie him down, what effect would a threat to Ankara have on the Ottoman? So, leaving strong outposts at Sivas, he withdrew his main army southwards and by a series of forced marches reached Caesarea, a distance of one hundred and twenty miles, within six days. Here he halted for four days, watering and feeding his horses and resting his men. The route he had taken was a rough one south of the River Halys. It never entered Bayazid's head that Tamerlane would either leave Sivas to its apparent fate or, if he moved, that he would take the circuitous route that he did. In military history there are many examples of the dangers of a preconceived idea as to an opponent's actions. Of all mistakes this can prove the most serious in its consequences, for not only does it give the enemy freedom from molestation but also results in one's forces being unbalanced and then having to dance to the enemy's tune. The American general Stonewall Jackson won an outstanding victory at Winchester because he advanced by the road up the Laurey Valley which Banks never dreamed he would take.

Bayazid was baffled; he waited for days, sending out strong reconnaissances to Sivas and the surrounding country. Unable to find any trace of Tamerlane's main army, they returned and their reports mystified the Ottoman, who was determined not to move until he had more definite news. The first contact came when unexpectedly a regiment of Tamerlane's raided his right wing and after taking some prisoners disappeared as quickly as it had come. Believing they had come from the south, Bayazid now sent out a strong cavalry column beyond the river and, though they searched

K

the country thoroughly, they found nothing. About this time he received reliable reports that Tamerlane was approaching Ankara and, thoroughly alarmed, he set out in pursuit. His road was far shorter than that Tamerlane had taken, but as his men were mostly infantry they could not move at the pace of the enemy. The weather was hot and water scarce so that, when Bayazid arrived near Ankara, his men were tired, thirsty and bewildered.

Tamerlane for his part, after resting at Caesarea (Kayseri), had pushed on to Ankara. His march had been carried out with his customary caution and care for detail. He sent a cavalry division ahead to act as a screen, to search for water and gather grain, so that on arrival at their camp each evening his troops and animals could be watered and fed in security. It had been his object to get across his enemy's communications and to force the battle well inside enemy territory, as he had done in his war against the Golden Horde. On arrival at Ankara, he found Bayazid's base which he seized, using the Ottoman tents for his men.

Ankara lay in the centre of a wide plain, ground eminently suited to cavalry action yet offering little cover or encouragement for infantry operations. There was a small stream flowing into the area which he diverted by damming so that it ran into his lines, thus ensuring water for himself while denying it to Bayazid's men, a factor that in the battle was of considerable importance and almost decisive in its effects.

Ankara, which was walled, stood out against him, but before his men had succeeded in making a breach his cavalry reported Bayazid to be about twelve miles away. Even although some of his men had successfully stormed one of the bastions, Tamerlane withdrew into the defensive perimeter. Everyone was alert in his camp, which by now was well entrenched. Throughout the night camp-fires were kept burning, while the whole front was continuously patrolled by his ever-vigilant horse.

However, Bayazid did not close; indeed his men were too exhausted to do so, after a long march of over two hundred miles with little water and in the burning sun, only to find themselves denied their own camp and the water supply they had expected to find. But what of the future? He and not his enemy would have to attack and so he found himself forced to do what he had most dreaded—to assault with his infantry over open ground against defences behind which stood a mass of the finest horsemen Asia could produce. Any superiority he had in numbers was outweighed by the state of his troops, the shortage of water and the strength of Tamerlane's position.

Neverthless, at ten o'clock on the morning of 20th July 1402 the Ottoman attack was launched. With their drums thundering and cymbals playing they advanced on the impressively silent enemy. The first contact was made by Suleiman, Bayazid's son, who, with his horsemen from Asia Minor, charged Tamerlane's right. He was met by a shattering hail of arrows and flaming naphtha, horses and their riders falling in the dust and smoke. Nur ad-Din, one of Tamerlane's most able and experienced generals, counter-attacked with such effect that Suleiman's men were thrown back in disorder.

It was at this stage that some of the Tartars serving in Bayazid's army deserted and joined the enemy. This disloyalty in the Ottoman ranks was probably due to Bayazid's arrogant conduct in the past, which had contrasted so much with Murad's patient and wise command. Seeing the success on this part of the front, Tamerlane now edged his other wing forward, and this, breaking through the Turkish skirmishers, put the poorly mounted horsemen of Bayazid to flight, leaving his infantry in the centre unprotected.

At this juncture Tamerlane made an important decision that settled the final issue. His grandson, Pir Muhammad, seeing the situation of Bayazid's infantry asked that he might be permitted to attack them, and this the Emir refused. In war it is generally considered a first principle to reinforce success and this is what Tamerlane did. He ordered Pir Muhammad, with the Samarkand corps and his favourite Bahadurs, to support the successful left wing. Charging with the verve for which they were so famed, they struck at the stalwart Serb cavalry and European infantry, who, holding every hillock, tried in vain to stem the mad onrush. King Peter of Serbia lost his life and Bayazid's whole right wing was decimated. There in the centre stood the flower of the Ottoman army, the tried Janissaries, who had not struck a blow, their flanks exposed and the cavalry protection gone. Tamerlane now took command of the Tartar centre and advancing with his elephants he crushed the powerless infantry of the enemy, pouring down a stream of fire from the howdahs of his elephants. As Lamb aptly put it: 'In a wrack of dust

and din, on that sun-tortured plain, the weary Turks died.'[1] Bayazid
with great gallantry fought on; but, wounded and exhausted, he was
eventually captured.

The well-worn story that Bayazid was put in a cage and taken
round like an animal has been rightly discredited. Bayazid was by
this time a sick man and had in fact to be carried in a litter, which
may have given rise to this tale. Indeed Tamerlane sent doctors to
attend him and appeared to have acted with every courtesy.

After this, Bursa fell and the Emir celebrated a great victory
with a suitable banquet which Bayazid attended, but at which he
was too ill to eat; his strength had been sapped by the ordeals of
battle and, as the less charitable said, by his past debaucheries. In
this campaign he seemed to have lost the great powers of generalship which in the past he had consistently shown. He had been forced
to march and counter-march, to fight where he least expected, as well
as in circumstances that could scarcely have been more unfavourable.
In fact he had been out-generalled by a greater man and that really
is the truth of his downfall.

Tamerlane marched on to Smyrna, which was still held by the
Hospitallers and which Bayazid had never succeeded in capturing.
The Hospitallers would not surrender; they had, after all, withstood Bayazid's attempts over the past six years. Tamerlane constructed wooden platforms out over the water beyond which the
Christian fortress was perched high upon a rock. The Emir next
started to build a mole in order to close the narrow entrance to the
bay. Eventually some three thousand of the knights, fighting their
way down from the heights, boarded their galleys. Nevertheless
when the Tartars eventually departed from Smyrna they left behind
a monument of two pyramids of heads. Tamerlane went on to
Ephesus, where, on his orders, his horsemen rode down the little
children who had come out into the streets to sing his welcome. He
finally revisited Georgia which again he pillaged on the pretext of
another Holy War.

Bayazid's eldest son and successor, Suleiman Chelebi, had to
pay homage to Tamerlane; but, with diplomatic cunning, the Tartar
encouraged each of the other sons to aspire to the throne and by so
doing sowed the seeds of future discord in the hope that it would
strengthen his own position.

[1] Harold Lamb: *Tamerlane—the Earthshaker.*

Tamerlane never set foot in Europe, for his interests lay not here but in the East. The monarchs of the West, until so recently fearful of Ottoman penetration, were irresolute; now it would seem, was the opportunity to drive the Muslims out of their countries; but they neither seemed to have the sagacity nor the courage to act and in the meantime Venetian and Genoese sailors earned good money for their kings by ferrying the remnants of Bayazid's army across the Dardanelles. In France and England alone was his victory acclaimed, both Charles VI and Henry IV sending him letters of congratulation. Charles recalled the visit of Bishop John of Sultaniah whom he summoned to his presence giving him gifts with his letter. As Constantinople was now freed from the terrible Ottoman threat, Manuel returned to his capital. Although Tamerlane had not raised a finger for this great city, the irony of fate was that it was by his victory that she was now to enjoy freedom for another fifty years. In Egypt and Syria the Mamluks recognised him as their lord and the name Timur was engraved on their coinage. In Cairo lay Egypt's wealth and from the treasury there he received precious gifts as well as the tribute which he demanded.

Such were Tamerlane's formidable successes in this latest campaign. In all, his writ henceforth ran from Delhi to the borders of Eastern Europe, from Russia to Cairo and eastwards in Central Asia to the Altais. He was, however, still restless and his intention to invade China was as strong as ever.

From Samarkand to Peking was over three thousand miles across deserts and over mountains. His energy was unabated and with his customary eye for detail he organised this, his last expedition. The arrangements included the deployment of garrisons to ensure the security of his empire and his capital at Samarkand, for he knew he would be absent for many years.

Eventually, in December 1404, he set out and by January had crossed the frozen waters of the Syr-Darya at Otrar. Here he was taken ill, an illness from which he did not recover. At the height of his career, in his seventieth year while at the head of his army, on the 19th January 1405, he died. It was the passing of one of the greatest men of history. Had death not snatched him away it is impossible to say what further conquests would have been his.

To assess Tamerlane as a man is not easy; there were such differences in his behaviour, contradictions that are not simple to explain

away. Power he sought and power he gained; but what of his use
or misuse of it? That he was intelligent there is no doubt. He was a
man of letters and had scribes who kept daily records of events. With
great patience he read their work which he took infinite care to
verify, correcting and altering as he deemed fit. Nazim-i-Shams, a
member of his court, was the man he first entrusted with this work
which, when he had completed it, was called *Zafar Nama*, the *Book
of Victory*. A second history was written by Sherif ad-Din which
brought events up to the date of his death and which is known under
the title *The History of Timur-Beg*. Tamerlane is also alleged to
have written the '*Institutes*' and these, called the *Malfuzat Timuri*,
contain much that give insight to his character and thoughts. From
all this one gets the impression of a man who was not only a warrior
but a man of learning who esteemed and enjoyed the company of
wise men.

He loved the fine arts and in his buildings he showed origin-
ality and imagination. His true love was for Samarkand, and Babur
in his memoirs, written over a hundred years after Tamerlane's
death, bore witness to the splendour of the architecture. At the time
of his visit to the court of Tamerlane, the Ambassador from the
King of Spain, Ruy Gonzalez de Clavijo, refers to the 'grand
edifices . . . very skilfully ornamented with mosaics and blue and
gold work'.[1] Tamerlane loved splendour and gave to the occasion
the dignity that was its due. Yet, this lover of art and beauty, this
king in whose court the rules of etiquette were jealously adhered to,
this man who could be charming to foreign visitors, could also be
cruel and barbarously vindictive. He said he believed in justice and
that was his reason for ruthlessly punishing tyrants. After his early
experience in a loathsome dungeon he vowed that though he might
be obliged to kill either as a punishment or in self-defence he would
never keep a human being in prison. He could appear urbane, but
as he wrote, 'The art of government consists, in part, of patience
and firmness, and in part of simulated indifference with a talent for
seeming not to know what one knows.'[2]

Loved by his army and his followers he was hated and feared by
those whom he conquered. He never seemed to have the knack that
Jenghiz Khan had of winning over the affection of those whom he had

---

[1] Narrative of the Embassy of Ruy Gonzalez de Clavijo.
[2] *Malfuzat Timuri* or *Institutes*.

beaten in battle. He ruled by fear and it would seem fear alone. His administration of conquered countries was designed to bring in taxes, to ensure law and order and the proper upkeep of important roads; in no sense was it aimed at colonisation as was the case with Murad. A rule built on fear could only last as long as the King lived; with his death the fear vanished, and with it law and order. Though Tamerlane may have been a man of letters he was one destitute of true philosophy or understanding of ultimate reality. Posing as a devout Muhammadan he made war on Muslim states whenever it suited his ends. As a young man he may have been genuine in his beliefs, but as he grew older he trimmed his sails more to the winds; professing adherence to the Koran, he was at heart a Tartar. That he endeavoured to build up a lasting Islamic empire must be open to doubt, though many of the true followers had placed their faith in him. With his passing the dream of a universal caliphate ended for those imams who had so hopefully trusted the words of a Tartar. Though he talked and discussed with them, Tamerlane never shaped his plans to their wishes. In fact he had cared very little for them, always placing his personal ambition first. This self-interest was the dominant theme of his life.

How, in the cold light of historical analysis, does he stand in comparison with Jenghiz Khan and Qubilai Khan? By some he has been likened to the former, but no one seems to have contrasted him with the latter. Let us for a moment consider these three men, first as soldiers and then as statesmen.

That all were great generals there is no doubt; success did not come to them through sheer weight of numbers and brute force, but from a strategic and tactical skill, an instinctive knowledge of the art of war and from an ability to learn from experience. Both Jenghiz Khan and Tamerlane suffered early defeats, both were thrown into the wilderness and both fought back. While Tamerlane owed his come-back to political sagacity, Jenghiz Khan owed his to the slow build-up of life-long friendships. During this period of trial the Yasak was born and a philosophy that far outlived its author. In the exercise of generalship there was more in common between Jenghiz Khan and Qubilai Khan than between these two and Tamerlane. The canvas on which the two former worked was broad and their widely dispersed sweeping movements displayed a tactical concept on a grand scale. It postulated a complete confidence in subordinates on whose initiative and skill the supreme commander could and did rely. This was manifested in Jenghiz Khan's invasion of China, in his campaigns west of the Syr-Darya, and again in the wide sweeping operations of his general Jebei and the wise Sübetei; and with Qubilai Khan it was exemplified in his broad encircling movement into southern China and the latitude he allowed his general Bayan.

Tamerlane, on the other hand, exercised a more rigid control, concentrating rather than dispersing his armies. It was with a concentrated army that he pursued the Golden Horde and outwitted the Ottoman, Bayazid. He exercised a personal control of the battle more reminiscent of Napoleon than of his illustrious forbears. These two conceptions of war came not just from the influence of circumstance, they stemmed from two basically different philosophies. The one was that of men who stood back, directing and not interfering, and only intervening on rare occasions; the other was based on a personal direction, an intimate control and the exercise of detailed command. In modern war these were part of the differences dividing Eisenhower and Montgomery.

As a general Tamerlane's greatness remains unassailable. His invasion of Russia with all the calculated risks involved was the exploit of a giant; and his handling of Bayazid, a formidable warrior indeed, forcing this hitherto undefeated general to run hither and thither was a display of tactical genius, equalled perhaps only by Marlborough in his campaigns against Louis XIV. Tamerlane and Marlborough never allowed themselves to be caught off balance. Tamerlane was always assiduously careful of the security of his army and he evinced this before Delhi, just as he did in his advance through the Lands of the Shadows.

It is, however, as statesmen that these three men show the greatest differences; their use or misuse of power marks a difference that was fundamental. What was this? Victory in battle has great potential but only as great as the ability or genius of the victor to exploit with wisdom the vista that it opens. Jenghiz Khan repeatedly tried to win over the people of the lands he conquered. His aim was to gain co-operation, and this was why he enlisted their men into his army and gave to the elders positions of trust. Thus did he treat the people of Khwarazm and it was only through the duplicity of the emirs that his policy here broke down; to this and to this only was the remorselessness of his future campaigns due. His policy in China resulted in his having over twenty divisions of loyal Chinese troops and engineers and, at his court, he had Chinese men of learning in whom he trusted. He thought of the future and endeavoured to lay foundations on which his sons could build. Though not making any professions of faith as Tamerlane did, he could never deceive and with the Taoist monk tried hard to find eternal truth.

Qubilai Khan, too, was a politician of outstanding ability. His understanding of the Chinese and sympathy with them drew their people to him. Though he conquered the land he was not hated as he might have been; he was in fact more respected than feared. Marco Polo leaves a vivid impression of the Great Khan and, though perhaps biased, his descriptions are in the main accurate. Although later, outside China, Qubilai Khan showed greed and unreasonableness in Thailand and in Japan, in spite of this his general use of power was for the good of the people whom he justly ruled.

What of the political wisdom of Tamerlane? In his youth, his handling of Tughluk, Lord of the Chaghatai, had shown a political awareness which brought him immediate rewards; but his later foolishness lost all that he had gained, when he bit the hand that fed him. In contrast, though Jenghiz Khan was forced to fight his friend, the Khan of the Keraits, this was due to no fault of his and, once having sworn loyalty, he did not break his vow. Tamerlane's wars in Fars, Iraq, Georgia, Afghanistan and in India had neither strategic nor political justification. They evinced a desire for power without any deep sincerity of purpose. Though he left governors and emirs in charge, he gave no political power, neither colonising nor incorporating into a commonwealth of nations; the people conformed from fear and nothing else. The political vistas that his victory over the Ottomans opened, he never seemed to see. He could have had the Christian world behind him, but he failed; that he was not unfavourable to having political relations with the Christian people is evidenced by his correspondence with Charles VI of France, and in his capital and at Tabriz Christians lived in security. But when Constantinople was prepared to work with him and to make the movement of Bayazid's army across the waters impossible he failed to take advantage of this freely offered friendship. Tamerlane was not a great statesman and what political philosophy he had was devoid of depth; a man of the moment, when he died nothing save bricks and mortar remained. Thus, one is left with an admiration for a great general, combined with a feeling of nausea for a cruel, ambitious man, who, having gained power, seemed incapable of using it for good.

Although the Empire of Jenghiz Khan lasted in one form or another for many centuries, that of Tamerlane fell to pieces after his death. Samarkand ceased to be the capital when Shah Rukh, his fourth son, removed his capital to Herat; Transoxania fell into a state of ferment; little kings and petty chiefs made hay while they could, and in the meantime the Uzbeks grew in strength. There was little stability. It was into this maelstrom that the boy Babur was thrown at a tender age. In his memoirs Babur succinctly wrote: 'In the month of Ramazan, in the year fourteen hundred and ninety-four, in the twelfth year of my age, I became King of Fergana.'[1]

It is incredible and yet a fact that this man, succeeding to king-ship as a mere child in the most unpropitious circumstances, should ultimately found a dynasty that was to rule in India for three hundred years; should be famed as the author of memoirs that have been described as *littera scripta*[2] and which remain immortal; and who left a justifiable reputation as one of the greatest gardeners of his-tory. Many kings have been great soldiers; many have combined these qualities with outstanding administrative ability; but few have possessed such a combination of qualities as did this happy warrior.

The little kingdom of Fergana, whose ruler he was to be, nestled

[1] *Memoirs of Babur.*
[2] Stanley Lane-Poole: *Babur.*

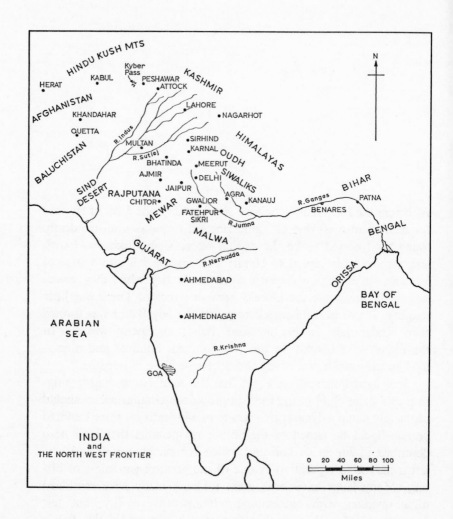

INDIA
and
THE NORTH WEST FRONTIER

in a beautiful hilly landscape; on the north bounded by the Tian Shan Mountains and on the south by the Hindu Kush. This lovely land was the source of the two great rivers, the Syr-Darya and the Amu-Darya. Some two hundred and fifty miles to the west was Samarkand and about the same distance beyond that lay Bukhara. Across the Hindu Kush was Kabul and the Khyber Pass leading to the arid plains of Hindustan. In this tangle of mountains and rushing streams, with its orchards and its gardens, Babur was destined to fight and roam and fight again. This was his native home and he loved it dearly. Its capital was the little town of Andi-zhan, the gardens of which were profuse with flowers. By its streams grew tulips and roses. The country was noted for its fruit, particularly its grapes and melons, while in the meadows were many birds. The pheasants were so fat that four hungry men could dine off one. The venison was excellent and the hunting of the wild deer a popular sport. Hawking was another pastime and polo was played on the flat areas of ground. All was gaiety, the people wearing brightly coloured clothes with purple as their favourite colour. The men were wild, impetuous, intensely clannish and politically unstable; but they all had impeccably good manners.

Babur's father, Omar-Sheikh-Mirza, had been an ambitious man who had made many enemies among the neighbouring chieftains. He was blessed with exceptional strength and if he hit a man he generally knocked him to the ground. He loved all forms of good living, but was particular neither about his dress nor his appearance. He was generous, humane, magnanimous and was as brave as he was manly. He was very fond of pigeons and it was his love of these that led to his untimely death. For one day, when tending a loft on the outer wall of the fort at Akhsi which overlooked a precipice, the wall gave way and, in the words of his son, he took his flight to the other world.

Babur, the eldest of eight children, had been named Zahir-ad-din, but because his mother's father was a Mongol and could not pronounce the letter Z he was called Babur, which in English means Tiger. The boy had every right to such a name for something of the tiger was in him. On his father's side he was descended from Jenghiz Khan and on his mother's from Tamerlane. This factor influenced him throughout his life, but he always had the greatest admiration for Tamerlane. Even as a boy he received the Sultan Masud Mirza 'sitting on a cushion, according to the custom of the sovereigns of the house of Taimur'.[1]

Of all the members of his family he had most respect for his maternal grandmother, who on more than one occasion helped him in the early and difficult years of his reign. Of her he tells the following anecdote. Having fallen into the hands of an enemy of her husband she was given by her captor to one of his officers. At the time she made neither remonstrance nor lamentation, but when the man entered her room she killed him and she and her maid threw his body into the street. She sent word to the man's master to say she was the wife of Yunis Khan; she had been given to another man which was against the Law of the Prophet, so she had killed him. 'Come, kill me if you choose,'[2] she said. She was not killed but was immediately released. She was a formidable woman.

For this and indeed for all the main details of Babur's life we are indebted to his memoirs from which I have quoted frequently. As one reads these one cannot help developing an admiration for and a sympathy with this remarkable character. The frankness with which he states his opinions, his likes and dislikes, his assessment of those who were around him, and the reasons for his actions dispel any doubt as to their veracity. For example, of India he wrote: 'Hindustan is a country that has few pleasures to recommend it.[3] Devastating and surely unjust, but in a few words one has his opinion. In these writings he makes life around him live and in so doing unconsciously throws light on his own attractive personality. Although courage and will-power were among his assets, one of his greatest gifts was his ability to assess the characters of those around him. His comments on these men, their strong points and their weaknesses, are as discerning as they are witty. He dismissed Kamber Ali, a Mongol, as 'A man of narrow capacity and muddy brain'.[4] Ahmad Beg, one of his nobles he said 'was an admirable horseman and kept excellent horses that he bred himself. Though a brave man his generalship was not quite equal to his courage. He was carefree and left the conduct of his affairs to his servants and dependants.'[5] He made a certain Baba Kuli a governor because of his ability to

[1] *Memoirs of Babur*.
[2] Ibid.
[3] Ibid.
[4] Ibid.
[5] Ibid.

maintain discipline among his troops and because 'he kept a watchful eye on his servants'.[1] Of the people of Fergana and their habits he wrote that they 'have a way of taking stones out of apricots and putting almonds in their place, which is very pleasant'.[2] He wrote of the lovely meadows where men used to rest, describing them as being like a mantle of lambskins to the weary traveller. His love of birds and animals was combined with a keen hunting instinct as is evidenced by his writing of Fergana as good sporting country.

Nevertheless, he was more than a writer and philosopher; he was a soldier who had to fight hard to hold his own in a world where might was so often right. In later life his generalship in his campaign in India was outstanding. At the time of his father's death Sultan Muhammad Khan and his uncle, Sultan Ahmad Mirza, had contracted an alliance and were marching on the capital. Neither of these threats was serious and both for different reasons withdrew. But he had to face revolts in all quarters, losing the important towns of Khojend, Marghinan and Urakipa; however by skilful negotiations he managed to retain control over the rest of the land.

He now devoted his attention to the problems of administration of his kingdom, a forbidding task for a boy scarcely out of his twelfth year. Helped by his maternal grandmother and other advisers he wisely contented himself with confirming most of his father's appointments, among which was Hasan Yakub whom he retained as governor of the capital; yet of the many who ultimately defected Hasan Yakub was the first to go. Nevertheless, the black clouds of the future had as yet not darkened his horizon and in these early days he received promises of loyalty over the greater part of his realm.

It was in this atmosphere of apparently justified confidence that he now looked across his borders and his eyes were soon directed at Samarkand. The capital of his forbear, Tamerlane, this glittering city acted like a magnet. The place was, moreover, ripe for the picking; but whereas taking was one thing Babur was to find that holding was another. At first he led an assault in co-operation with his friend Sultan Ali of Bukhara; but when Ali became involved in his own problems Babur continued on his own. Eventually in 1497, two years after setting out, Samarkand fell; its ineffectual king,

[1] Ibid.
[2] Ibid.

Baiesanghan Mirza, deserted by many of his troops, was forced to flee.

Babur was fascinated with Samarkand. He wrote that of the whole habitable world there must be few cities so pleasantly situated and described in detail its many beautiful buildings. Of those that attracted him most he loved the stately palace known as the Gok-serai which Tamerlane had erected. There was also the Grand Mosque which had been constructed by stone-cutters from Hindustan and decorated with inscriptions from the Koran. And Tamerlane had, in addition to the many other buildings, built a large observatory that he had equipped with the most up-to-date astronomical apparatus.

To add to his delight he found the climate stimulating, the appearance of the surrounding country beautiful and the many gardens a constant pleasure. The latter had been tastefully laid out on a regular plan and here were born the ideas of the formal gardens for which in later years he was to become so famed. Elms, cypresses and white poplars grew in profusion and all these had been systematically laid out. At the foot of the Hill of Kojak was a particularly exotic garden in which were fine buildings, the most interesting being the Chinese House, the walls of which were overlaid with porcelain brought specially from distant Cathay.

At first Babur was able to reward his soldiers with loot; but soon the deprivations of war both within the city and in the surrounding country made it impossible to provide adequate supplies of food for his men or fodder for his horses. Many of his following departed until finally he found himself alone, save for a mere handful of loyal troops. As though this were not enough, he now heard of revolts in his own kingdom. Leaving Samarkand he set out for Fergana; but when he reached Khojend news came that Andizhan had fallen.

A nominal king at Samarkand, he had in the process of conquest lost his own country. In his memoirs he particularly wrote that he had lost the one without preserving the other. Many begs and soldiers who had their families in Andizhan deserted him, only some two hundred remaining loyal. Babur blamed the dissident nobles, yet surely the fault was his. Immature judgement had led him to grasp at things beyond his compass and in so doing to lose the substance for the shadow. Youth and impetuosity, inexperience and unfounded optimism were the root causes of his distress.

With no little courage, great tenacity and much skill he fought back, attacking and retaking Samarkand; but the odds were too heavily loaded against him and so once again he was forced to retreat. With only a handful of men he eventually found himself a fugitive in his native land, forced to live in the hills, dwelling in shepherds' huts and having to suffer the ill-concealed ungracious protection of his Mongol relatives. In 1504, when he was twenty-two years of age, he crossed into the Hissar territory of Bukhara with about three hundred faithful adherents. Such was his predicament that between them all there were but two tents, one of which he gave to his mother. In his struggles for his country his arch-enemy had been Shaibani Khan who by now was master of Samarkand and all Fergana. Happily for Babur as each day passed his ranks were swelled by men who, discontent with conditions in Hissar, were seeking a new leader. Among them were bands of Mongols who had defected from Khusrau Shah, a bullying adventurer who had seized control of the country and whose cruelty was a byword. Finding himself deserted, Khusrau Shah threw himself on Babur's mercy making over to him his arms, some seven or eight hundred suits of armour and quantities of other equipment. For Babur the tide was beginning to turn.

Though his following was growing his position in Hissar was insecure and so he naturally looked south to Afghanistan where the pleasant city of Kabul lay. Always influenced by the astrologers, he was encouraged by the sight of the star Canopus which lay low on the southern horizon; here he said was a sign he should not ignore. It is strange; but this idea, born of a superstitious belief, marked the turning point of his career and indeed ultimately settled the fate of India for several hundred years. He marched to Kabul and from there mounted his invasion of Hindustan. The Afghans had little stomach for fighting and so he was able without serious opposition to take possession of both Kabul and Ghazni. That he had a low opinion of the Afghans there seemed little doubt, for of them he said, 'a narrow place is large enough to the narrow-minded'.[1] Although, by comparison with his own sparsely populated hills, the country was thickly peopled, his first impressions were not favour-

[1] Ibid.

L

able. This was strange because eventually he developed a love for Kabul, far greater than any affection he could muster for India. At his death he was at his own wish buried by the spring in the gardens on the hillside at Kabul, of which he had said, 'When the aarghan flowers are in bloom, the yellow mingling with the red, I know no place in the world to compare with it.'[1] Afghanistan was not easily accessible and for five months of the year Kabul was snow-bound; nevertheless in the meadows of Chalak there was lush grass although in the summer mosquitoes abounded to the discomfort of both men and horses. Fruit was plentiful but grain was scarce. Always a horticulturist, Babur discovered no less than thirty-three kinds of tulip and noted the beautiful aarghan to which reference has already been made. Grapes were plentiful and particularly good, as were the peaches, apricots, almonds and walnuts. In the spring when these trees were in bloom their delicate colours gave beauty to the otherwise drab colours of rock and stone.

Kabul was a great horse-dealing centre and from Hindustan large quantities of cloth were imported from the sale of which merchants made enormous profits. This romantic city was an *entrepôt*, a meeting place for many people, and no less then eleven languages could be heard in its bazaars. Babur originally had great hopes of raising large quantities of grain from here and Ghazni, but soon discovered he was aiming too high; nevertheless, in spite of this the revenues he obtained were considerable. From the merchants and the caravans he heard of the lands beyond the Khyber which stirred his ambitions. He thought of Tamerlane and like Tamerlane he decided to invade the country. At first there was no question of conquest and he was animated by no other thought than loot, mingled with a not unnatural curiosity. When the sun was in Aquarius he set out from Kabul. In the rock-strewn Khyber the scenery was magnificent in its barren grandeur, but as he descended into the plain beyond he found himself in a new world, a place of warm temperatures with new grasses, new trees, unknown animals and strange and beautiful birds. Here there was game in plenty as well as plunder for his troops. He marched on Kohat which for two days he plundered and thence proceeded to Bannu. Passing along the Indus he reached Dera Ghazi Khan and, turning north, entered the Gomal Valley. By the lake at Ab-i-Istada observed what

[1] Ibid.

appeared to be a reddish twilight which, when he got closer, he found was an immense flock of flamingos; as they moved their wings in flight the red feathers, at intervals seen and then hidden, gave the illusion of the ruddy crepuscule. Here, too, he saw flocks of every species of bird and along the banks of the river were the eggs of countless fowl. Crossing the Ghilzai Mountains to the north he reached Ghazni at the close of the year 1504, the year he had first entered Kabul.

Two years later he set out for Khorasan with the object of checking Uzbek aggression in that area. Although he moved with great rapidity, discarding his baggage and camp-followers with all their paraphernalia, he never in fact got to grips with the Uzbeks. He was met by the Mirzas who had come out to greet him and here one gets the first impression of his assessment of his own importance. He had not, he felt, been received with the respect that was his due. 'Though but young', he wrote, 'I was of high extraction and when a prince had done what I had done to show me any want of respect was not quite commendable.' His rebuff was well received and there followed a series of drinking parties and much gaiety, to which Babur at this time was unaccustomed. But this, before his stay was over, seems to have been put right as from this date until his battle against the great Rajput general, Rana Sangrama, in 1526, he was a heavy drinker and his memoirs abound with stories of gay drinking parties. It was prior to this battle that he renounced drink for the remainder of his life. Among the Mirzas there was little talk of war and, as time dragged on, Babur began to fret about affairs at Kabul. Deciding it was time to leave, and not wishing to divulge his real reasons, he pleaded the necessity of going into winter quarters.

He gives a vivid description of the march back over the mountains through the deep snow and in the bitter cold. At times the road completely disappeared and, snow-bound, they were forced to halt. Their pace of advance slowed down to two or three miles a day as with every step, they sank up to their chests in snow. It was in these circumstances that Babur displayed the best of his character. This was no time, he said, to plague the men or for the display of authority; each must show his spirit and endeavour to emulate the courage of the other. On reaching a small cave one evening he prepared for himself a small area on which to rest, no larger than a prayer mat. His men desired him to take shelter in the cave but he would not go, feeling that for him to be in the warmth while his men were in the bitter cold would scarcely be consistent with what he owed them. Comforting himself as he shivered in the cold he thought of the Persian proverb—death in the company of friends is a feast. The qualities of leadership are many; but of them all this one is the most important: nothing will draw troops closer to their general than the genuine sharing of hardship.

Eventually they got beyond the worst of the conditions only to run into new dangers. Their advanced guard was halted by a body of Hazaras who were holding a prominent hill covering the road to Kabul. Babur, seeing this, ordered his men to push on, but on observing their unwillingness to do so led them himself. They followed him, some on foot and some on horse, and the position was quickly taken. The Hazara leaders taken prisoner were set free as were the remainder.

As he approached Kabul he realised the place was already under siege. Muhammad Husain, whom Babur described as a blind and confirmed heretic but a brave and courageous warrior, with Sultan Birlas, both of whom Babur regarded as his friends, had in his absence proclaimed his cousin Khan Mirza as King of Kabul. They had been joined by a large body of Mongols whose loyalty Babur had not hitherto questioned. Nevertheless most of the inhabitants had remained true to him and were doing all in their power to put the defences of the fortress in good order. To them he sent a message appraising them of his plans for their relief. His intention was to approach by the pass through Ghuband and he would, when he was ready to assault, light a fire on a certain hill in reponse to which the garrison were to light one on the citadel. When he saw this he would attack. In due course the fire was seen and, spurred on by the necessity for speed, he personally led the attack. Those who attempted to withstand him were overcome and, retreating through the narrow streets, were thrown into confusion. However, though he eventually entered his capital in triumph, the disloyalty that he found even among his own family affected him deeply.

In the palace he immediately went to visit his relatives, the Shah Begum and the Princess, whom he saluted with the same respect he was accustomed to show, notwithstanding the fact that they had sheltered the usurper Khan Mirza. Such was their embarrassment that they could neither speak nor stammer an excuse and so they sat silently before him. All this made him very sad, but not vindictive; even though in searching through the Princess's rooms he found Muhammad Husain, the instigator of the revolt. Magnanimously, on account of his blood relationship, he allowed him to go free to Khorasan. He sent men in pursuit of Mirza, who, when he was captured, was also permitted to go to Khorasan.

Although in dealing with his peers Babur had insisted on the respect that he considered his due, in victory he showed clemency to captives. When his men were suffering hardship he shared their miseries with them, and when they wanted leadership in battle he gave it. While Tamerlane certainly had these same qualities of leadership he did not possess the magnanimity of Babur.

In 1507 he again raided northern India. He pillaged the Ghilzais and marched on Kilat which fell with no resistance. The merchants were taken by surprise and the temptation to the soldiers to pillage was great; but Babur would not permit this, contenting himself with levying a tribute. Turning north he moved on Kandahar and here the riches were such that the temptation to stay and enjoy the rewards were strong, However, his friend, Kasim Beg, strongly urged him not to tarry and this advice, after distributing the prizes to the soldiery, he took. They had not the time to count out the money and had to use scales to weigh and divide it and their animals were borne down with the sheer weight of treasure. When they reached Kabul the rejoicing was great and Babur's reputation high. Within a few days he learned that Shaibani Khan with a large army had laid siege to Kandahar and he realised now the wisdom of Kasim Beg's advice.

Babur's troubles were, however, by no means over for he was still threatened by disloyalty. Kuch Beg, a hitherto reliable and gallant soldier, with Fakir Ali and Baba Chehreh, formed a plan against him; but, caught in the middle of the enterprise, they were frustrated and imprisoned. Next he heard of a large-scale Mogul design to kill him. The clouds of disappointment were temporarily lifted when on the fourth day of the month of Zilqa'deh, when the sun was in Aquarius, a son was born to him whom he called Humayun. Early the following year he faced yet another revolt, the number of rebels being estimated at thirty thousand. In circumstances that would have daunted a less staunch character, discarding any idea of defensive tactics, he sought out his opponents wherever he could find them. Exposing himself to every danger, attacking when opportunity presented itself, he drew forth the admiration of all. His followers steadily grew as success followed success. Just at this moment an unexpected event played into his hands. His friend, Shah Ismail, the King of Persia, attacked his old arch-enemy Shaibani Khan whom he utterly routed and killed in the battle. From now Babur's position rapidly improved; soon he was in possession of Hissar, Bukhara and his beloved Samarkand.

When all seemed so propitious events outside his control once again upset his hopes. The ever-growing power of the Uzbek tribes was making itself felt. Coming down from the north they overran Transoxania and by 1515 had occupied Samarkand. The force of this invasion was more than Babur could withstand and so, once again, he moved to Kabul. This was the point at which he had to make a decision. Was he to fight back for what he had lost or were the odds too great? Facing up to the realities of the situation he made the fateful and hard decision to give up once and for all any idea of trying to regain that which he held so dear, his own country of Fergana. So, realising that he must discard an emotional dream for reality, his eyes turned east. Tamerlane had shown the way. Babur has seen enough of Hindustan, as he called it, to realise that here was a jewel the possession of which should not be beyond his compass. Here he would have nothing to fear from the Uzbeks nor would he be dependent on followers he had learned to mistrust. Those who were staunch and loyal could and would come with him. Kabul, an easily defensible place, would make an excellent spring-board for his enterprise and a firm base from which he could operate, south and not north.

Thus was the dream of India born. Babur was in his thirty-sixth year and Humayun was eleven. The callow young King of Fergana, who had made mistakes, was now an experienced man. He had never lacked courage; but wisdom he had been forced to fashion on the hard anvil of experience. He had learned how to handle men, he knew when to be strong and when to yield. He was not frightened of being magnanimous when he believed this to be right. He had learned whom to trust and whom he could not trust. Although it was a bitter blow to give up Fergana and dreams of Samarkand, he was aware of the true odds against him, and courageously he did not shrink from making a distasteful decision. He was always aware of the great house to which he was proud to belong and he would not tolerate any slight to his dignity. At this period of his life he was still a fairly heavy drinker, but he drank for the pleasure of the company and the occasion, and not from vice. He had a son and heir in whom he had confidence. In the prime of life he looked forward and not back; yet all the glittering jewels that lay ahead could never diminish his love of nature, of flowers and of the birds of the air and beasts of the field. He composed poetry, wrote beautiful prose and was a philosopher. He was, as well, a devout Muslim. Such was the future Emperor of India; such the man whom history has rightly called 'The Great Moghul'.

15 Babur—The Emperor

Tamerlane, when he left India, bequeathed nothing of permanence and the country degenerated into a series of petty states. As many of the Muslims grew soft in both a climate and conditions to which they were not accustomed, the once sturdy race of conquerors was fast becoming little more than a jostling crowd of place-seekers. The respect in which they had been held to a great extent evaporated. However, when in 1451 anarchy paved the way for the Lodi Afghan, Bahlol, to seize the throne at Delhi there was once more strong rule and something of the glory returned; but later, his successors, sometimes from necessity and at others in an attempt to strengthen their position, committed the government of the provinces to their countrymen and power once again became dissipated. Each governor, according to the Afghan way of thinking, considered his office as his right rather than due to the bounty or liberality of the sovereign. There was thus little cohesion and the people naturally tended to look to their immediate governor, in whose hands their happiness or misery lay, rather than to the distant and little-known sovereign at Delhi. Furthermore, Afghans resented any undue assumption of sovereignty and only with difficulty could they tolerate the rules of etiquette and the tedious customs of a formal court. To them a king was little more than a chief or comrade-in-arms, who must not show airs or want of respect to the chiefs upon whose swords his dominion ultimately rested. At the time when

Babur contemplated his invasion of India the Lodi emperor, Ibrahim, was a man who delighted in formalities and to whom etiquette meant much. Although Ibrahim styled himself emperor, it is not surprising that between the Khyber and his capital there were large stretches of country in the hands of local chiefs or governors, the most important being Daulet Khan at Lahore.

What, however, of the rest of India? Where were the famous Rajputs and the fighting Jhats? Where were the lords of Marwar Amber, Gwalior, Ajmir and many more and who, if anyone, was at their head? Some of the Rajputs were in fact led by one worthy of the task, the great Sangrama Singh, of whose bravery we will hear more later; but, among others the old jealousies had once again reared their heads. Many Hindus had accepted office under Muslim lords and many others had even accepted the Islamic faith. Indeed, the body politic of northern Hindu India, save for some Rajputs and the Jhats, was without leadership and lacked any form of national unity.

To the south-east of the Delhi kingdom lay the predominantly Hindu areas of Bengal, Jaunpur, Gujarat and the Deccan, all of which were ruled by Muslims. Thus, the impression that Islamic domination was confined to the north is not founded on the facts; a point that Tamerlane seemed to have ignored. When Muhammad Ghuri appointed Kutb-ad-din Aybak as his viceroy at Delhi another of his generals, Bakhtiyar Muhammad, founded a kingdom in Bengal and from that date, 1202, until it was finally conquered by the son of Babur in 1537, Bengal retained its independence. Jaunpur, the 'Kingdom of the East', lying between Bengal and Delhi was founded by Khwaja-i-Jahan in 1394 and lasted until, nearly a hundred years later, it was brought under the sway of Delhi by the Lodi, Bahlol. From the middle of the fifteenth century the kings of Malwa had been Muslims. In 1397, a year before Tamerlane's invasion, Firuz Shah of Delhi granted a fief of Gujarat to Zafar Khan, the son of a converted Rajput. The importance of Gujarat lay in its sea trade, for through its ports the bulk of Indian trade with Persia, Arabia and the Red Sea passed. The Muslim rule in the Deccan was found in 1347 by Husan Gangu who was granted this independent kingship by Tughlak, then King of Delhi.

This was the India to which Babur's eyes were turned. What

were the factors that drove this descendant of Tamerlane to look south and to make his eventual home far away from the land of his forbears?

Whereas earlier Muslim invaders had been impelled by thoughts of a Holy War against an idolatrous people and the desire for loot, Babur's avowed intention was to take over and govern a country which he believed was his by right, and this conviction was apparently quite genuine if one can accept what one reads in his memoirs. But was this sheer invention and just the excuse of an adventurer who sought power where he felt it could be most easily gained? What, in fact, drew him to India?

India was strange to him and was a country that he really did not understand. He was a man of the hills, whose home was in the mountains of Fergana which he dearly loved. Between here and the arid plains of Hindustan lay Badakhshan, the Great Pamir Range and Hindu Kush, the countries of Chitral and Tirah. His antecedents and racial affinities were on the Amu-Darya. Why then did he look to the hot, dry plains that lay south of the Indus, to the Ganges and swamps of Bengal? The country never really appealed to him, neither did he admire its people of whom he wrote: 'They have no idea of the charms of a friendly society, of frankly mixing together, or of familiar intercourse.'[1] This is readily understandable, for among the people from whom he sprang there was a courteous way of life that was peculiarly attractive. The formalities of greetings were strictly observed and a high standard of polite behaviour was generally accepted. A person, though he or she may have plotted, was treated with courtesy; as for instance when Babur found the Shah Begum and the Princess had fostered a revolt against him. He greeted them 'with the same respect and form as I had been accustomed to use'.[2] A prisoner of family would be set free although he could never be fully pardoned; thus was Muhammad Husain set at liberty and allowed to go to Khorasan in spite of his 'having conducted himself in such a criminal and guilty way'. There were, of course, codes of behaviour among the Hindus, but these Babur did not seem to understand. He regarded them as idolaters and infidels and a people quite incapable of national loyalty or cohesion. Their caste system, which he probably never understood, baffled him. In

[1] Ibid.
[2] Ibid.

fairness, however, much that he wrote of a disparaging nature was done before he had been confronted by the Rajputs. When faced by them in their last stronghold, he paid great tribute to them as men and soldiers. He later also fully recognised the skill of the Hindu workmen whose ability as craftsmen he loudly praised.

If India as a country did not draw him what then were the compelling factors? The wealth that he ultimately found was incidental and, although this factor may have been in the background, it was not the predominating influence. This could be obtained by raids; the dominion which he sought had other root causes. There were three. First, that his own country was barred to him; second, his admiration for the Turkish as opposed to the Mongol way of life; and, third, his desire to emulate Tamerlane as he imagined him to have been.

The hard facts were that from bitter experience he had at last realised his own country was forbidden him. It, Samarkand, Bukhara and the surrounding areas were in the hands of the Uzbeks. A long struggle to re-establish himself there had only resulted in repeated failure and so he had been driven to Kabul. He knew he could no longer have hopes in the north; but in Kabul he was strong and the Afghans, who surrounded him, he held in contempt; experience had taught him that they had feet of clay. He had raided the lands over the Khyber Pass up to the line of the River Indus, raids that had added to his prestige but done little else. He could and indeed did raid further south; but these early forays did not as yet infer any idea of conquest and neither were they particularly lucrative.

Much of what he subsequently did stemmed from his dislike of the Mongols and its corollary, his admiration for the Turks. It is, therefore, strange that history should call him 'The Great Moghul'. Though a descendant of Jenghiz Khan on one side of his family and although his organisation and basis of his military thought was the ancient Yasak, he heartily disliked the Mongol race. Their perfidy had sickened him and their uncouth behaviour was foreign to his sensitive nature. Even members of his family had proved unreliable and at Kabul it was his Mongol aunt, Shah Begum, who had sided with those who had revolted against him in his absence. As a young man he had written in his diary: 'Such is the uniform practice of these wretches, the Mongols, if they defeat the enemy they instantly seize the booty; if they are defeated they plunder and dismount their allies.'[1] He penned the following couplet:

'If the Mongol race were a race of angels it is a bad one,
and were the name Mongol written in gold it would be odious.'[2]

Nevertheless, when he set out to conquer India his army included Mongol troops who, as part of Humayun's army, came from Bukhara. Be that as it may it was in this frame of mind that he was drawn to his Turkish extraction and in particular to Tamerlane, for whom from childhood he had always had a deep admiration. When, as a fugitive, he had been living with the shepherds in the hills of Fergana, he had sheltered with a headsman whose mother was said to have been a hundred and eleven years of age. She was a vigorous and talkative woman and her constant theme had been of the conquest of Hindustan by Tamerlane. One of her relatives had served in his army and Babur wrote that she often told stories on this subject, stories that added fuel to his admiration for his great ancestor. Thus, priding himself on his Turkish antecedents, he despised the Afghans and considered their rule in India as unlawful. Believing that the country properly belonged to Tamerlane and his successors he eventually persuaded himself that by invading India he would be fighting for the liberation of his people from a foreign yoke. The fact that they were predominantly Hindu and for the most part already ruled by Muslims, who were not even of Afghan extraction, never entered his calculations.

So, when in 1519, he set out to invade the country he sent an ambassador ahead to demand of the Emperor Ibrahim, that the countries which from old times belonged to the Turks[3] should be given up to him. He also sent letters to Daulat Khan, the governor at Lahore, in an endeavour to undermine his loyalty to his lord the Emperor. Ibrahim ignored his ultimatum and the vacillating, treacherous subordinate at Lahore prevaricated. As the season for operations was passing Babur returned to Kabul. In the following year he came again and this time at Sialkot he gained a success, the city surrendering with little or no opposition. Much to the relief

1 Ibid.
2 Ibid.
3 Ibid.

of the local inhabitants Babur had many Afghans put to death. Babur now heard that his Kabul kingdom was threatened by an invasion from Kandahar, which brought home to him the necessity of providing proper protection for his base before venturing on foreign enterprises. Among other precautions he placed the country of Badakhshan under his son, Humayun, to whom he allotted an adequate army.

Unrest and disloyalty in Ibrahim's kingdom played into Babur's hand. Once again he invaded the country and at Lahore he defeated Ibrahim's army, which had had to fight without Daulat Khan. Babur now found himself undisputed master in the Panjab. Leaving a strong garrison he returned to Kabul to make the final arrangements for the last and permanent occupation of Hindustan. This took place in the winter of 1525, on Friday the first of the month of Safar when the sun was in Saggitarius, an omen which as an astrologer he regarded as important. Of his army he wrote 'Great and small, good and bad, servants and no servants, the force numbered twelve thousand persons.' Humayun was to join him with his army from Badakhshan. He was, however, forced to write to his son very sharply for his slowness. In addition to Humayun's force Daulat Khan with his son, Ghazi Khan, had promised to join him with a motley crowd of thirty or forty thousand followers. But, recollecting that as the old proverb said 'Ten friends are better than nine'[1] Babur judged it advisable to wait for further reinforcements of his own from Lahore.

On his advance south he was attacked at Sialkot by parties of Jhats who swarmed down from the hills, but this he was able to cope with. He disliked the Jhats and did not seem to realise what a splendid potential as fighters they had. Following on this he heard that Daulat's son, Ghazi, had fled with most of his followers and, resisting the temptation to go off in pursuit, he 'placed his foot in the stirrup of resolution' and marched on Delhi. A successful brush with the enemy in the vicinity of Ambala earned Humayun his spurs. This is of interest as years later after his father's death Humayun added a note to Babur's memoirs to state that he remembered the occasion as he used a razor for the first time on that day. He was, in fact, just eighteen years of age.

Babur's intention was to meet Ibrahim on the field of Panipat,

[1] Ibid.

the battlefield of so many past glories. The details of this occasion
are interesting as a classic of a defensive-offensive operation, the
very core of which was an accurate assessment of the enemy and
his reactions. It was a superb case of an action in which every
detail was pre-planned, of a commander placing himself so that he
and not the attacker had the initiative. Though the causes of Ibrahim's defeat were different there was a striking similarity between
this action and that of Saladin at Hattin. Babur's success was not
just a matter of superior strength or of fighting quality, as this narrative will show. His estimate of Ibrahim was that he was impetuous
and negligent of detail, and that he was one who would march without order or plan and engage in battle with little foresight.

His dispositions were, therefore, designed to draw Ibrahim on
to attacking him and then, when he was at close quarters, to surround
him and counter-attack in sufficient strength to annihilate him.
Panipat with its buildings and suburbs was to form the pivot of his
manœuvre. His main defence was based on the 'Custom of Rum',[1]
an Osmanli order of battle by which the guns and gun-carriages
were connected together with twisted bullock hides and chains. The
matchlock men took station behind the guns and breastworks, which
were erected between each pair of guns, from where they were to discharge their matchlocks. He dug ditches and erected abatis of felled
trees and thorn, through which spaces were left large enough for a
hundred or a hundred and fifty men to issue forth for counter-attack.
Babur's advisers, criticising him for the strength of the defensive
posture that he had decided to adopt, said no man in his senses
would attack such a position, to which he replied that he was not
fighting the Uzbeks who, if they came up against such a problem,
would withdraw; rather was he facing a man who, heedless of the
odds, would attack and, not having the courage to withdraw, would
vacillate in the emergency.

When he had completed his preparations he despatched a party
with instructions to close with Ibrahim in the hope of drawing him
on to attack. As this was not successful he sent a larger body of
between four and five thousand men with orders to carry out a night
attack and, again with the hope of drawing Ibrahim, in the morning
they were to feign withdrawal in disorder. This time the enemy
kettle drums were soon beating as they advanced on the withdrawing

[1] Stanley Lane-Poole: *Medieval India.*

troops. Babur now sent Humayun's division to cover the retiring of his probing party while he himself prepared for the main battle. Though Ibrahim's men came on they did not close, and during the night Babur's soldiers stood to for what turned out to be a false alarm. Babur at this point states that he was worried about the morale of his men as he observed that those who had as yet not been in serious battle were getting jumpy. This preoccupation with the state of his men indicated a shrewdness of judgement, for to a commander nothing is more important than the factor of morale.

On the following morning when the light was such that one could just distinguish one object from another his dawn patrols reported that Ibrahim was advancing. All now braced on their helmets and armour and stood by their horses. The right division was commanded by Humayun and the left by Muhammad Sultan Mirza. The left and right centres were under Chin Taimur Sultan and Khalifeh respectively, while Abdul-Aziz, the master of his horse, commanded the reserve. On his right flank he stationed the Mongols under Wali Kazil and on the extreme left he placed Kara-Kuzi with instructions to encircle the enemy when they came close to the main position. As Ibrahim advanced Babur noticed the bulk of his force was concentrating on his right flank; he therefore moved his reserve under Abdul-Aziz to this area. As he drew near Ibrahim hesitated, uncertain whether to continue or to withdraw. Seeing this not unexpected vacillation Babur now instructed the flanks to wheel behind the enemy and attack Ibrahim in the rear. At the same time Humayun and Muhammad Sultan Mirza were ordered to charge. As Ibrahim's confusion was now obvious the centre was instructed to advance under the fire of its guns.

The sun had mounted spear-high when battle was joined and by midday it was over. The conflict had gone exactly as planned, the enemy was routed and their king slain. The estimate of the dead on the battlefield was between fifteen and sixteen thousand; but later the local people reported the losses as far greater. Thousands of men, animals and many elephants fell into Babur's hands.

Humayun was sent to Agra with instructions to travel light in order to seize the treasure there. In the meantime Babur advanced on Delhi which he seized without opposition, and a few days later he moved to Agra himself. Here the Bikramajit family were caught trying to escape by Humayun's guards. Humayun did not permit his men to plunder them and, of their own free will and out of gratitude, they presented him with their personal jewellery. Among this was the famous diamond known as the Kuh-i-nur or Mountain of Light, said by Babur to weigh three hundred and twenty ratis, the equivalent of about one hundred and eighty-seven carats, but more recent estimates place it at one hundred and two. It was for a long time in the possession of the Moghul emperors of Delhi and it was here that in 1665 the famous voyager, Jean Baptiste, travelling as a merchant in precious stones, saw it. In 1739 it went to Persia, thence through Afghanistan and once again it found its way back to India. Then, on the annexation of the Panjab in 1850, it became the property of the British Crown. On his arrival at Agra Humayun presented the Kuh-i-nur to his father.

It is at this point in his memoirs that Babur wrote that his desire to conquer Hindustan dated from 1504, but although the germ of the idea could possibly have been there his main objective at that time was not the conquest of India; it was to regain his kingdom in Fergana and Samarkand, and it was not until his dream was finally shattered that his eyes were turned southwards.

The treasure resulting from his victory was, of course, great. To Humayun he gave £20,000 and a palace and to all his chief officers he made large gifts; each individual who had fought with him also had his share of the prize money; and his daughter, Gul-badan Begum, tells how the royal harem were summoned to the audience hall to receive their gifts of jewels and brocades.

The hot season in Agra, always trying, was this year particularly oppressive and many of the soldiers suffered from heat exhaustion and, growing homesick, longed for the hills of their native lands. For Babur, however, this was no time to turn back so he summoned a council of his chiefs to put before them his future plans. Concluding, he said, 'If there is any among you who cannot bring himself to stay, let him depart.'[1] All but one khan remained.

Although he was now King of Delhi, he was by no means Emperor of India. His next problem was to deal with the Rajputs under Rana Sangrama who were determined to resist. Heretofore Babur had fought Muslims, the fierce Uzbeks, the Afghans with their motley crowd of followers, and he had warded off an attack by

[1] *Memoirs of Babur.*

the Jhats; but now he was faced with a true 'Jihad' against an opponent who would be a worthy antagonist.

Rana Sangrama of Mewar, the State of Udaipur of today, was known as the 'Sun' of the Hindus. He had defeated the Lodi rulers in eighteen pitched battles and was now laying siege to Bayana. His army included eighty thousand horse and five hundred elephants and he was supported by seven rajas of the highest rank, nine raos and one hundred lesser chieftains. Rana Sangrama himself was of formidable appearance and though of medium stature he possessed great muscular strength; he was fair-skinned, with large eyes (one of which he lost in a brawl); he was crippled in one leg from a cannon ball and had on his body eighty wounds from sword and lance. This was the man Babur was to meet.

As at Panipat his gun-carriages and wagons were chained together. Among the Muslim guns was an enormous cannon called Malik-i-maidan, which the chief artillery officer distinguished himself by firing. In a preliminary skirmish the Rajputs had shown that they were a very different matter to the rabble Babur had met at Panipat. Morale among his men sank and disorderly panic was only averted by a fighting speech from the King. Babur, who up to this point had been a heavy drinker, now swore he would abstain and in fact never drank again. He called on all to give of their best and to be prepared to die for their religion. 'How much better is it to die with honour than to live in infamy . . . if we die in the field we die as martyrs, if we survive we rise victorious'.[1] His words appealed to the hearts of every man and all vowed to conquer or to die. Today, as in the past, there always comes a time when a commander must put himself over to his men in language they can understand; this Babur did. On 16th March 1527 the two armies faced one another. Babur, now in his forty-fifth year, rode up and down the ranks reviewing his troops. Opposing him were the saffron-robed Rajput horsemen, their helmets garlanded with the bridal coronet, their eyes reddened with opium and their lances and swords glittering in the sun.

The Rajputs opened the attack by charging the centre and right wings of Babur's army but his men held their ground. The chained guns and abatis were too much for the Rajput horse, who again and again assaulted without success. Ustad Ali's great gun belched

[1] Ibid.

M

forth its missiles which ploughed their way through the charging ranks; casualties mounted up and the gallant Hindus were scattered like teased wool and their ranks broken 'like bubbles of wine'. Devotion was never more manifest and Rana Sangrama's soldiers gave their all. As the relentless battle raged it slowly drew to its inevitable conclusion, which was hastened by the perfidy of one man. While the issue could still be said to be in the balance a chief, Sillaidi of the Tuar tribe, who was leading the van, treacherously went over to the enemy. From the field on which Rana Sangrama staked and hoped so much this gallant warrior was forced to retreat. He withdrew to the hills of Mewar where he died of grief within the year.

Babur next attacked the Rajput fortress of Malwa near Chanderi. The siege was a bloody conflict but the end inevitable. In their desperation the garrison killed their women and children before rushing out naked to throw themselves on the Muslim swords. It was a terrible victory, but it was complete. Babur's admiration for the gallant bravery of the Rajputs comes out clearly in his description of the fighting. He tells how the last three hundred of the defenders slew one another, one person taking his stand with his drawn sword while another stretched out his neck to die. They were, indeed, as brave as lions.

Babur now built a road from Agra, where he had decided to make his capital, to Kabul with towers twenty-four feet high at every sixteenth mile where post houses for rest and stabling of horses were provided. The cost of building and maintaining the road was partly borne by the more wealthy landowners through whose properties it ran. Up to this point the Indians regarded Babur as they had all other invaders; one who, like a fierce wind, would come and go. But when they discovered that he intended to stay they reconsidered their policy and, out of weariness of incessant wars, saw the advantage of having a permanent and strong ruler. Three thousand from the Doab were the first to come over voluntarily to him and these, many of whom were Afghans, were rewarded with plots of land in Oudh.

Babur still had trouble to solve. The Lodi leader, Mahmud, was now joined by Jaunpur and Bihar. Although Mahmud was said to have had one hundred thousand followers his army melted away at Babur's approach. The Lodi now sought refuge in Bengal which up to this moment Babur had no intention of attacking, provided it did not threaten him. The protection Bengal was giving to the Lodi he considered as an unfriendly act, and so he determined to stamp out this last flicker of Afghan resistance, even if it involved war with Bengal. On 6th May 1529 he fought what was to be his last battle; it was an engagement fought over and across the Gogra River at a point near its confluence with the Ganges. Babur decided to force the passage of the Gogra in the face of the Bengal army. His arrangements were characterised by his customary elaborate preparations. Much of his success was due to his skilful handling of his artillery the bulk of which, under Ustad Ali, he placed on the high ground between the two rivers. Another commander, Mustafa, was to direct the remainder of the artillery on to the Bengali flank and their flotilla of boats that lay in the river. Babur's army was in six divisions of which four under his son, Askari, north of the Ganges were to engage the enemy in order to cover the other divisions that were later to cross the river. These were the fifth under himself, which was to support Ustad Ali's batteries, and the sixth which was to do the same for Mustafa's guns. As the Bengal army moved up to meet Askari, as Babur had anticipated it would, the fifth and sixth divisions were ordered to cross by swimming, using boats and even bundles of wood and reeds and then to attack the enemy in rear. Surprised by these combined assaults, and with artillery blazing away into their exposed flanks, the Bengal army was soon overpowered. Thus ended the so called Afghan revolt and Babur, who had no wish to continue hostilities with that country, now concluded a peace treaty with Bengal.

His position assured, he was now entitled to be called emperor, for his writ ran from Kabul to the borders of Bengal. Rajput resistance had been crushed and the incipient Lodi revolt had collapsed. This was the last military exploit of the 'Great Moghul', and the year and a half of life that was left to him was spent in Agra. He occupied a great deal of his time at the fort where, shortly after his arrival, he planted gardens and the methodical way in which he approached the task comes out in his memoirs. 'I first of all began to sink a large well which supplies the baths with water; I next fell to work on the piece of ground on which are the tamarind trees, and the octagonal tank; I then proceeded to form the large tank and its enclosure; and afterwards the tank and grand hall of audience that are in front of the stone palace.'[1] He then proceeded with the erection of edifices and symmetrical gardens, and in every garden he planted roses and narcissi; the water-runs were in white stone and the rest was in red. This, however, was not the present Fort at Agra which was constructed by his grandson Akbar.

Babur was intensely fond of Humayun. When in 1529 Humayun, hearing that his father was not well, returned to Agra Babur's pleasure was unfeigned. 'I was talking with his mother about him, when in he came. His presence opened our hearts like rosebuds and made our eyes shine like torches.'[2] This charming turn of words depicts vividly the happiness of the occasion. But the end was not far off. Humayun left only to return as a very sick man himself. He was, in the opinion of his doctors, in the last stages of a serious fever, from which his only chance of recovery was some supreme sacrifice. Babur, who was horror-struck, volunteered to give his own life. In vain it was suggested that he should sacrifice the Kuh-i-nur. 'Is there a stone that can be weighed against my son?'[3] he said. Rather he would be prepared to give his own life. Whatever the truth was, it is a fact that as Babur's life ebbed Humayun recovered. Babur died on 26th December 1530 at the age of forty-eight. He had been a king on and off for thirty-six troublesome years. He was buried at his own wish in the garden that he had loved on the hillside at Kabul.

He had crammed a great deal into a short life. He had established an empire in India that was to last until, by then sadly reduced in importance, it gave way to the British East India Company. He died a young man and one wonders what he would have done had his life been spared. He had shown all the signs of latent wisdom, of a kindness of heart and of a strong sense of justice. He had sought power and he had gained it. If he had achieved his successes by an outstandingly high standard of generalship, he had exercised the power he had gained with tolerance and he ended by having friends among those whom he had conquered.

[1] Ibid.
[2] Ibid.
[3] Ibid.

Babur died before he had time to consolidate his new-found kingdom in Hindustan; he thus left for his son a somewhat untidy realm, a situation that called for resolution and, when necessary, the use of military force. In extent that part of the country where he held undisputed power did not include much more than the North West Frontier and the Panjab. The chiefs of Rajputana were cowed but not subdued, and many fiefs were held by unruly Afghans. Bihar and Bengal had not been annexed. Though relations with these states were friendly their governors owed a certain degree of allegiance to Delhi.

Humayun, although not without merit, was not a strong character; addicted to opium, and often not fully master of himself, he could scarcely be expected to control a people of diverse religions who were led by capable and ambitious men. The first to revolt was a bold Afghan, Sher Khan, then Governor of Bihar, who succeeded in driving Humayun out of the country. Within two years, in 1542, Sher Khan formally mounted the throne at Delhi under the name of Sher Shah.

Humayun, a fugitive, wandered in Persia and Afghanistan, seeking help with little success. However, in 1555, after the death of Sher Shah, he was able to return; but one year later he died as a result of a fall. He left his kingdom to his son, Akbar, who at the time was a boy of fourteen. He was enthroned at Kalanaur in Gurdaspur where the ancient kings of Lahore had been crowned. The lands Akbar inherited consisted of little more than the Panjab, Delhi, Ajmir and Agra. As was only natural the boy king was subjected to petticoat government; but, as time went on, he discerned that those in whom he had placed his trust were unworthy and, when he reached his twentieth year, he rebelled. Disillusioned, he wrote: 'On the completion of my twentieth year I experienced an internal bitterness, and from the lack of spiritual provision for my last journey my soul was seized with exceeding sorrow.'[1] He knew that from now he must rely, not on human help, but on divine guidance and henceforth never allowed himself to be beholden to others. The Jesuit father, Peruschi, who met him some years later, said in this connection 'He is willing to consult about affairs, and often takes advice in private from his friends near his person, but the decision, as it ought to be, always rests with the King.'[2]

Akbar's reign lasted for almost fifty years, from 1556 until 1605. It was a period of greatness for India and contemporaneous with the glorious reign of Elizabeth I of England. His achievements were great in the military field, in the realm of administration, in the arts and in matters of religion. This chapter will deal with him as a conqueror. This is for simplification of presentation, for the remarkable thing is that almost up to his death he was on one campaign or another without ever losing his grip on either the administration and government of his country or of his searchings for religious truth and enlightenment.

Akbar gained great power which he unashamedly sought; but he used it for the good of the people over whom he ruled. That he was ambitious there is no doubt and he never felt any scruple about starting a war. Although once he had put his hand to the plough he would pursue his campaign without mercy, yet his better nature always made itself felt after victory had been achieved. In considering his attitude towards war one must bear in mind the age in which he lived, the rebellions he had to face and the somewhat tattered kingdom which he inherited.

As to the fact that a man who was as strong minded as he, and who achieved military success after military success, should be faced with almost continuous revolt one might be surprised; yet this was

---

[1] Abdul Fazh Allami: *Ain-i-Akburi*.
[2] Vincent A. Smith: *Akbar*.

the case. Even five years before his death he had revolts in Bengal. Neither Jenghiz Khan nor Tamerlane would have tolerated this and in their times none would have dared to do so. Why was this not the case with Akbar? If one answer lay in the policy of tolerance he habitually pursued, a policy that nevertheless meant in the end his leaving a united country, another and more likely one was his attitude, ultimately hostile, to his Muslim brothers. This, however, we must pursue in the next chapter.

Akbar's military successes were astounding and, if these alone are taken, history would hold his name in high esteem. Chronologically, these were his achievements. In 1567 the Rajput stronghold of Chitor fell and Ajmir was annexed. In 1570 he took possession of Oudh and Gwalior and two years later himself led an expedition into Gujarat, defeating the last of the Sultans of Ahmedabad. This great province was then incorporated into his kingdom. In the same year his generals drove out the Afghans from Bihar and Bengal. By now he was undisputed ruler over a larger part of India than any had been before. In 1578 he annexed Orissa, joining this state up to Bengal. Kabul fell to him in 1581, Kashmir six years later and in 1592 he took Sind, whilst Kandahar fell in 1594. Finally, he wrested an important part of the Deccan from its hereditary Muhammadan rulers. At his death his kingdom extended from the Bay of Bengal to Afghanistan and from Ahmednagar in the Deccan to the Himalayas and Kashmir.

Of all these enterprises that which most touches the imagination was his siege and capture of Chitor, both on account of its tragic circumstances and of its effect on his relationship with his Hindu subjects. When Rana Sangrama, after his heroic fight with the Emperor Babur, fled to Mewar, the Rajputs rallied to their defeated hero; but his life was short and in the following year, the year in which Babur died, he passed away. Akbar was early anxious to heal Rajput wounds, to gain their confidence and support. He had taken as his wife the daughter of the Raja of Jaipur, intending by this act to demonstrate that he considered himself padshah (or king) of his whole people, Hindu as well as Muslim. This princess, whose posthumous name Maram-zamani is translated as 'The Mary of the Age', became the mother of Salim, who, as Jahangir, succeeded his father. Her brother Bayan-das and her cousin Man Singh both held high posts in Akbar's army. But the policy of paternal friendliness did not take root in the Rajput stronghold of Mewar, and in the fortress of Chitor, these stalwart people adopted a defiant attitude. To Akbar this was revolt and with scant justification he marched on the sacred city.

Chitor was situated on a rocky hill which rose steeply from the plain and was some eight miles in circumference. It also had an ample supply of water. It presented a problem that could only be overcome by mining. The first attempts were unsuccessful and although the Muslim writers give the impression that there was only one attack, the local annalists affirm that there was at least one other unsuccessful attempt which was repulsed by the bravery of the absent raja's queen. The wretched Raja Udai Singh had taken flight. Eventually Akbar's miners, under Raja Todar Mal, competed another covered way or 'sabat' and by 23rd February 1568 all was ready for the final assault. That night Akbar, on taking a last look at his arrangements, saw by the flare of a torch in the ramparts, what appeared to be a Rajput officer also going his rounds. Seizing a matchlock, he fired and the man fell. In the event this unknown person turned out to be Jaimal Rathor, who with Prince Patta, commanded the fortress. Less than an hour later Akbar received reports that the defences appeared to be deserted and that somewhere in the fort three fires seemed to have broken out. The ghastly truth was that Jaimal's death had been the signal for the 'Supreme Sacrifice' of the wives and families of Chitor. Separate fires had been kindled for the Sisodia, Rathor and Chaudhan clans and into the flames of these nine queens, five princesses, all with their daughters and infant sons, walked to their death. It was recorded that three hundred women perished in this way rather than give themselves to the enemy. On the next morning when the soldiers made their entry eight thousand Rajput soldiers sold their lives, all perishing to a man. In all thirty thousand men lost their lives in this terrible holocaust.

Although the gates of the fortress were torn from their hinges and taken to Agra, and the ceremonial kettle-drums and great candelabra removed, no structural damage to the buildings was done. The fall of the sacred city deeply wounded the Rajputs and no successor of Udai Singh ever dared set foot within its precincts. Chitor remained desolate. However, the valiant Rana Partap Singh, successor to Udai, fought more or less continuously with Akbar, eventually winning back a large part of his state.

Deep though the resentment was Akbar finally succeeded in overcoming this and in the end received from millions the praise that no other of his race had ever obtained. One of the acts that helped to achieve this was his erection of statues in honour of Jaimal and Patta. Even Tod, the great protagonist of the Rajput cause, conceded that the gallant resistance of the defenders of Chitor as well as the exceptional character of Rana Partap Singh touched the Emperor's heart; yet, somewhat contradictorily, the Muslim and Jesuit writers claim that to the end of his life Akbar appeared to have been determined to destroy Partap Singh, a desire that he was only refrained from putting into effect by the refusal of his son and his great officers to take part in another campaign into the heart of Mewar.

Akbar's next venture in which he took a personal part was in Gujarat, that extensive region lying between Mewar and the Arabian Sea. With its ports and maritime commerce it was one of the wealthiest kingdoms of India. Its capital at Ahmedabad was reputed to be one of the finest cities in Asia, with a vast wealth that it owed to its salt, cloth and paper trade. It was, therefore, a tempting place to an avaricious man of Akbar's character. Nevertheless, there were other reasons, perhaps more compelling, that drew him on to embark on the conquest of Gujarat. First, it had been occupied by his father, Humayun, and could, therefore, be regarded as a lost province; second, the government was unsettled and the country divided into several warring principalities, conditions that demanded the interposition of a power capable of enforcing law and order.

Having made up his mind to annex Gujarat Akbar on 4th July 1572 marched out of Fatehpur-Sikri with all the normal military precautions. His advanced guard consisted of ten thousand horse, while special arrangements were made for the protection of his flanks. By the middle of the following February Surat had fallen and Akbar felt himself able to return to Fatehpur-Sikri to attend to the business of state. However, a revolt in August brought him back and, after an incredibly swift march in which he covered nearly fifty miles a day, he reached and attacked Ahmedabad. On the 22nd September this great city fell. The conquest of Gujarat was now final, the province was placed under a viceroy and an administrative organisation established. So effective was this that the revenue from Gujarat yielded no less than five million rupees to the treasury annually. The details of this administrative miracle, for which Raja Todar Mal was to no small extent responsible, will be dealt with fully in the next chapter.

It was during the campaign in this area that Akbar first came into contact with the Portuguese, who had come up from Goa with the apparent object of assisting the defenders of Surat; but, coming to the conclusion that Akbar was too formidable a foe, they decided to make friendly overtures to him. Accordingly they offered presents which were graciously received. Their respect was mutual and in Akbar's case was influenced by his regard for Portuguese naval power, for he was at the time concerned about the safety of the pilgrimages to Mecca. A peace treaty was made, the negotiations for which were carried out by Antonio Cabral, the Portuguese viceroy at the time.[1]

At the time of his accession Akbar found that Afghan chiefs had control of the states of Bihar and Bengal. Since the twelfth century the Muslims who had ruled here had been loosely dependent on the Kings of Delhi. Now, in Bihar, which bordered on Akbar's kingdom, the governor was one Suleiman Khan, who in 1564 had moved into Bengal, setting up a capital at Gaur. Akbar's relations with Sulaiman were that of cat and mouse, the latter finding it generally advisable to recognise Akbar's authority. When Sulaiman's younger son eventually succeeded his father he forsook the more prudent policy of his forbear and, assuming all the insignia of royalty, even went so far as to order the coins to be stamped with his name. This assumption of kingly state, coupled with the flagrant oppressive measures of Daud, was in Akbar's eyes sufficient justification for his intervention.

Although he left the operations to his general, Munis Khan, Akbar sent Raja Todar Mal to assist him and particularly to assume responsibility for the operations in Bihar. The Emperor personally took command of the attack on Patna which had to be carried out in the difficult conditions of the rainy season. This was typical of Akbar, who allowed neither climate nor terrain to deter him, and his handling of the crossing of the swollen rivers in the most appalling conditions was a classic of determination and skill. Patna fell and then Akbar returned to Fatehpur-Sikri after an absence of seven months. The rest of Bengal gave in with little resistance and Daud

[1] Ibid.

withdrew to Orissa on the shores of the Bay of Bengal. There, at the Battle of Tukaroi in March 1575, he was finally defeated, and so, after a life of two hundred and thirty-six years, the hitherto independent kingdom of Bengal finally perished. Little regret was felt for this as the Afghan jagirdars, among whom the land had been parcelled out, had no sympathy for the wretched Hindus whom they had bled and over whom they held sway.

Akbar now entered what was to be the most critical period of his reign. His unorthodox behaviour in religious matters had upset the more rigid Muslims, who now began to plot against him. The rebels looked to Akbar's half-brother, Mirza Muhammad Hakim, who ruled at Kabul and who owed a nominal fealty to the Emperor at Delhi. In 1581 a conspiracy for Mirza Muhammad Hakim to seize the throne at Delhi was hatched. The plot received the support even of members of the court at Fatehpur-Sikri with whom Bengal promised to collaborate. With his excellent intelligence network Akbar heard of the scheme, intercepting letters from his finance minister to Muhammad Hakim. During raids by his half-brother into the Panjab, which were repulsed without difficulty, further documents which compromised the ex-finance minister, Shah Mansur, were found. Another attempt at invasion reached the city of Lahore where support was expected; however, notwithstanding precautions taken to avoid antagonising local feelings, no one stirred to help the invaders, who had to withdraw ignominiously. With real sincerity Akbar hoped to avoid war with his relative; but, eventually he was driven to open hostilities. With fifty thousand cavalry, many elephants and a large body of infantry he advanced on Kabul. Always meticulous in matters of detail, and realising what pay meant to the common soldier, Akbar advanced eight months' pay to all ranks from his treasury. While he was on the march northwards he obtained further evidence incriminating Shah Mansur who now paid for his treachery with his life. This execution put an end to the conspiracy and a general amnesty was promised to all who adhered to the Emperor. This story was described in detail by the Jesuit father, Montserrat, who remarked that throughout the whole camp the punishment of Shah Mansur was approved.

Akbar's advance on Kabul was methodical, and, although carried out in July when the rivers were in flood, went ahead without interference. Muhammad Hakim fled and on 10th August 1581 Kabul was entered without a fight. Akbar placed his half-brother's sister on the throne, informing her that he did not wish to hear Muhammad Hakim's name, that though he had placed her on the throne he would take the province back when it pleased him, and finally that if Muhammad Hakim misbehaved himself again he would not show him his clemency a second time.

In the space of ten months Akbar had retrieved a situation that could have scarcely been more dangerous. He had quelled a serious revolt, had defeated an attempted invasion of his kingdom, had retained the loyalty of the Hindus and won over the wavering Muslims. He had used his numerical superiority with skill and with firmness and without vindictiveness re-established law and order. By December his kingdom was secure and his power to do as he felt right was undisputed. From this moment he never looked back; he had successfully passed the watershed of his career. His war against his half-brother had been one he had not wished to undertake; but, once he put his hand to the plough, he did not turn back.

In 1585 Muhammad Hakim died and this finally freed the Emperor from anxieties concerning Kabul which he then incorporated into his empire. No question of annexation arose as Kabul had always been regarded as a dependency. However, a new danger threatened. Beyond the Hindu Kush in the neighbouring state of Badakhshan the Uzbeks had by now firmly established themselves. With good reason, Akbar regarded this as a positive threat and so thought it advisable to remain in the northern territories. Indeed, he did not see either Agra or his beloved Fatehpur-Sikri again for thirteen years. His next campaign was directed against Kashmir, which he annexed and placed under imperial administrative officers as a part of the province of Kabul, where it remained until the end of the Moghul Empire in the middle of the eighteenth century.

In Babur's time Upper Sind had been regarded as an integral part of Hindustan and Akbar, whose policy now was to bring all the provinces of northern India under his sway, decided on a plan to annex the whole of the province. By 1591 Sind and the greater part of Baluchistan had become an integral part of his kingdom. The year 1595 witnessed the completion of these conquests when Quetta, the rest of Baluchistan and Kandahar all fell to him. Akbar's kingdom now stretched from the borders of Persia to the Bay of Bengal.

His attention was now directed to the Deccan, that stony upland country lying between the Portuguese possessions on the coast of the Arabian Sea and Malwa. His object here was to obtain a foot-hold for a further advance to the coast and the Portuguese settlements at Goa. He had for some time resented their power and was particularly annoyed by their interference with the pilgrimages to Mecca. But this was a campaign he did not live to finish. His only gain was the important fortress at Ahmednagar and the surrounding country. The fort fell to him after a heroic defence by the Queen, Chand Bibi, her guns in their final salvo being loaded with her jewels.

This marks the end of Akbar's military achievements. But what of the man? His character, his administrative genius and his religious philosophies are dealt with in the following chapter. As one reads one cannot help but be impressed at this general, who seemed always to be away on one campaign or another, and who found time for the political, economic and spiritual sides of kingship. These duties he never neglected and in the end it was perhaps the way in which he carried them out that most endeared his memory to posterity.

If Akbar's ruling passion was ambition and a desire for power, was this of itself a bad thing? History will show the use to which the power he gained was put. Did it merely result in the extravagant building of cities or did it help to produce better conditions, security and tolerance for and towards his people? From time immemorial men have accepted a degree of oppression so long as they also had security from outside aggression and, from within, the deprivations of greedy overseers. Akbar provided all of this. In the first instance Hindu and Muslim under him were able to live together and this alone was an achievement; secondly, no longer were the people either robbed or oppressed by jagirdars who had been little short of kings in their fiefs; thirdly, Akbar's military strength meant the land was secure from threat of foreign invasion; and finally, the army was properly paid and did not rely on loot for the sustenance of the soldiers. Akbar, in fact, provided the cement of good administration which gave a security the land had not enjoyed before.

He displayed a mind capable of grasping broad principles whilst at the same time remaining alive to the importance of detail. This faculty enabled him to check and control laxity in the administrative machine. His system, however, depended on the ability and character of the autocrat working it. Rule by autocrats is today sometimes referred to as dictatorship. Mustafa Kemal Atatürk was an autocrat; but he understood his people and gave them a system they both understood and accepted. Stalin was a dictator who ruled through fear. In France in more recent times de Gaulle, though virtually a dictator, owed his position to the popular vote. It is as an autocratic dictator that one must view Akbar, and his ministers, with whom he worked in the closest harmony, were his pupils and not his teachers. One of the most outstanding of these was Raja Todar Mal, a Kshatriya Rajput, who had learned the elements of good administration under Sher Shah. Todar Mal was as able a soldier as he was an administrator, though it is in the latter category that he was best remembered in India.

One of the fundamental bases of Akbar's rule was that no stability could result from a system in which the indigenous Hindus were subservient to and persecuted by a Muslim minority, however powerful they might be. Thus, his first principle was that Hindus as well as Muslims should be considered eligible for the senior offices of state, both military and civil; his second and no less important principle was that every man, whatever his creed, should be free to worship after his own fashion. These two principles he maintained throughout his life.

Let us now examine what can best be described as Akbar's administrative genius. This was displayed first in Gujarat where with Todar Mal's help the first land and tax reforms were instituted. Whereas in the past the practice had been for land to be given as fiefs to nobles to be administrated by them, Akbar now converted all territories into crown lands, which were to be administered by officials directly responsible to the Emperor. These officials, known as Mansabdars, were graded as commanders of so many men, implying military as well as civil responsibilities. This centralisation of administration through men directly responsible to the Central Government might with some truth be said to be the beginning of the Indian Civil Service.

All land was now systematically measured and new measurements were introduced for this purpose. These included the gaz or yard, equal to forty-one digits and the tanab or chain which was of sixty gaz. Similarly square measurements were laid down. In addition all land, thus now properly measured, was classified according to its potential as a crop-producing element and, according to which category the land fell into, rates for taxation were fixed. All this eventually, throughout the whole of India, was recorded in what has been aptly named as a Doomesday Book. The area under each individual crop had its own rate and as the kinds of crop were innumerable the multitude of rates was prodigious; yet in a veritable maze of tables all this was recorded. The system, with modifications, was that which formed the basis of British land assessment three hundred years later.

Akbar simplified the whole system of taxation, abolishing innumerable vexatious minor duties including poll tax and pilgrim dues, in place of which he put a land revenue, which to an agricultural people was both understandable and reasonable. Middle-men were cut out and the agriculturist was recognised as the owner of the soil from which the state was entitled to its fair share of produce. The husbandman paid his tax himself, but was allowed to do so in kind for certain crops, and even to this day the separate piles of grain can be seen, some for the farmer and some for the tax. The rates of taxation were high, Akbar demanding one third; but he claimed this was not excessive in the light of the host of miscellaneous imposts that had been cut out. The greatest benefit to the cultivator was, of course, the elimination of the middle-man.

Rates of wages were laid down; that for the unskilled labourer being two dams or a penny and a half per day, while a first-class carpenter received seven dams. Small as this amount seemed, the price of food was remarkably low, a quart of milk, for example, costing less then two dams. In order to prevent the poor being cheated every item of food was priced. This included meats, all types of grain, white and brown sugar, clarified butter, oil and salt. The rupee was fixed at between two shillings and two and ninepence.[1] In regard to the cost of living it is interesting to note that a traveller, Tom Corygate, known by the name of 'the wanderer of the age' reliably recorded[2] that he had lived on twopence a day and at times only a penny.[2]

This highly complex yet detailed system has been criticised, and doubts as to the skill and honesty with which it was administered have been raised,[3] but it is forgotten that even in the times of the British Raj criticism of administrative honesty has, perhaps

[1] Ibid.
[2] Ibid.
[3] Ibid.

with some justification, been made. Moreover, when one com-
pares the system that Akbar did away with and the blessings
of that which he introduced, there can surely be little doubt of
the ultimate good he did. The India of his period was a highly
organised society on paper and in fact. Although there is always a
gap between governmental statistics and reality, and allowing for
the frailties of human nature, there is ample evidence that Akbar gave
to his country a government that neither they nor their neighbours
had ever experienced before.

In matters of foreign policy he was essentially insular. India was
his realm and nations that bordered on it had to recognise his
sovereignty; if, to his mind, they were in danger of becoming a
threat to this they had to be dealt with. The greatest danger came
from the Uzbeks and his campaigns in Afghanistan and Baluchistan
had as their objects the building up of buffers between India and the
warlike peoples on the North West Frontier and beyond the
Hindu Kush. Akbar had no fleet and understood little of sea power.
With those countries that lay beyond the seas he was prepared to
have friendly relations and seemed always happy to welcome their
envoys and missions, so long as no designs on India's soil was implied. It was the physical presence of the Portuguese that resulted
in his eventual quarrel with them; but in the early days and for the
sake of the seaborne pilgrimages to Mecca he was prepared to be
friendly. Another factor that held him in check was his desire to have
the advice of the Jesuit fathers on matters pertaining to the Christian
faith. It was later that his policy hardened; and, as we have seen, his
war against the Deccan was just to provide a springboard for an
attack on Goa, a goal he never achieved. In matters of foreign policy,
although Akbar's interests were superficially wide, his outlook was,
in fact, insular.

By far the most interesting and certainly the most unpredictable
of all his preoccupations were his excursions into matters of religion.
It has been said that he suffered from a form of megalomania, which
ultimately led him to think of himself as divine; but this savours of
superficial hindsight. If, in the end, this obsession was a form of
mental disease, it certainly was not the cause of his early curiosity
in matters of faith, for there is ample evidence that this arose from
a genuine interest and a mystic strain in his character. As a young
man he had found much that disturbed him in his Islamic faith.

N

Although born a Muslim he began to realise that in the kingdom he inherited it was vital to have the co-operation of the Hindu people over whom he ruled. His natural inquisitiveness caused him to delve into the intricacies of Hindu beliefs, and in these he discovered much that he understood and with which he was, at least, in sympathy. The big differences that divided Islam, resulting in the denouncement by one side of the other as heretics, gradually drove him to the conclusion that perhaps both were wrong. The truth, he felt certain, must be sought outside the range of their bickerings. No longer confining himself to what he now felt were vain attempts at arbitration between sects, he started to consult other religious teachers. This, naturally, brought him into conflict with the general run of Muslim opinion and was unquestionably one of the root causes of the revolts he had to face. The effect of these, rather than causing him to modify his conduct, made him the more determined to rely on and encourage Hindu support. The political wisdom of this, in the long term, was borne out by results.

But in his search after the truth he relied not only on studying Hindu philosophy, and he consulted Parsee, orthodox Jain and Christian teachers.

In regard to the mystic strain in his character, at the early age of fifteen he said that he was constrained by some influence which was stronger than himself, a God whom as yet he did not quite understand. One day, in a frenzy, he mounted a vicious horse named Hairan, forbidding anyone to follow him. The story went that he dismounted and under a tree, by which a memorial was ultimately built, he communed with God. In his twentieth year he went through a period of extreme melancholy. Again in 1578 when he was twenty-five, on a hunt which he had organised, he was seized by a frenzy and in his own words he 'came face to face with God'.[1] There is no reason to disbelieve these stories and there seems little doubt that he was both sincere and at times inspired. He struggled over many years to make contact with what he described as the Divine Reality and from time to time he believed he had succeeded. Sometimes during his fits of extreme melancholy he was in real danger of getting into a state of religious mania, from which only his interest in worldly matters saved him, bringing him back to the realities

[1] Ibid.

of everyday life. Throughout all this period he was conducting with consummate skill military operations of great magnitude and administering his realm with both wisdom and political ability.

During his war in Gujarat he met Dastur Mejerjee Rana, a leading theologian of the Parsees in India. The philosophy of the Zoroastrians was that in the world there were two groupings of power, the one for good and the other for evil. Light was the symbol of good, burning up evil with which were associated darkness and destruction. Riding between the opposites man was placed so as to be free to choose. The gods of vulgar belief were discarded and the basis of the philosophy was abstract, the abstractions being the ethical forces that dominated human affairs. This caught Akbar's imagination and he started a sacred fire which was prepared according to Parsee rules. From about March of 1580 he began to prostrate himself in public before the sun and fire. There were similarities, although the differences were fundamental, between some of these attitudes and the Hindu customs; as, for instance, when the ladies of the zanana had their offerings burnt according to Brahmanical teaching. Akbar undoubtedly received some Hindu support in his sun worship, notably that of Raja Birbal, who ultimately joined him in his 'divine Faith'. These two men were very drawn to one another and Akbar grieved when his friend was killed in the war with the Yusufzai on the North West Frontier. Nevertheless, Akbar never became a Zoroastrian.

The next sect to exercise an influence on him were the Jains. The Jains were essentially ascetic, believing that everything possessed a soul and, therefore, life. They would not take life and the Jains of today can be seen dressed in pure white with a cloth over their mouths and noses to prevent them from breathing in the insects of the air. Akbar's Jain advisers persuaded him to release prisoners and caged birds, also to prohibit the killing of animals on certain days. He himself now abstained from eating meat and went so far as to issue orders restricting to the narrowest limits the killing of any animals, a measure which, to the Muslims, presented many obvious problems and possibly hardships.

Finally we come to Akbar's contacts with the Christian Church, many of which were through the Jesuits. From Goa no less than three important missions visited him; the first was in 1580, the second in

N*

1591 and the third in 1595. However, his first conversations with
Christians on religious matters dated from his acquaintance with
some Portuguese traders whom he met in 1572; but these were dis-
continued when in the following year conflict with the Portuguese
seemed likely. Subsequently, this was only avoided by the diplomacy
of Antonio Cabral, who visited him at the time of the fighting round
Surat. Akbar sent an envoy to Goa in order, he said, to satisfy himself concerning the wonders of Portugal and the manners and
customs of other European countries. His interest in the Christian
Church was again stirred when he heard of the work of two priests
in Bengal, Anthony Vaz and Peter Dias, who had refused absolution
to some of their converts because they had committed frauds against
the inland revenue. To the Emperor's thinking, if a religion con-
demned dishonesty, even when practised against an alien state, it
must possess exceptional merits. His curiosity aroused, he sent for
Father Julian Periera, Vicar-General in Bengal, to question him
concerning his church's dogma. When he had tried to gain information from lay sources he had discovered these were not qualified to
satisfy his curiosity on deeper matters. His real interest in the
Christian way of life was somewhat similar to that which Qubilai
Khan had displayed; both men were genuine in their desire to know
more about the teachings of Christ; but neither ever embraced
Christianity.

In September 1579 Akbar sent his ambassador, Abdulla, to the
chief priest of the Jesuits at Goa. He asked that two learned
men should bring the holy books and particularly the Gospels for
him to study, stating that he most earnestly desired to understand
them. The Jesuits were only too anxious to accept this unexpected invitation, believing that the opportunity of winning over a king and so
extensive a kingdom to the Church, and incidentally for the benefit
of Portugal, was one that must not be missed. The mission included
two outstanding men, Father Rudolfo Aquaviva, one of the most in-
fluential nobles of Naples, and Father Antonio Monserrat, a Catalan
Spaniard. The third member was a converted Persian, Father
Henriquez who acted as interpreter but otherwise was of little
consequence. Aquaviva was a saintly man and dedicated to the
proselytising mission. Monserrat, also a good man, was quite
different to his companion. Zealous, his enthusiasm knew no
bounds, and his attacks on the followers of the Prophet were so

strong that the Emperor had to restrain him. In an historic and detailed account of northern India he gave minute descriptions of Akbar's campaign against Kabul in 1581, on which he accompanied the Emperor.

This first Jesuit mission coincided with a growing antagonism of the Muslim community to Akbar's religious thinking. His policy of religious tolerance was regarded as an affront to the Muham-madan religion and the fears they had certainly appeared to be justi-fied. In 1580, the year of the mission's arrival, he had in fact promulgated a document setting forth in unmistakable language that in matters of religion the King's authority was higher than that even of the Mujtahid, the Supreme Doctor of the Faith. The similarity between this and the acts of Henry VIII, though the motives could possibly have been different, is obvious. Akbar, in order to cut the ground from under the feet of the religious fanatics who might oppose him, was promulgating little short of the doctrine of imperial infal-libility. The outspoken antipathy to everything pertaining to the Islamic Church by the Jesuit fathers did not help matters, and this became an ever-growing source of anxiety to Akbar. It was, indeed, while the mission was at Fatehpur-Sikri that he was faced with the revolt in Bengal and the hostility of his half-brother in Kabul, both of which had their origins in Muslim unrest. The last of the debates on religious matters with the mission, which was intended to deal with the relative values of the teachings of the Koran and the Bible, broke down from lack of interest on the part of the people and be-cause by now the fathers thought Akbar was more interested in the promulgation of his own religion than in becoming a convert to the Church of Rome.

Whereas Akbar set out to satisfy his genuine curiosity, entering discussion with a reasonably open mind, the fathers had one object and that was to convert. They unquestionably took advantage of the Emperor's leniency over free speech and their utterances made in public were unreservedly hostile. Father Aquaviva, on his way back to Goa was murdered by Hindus who resented what he had said and this, to Akbar, was a grievous blow, for his liking for the priest had been genuine. In the meantime Monserrat was safely escorted back to Portuguese territory. Something of the hostility of Father Aquaviva can be gleaned from his written word. 'Our ears hear noth-ing but the hideous name of Muhammad . . . in honour of this infernal

monster they bend the knee, prostrate, lift up their hands, give alms
and do all they do.'[1]

After this the Jesuits paid two further visits, both at Akbar's
request. The second was between 1591 and 1592 and the third, led
by Father Jerome Xavier, left Goa in December 1594. Xavier in fact
stayed in India for twenty-three years, long after Akbar had passed
on. There seems little doubt that the Emperor was genuine in his
desire to learn more of the Christian teachings. In his letter asking
for the first of these two missions he wrote that he wished to 'be
taught many things concerning the faith of the Christians and of
the royal highway whereon they travel to God's presence'.[2] Akbar
was reported to have set up in an elevated position the picture of the
Virgin and to have called on his relatives and courtiers to kiss it with
due reverence. He was also alleged to have turned the mosques of
the city into stables on the pretext of preparation for war; but later
he pulled down the minarets saying that as the mosques were no
longer needed for prayer they were unnecessary. He showed every
honour to the Jesuits, who were not called upon to perform the ceremony of prostration, which was, however, rigorously exacted from all
others, even including the princes. Whatever justification the Jesuits
may have had for thinking they could convert Akbar, in fact he
never, as we have seen, embraced Christianity. Indeed, his mind was
by now set on a dream, that which he had cherished for years: to
found his own religion.

Akbar's heart was always in the fair city of his dreams, Fatehpur-
Sikri, and it was here that he thought of his 'Divine Faith'. The more
he delved into the details of the laws by which the two Muslim sects
were divided the greater became his doubts. In those endless discussions he had with the teachers and leaders of other religions he had
found much good, but also much that was lacking. There seemed to
him to be truth in all faiths, yet no one, in his view, held the
master key. Akbar was by no means the first nor indeed the last to
face this baffling problem, and there is no doubt that he passed
through an agony of self-examination. The questionings, the endless
discussions and the theological maze in which he found himself were
overwhelming; eventually leading him to the belief that he, and he
alone, could see through the glass clearly. He knew he had been

[1] Goldie—see Vincent A. Smith: *Akbar*.
[2] Vincent A. Smith: *Akbar*.—Pass granted to Leo Grimon.

born with a mystic strain and this characteristic remained with him to the end. His great problem was to find a satisfying answer to the age-old question, 'What is truth?'. Although he never found the answer, dying a baffled man, he nevertheless was sincere in his search for this elusive thing. To dub his 'Divine Faith' as megalomania is to do injustice to a thoughtful man.

It was as early as 1582 that he issued his long-cherished project, 'Din Ilahi' or doctrine of the 'Divine Faith'. It was drawn up by Muslims and signed, often against their will, by the divines and lawyers of the court. Its frightening assumption and, indeed, its cornerstone was the acceptance of the authority of the King over the Sublime Doctor of the Faith, the Mujtahid. It made the Emperor's decisions on religious matters binding on the Muslims of India, opposition involving both loss of goods and membership of the faith. And yet, in bizarre contradiction, Akbar as an old man still went on pilgrimages, which his Muslim subjects found strange. They naturally asked why he should visit the tomb of a good Muslim while rejecting the foundations of everything the Prophet had laid down. During this period he was consulting with the Jesuit missions and apparently at least keeping an open mind concerning the teachings of the Gospels. As his new religion developed it contained elements of Muslim teaching, for instance the infallibility of the one God, of Hinduism and Jainism, of Parsee Zoroastrianism and of Christianity; yet, increasingly it became based on his own infallibility. It had many weaknesses, as indeed do all compromises, and not the least was his belief that he himself was the mouthpiece of the Almighty. His whole outlook was influenced by his profound and honestly held belief in his God-given power. In his eyes it was he who had seen the weaknesses in all cults, he who saw how little reliance could be placed on the religious teachers, the mullahs and the priests, all of whom were to his mind influenced by political motives. It was he alone who had unravelled the tangled skein and found truth. The mystic in him eventually took control.

But this new cult, save for court followers, had few disciples. Although some boldly refused to accept the new faith, others temporised for fear of losing favour. When Akbar died, his religion passed away with him. Yet the broad-minded sympathy and vision of Akbar left a lasting impression. A country of warring religions, of different races and differing philosophies that had heretofore been split from top to bottom had been made into a united nation.

While all these heart-searchings on matters of faith were going on Akbar retained his grip on military operations as well as the administration of the realm. Sufficient has been said of both to indicate how successful he was. This religious mystic possessed a fund of sound commonsense and it is this that has possibly made some commentators doubt his sincerity. He was, it has been said, a master in the art of dissimulation. The Jesuit, Bartoli, wrote that 'He never gave anybody the chance to understand rightly his inmost sentiments . . . a man apparently free from mystery or guile, as honest and candid as could be imagined; but in reality, so close and self-contained . . . that even by much seeking one could not find the clue to his thoughts.'[1] If it is true that Akbar was seeking after the ultimate truth, this was not dissimulation so much as uncertainty. In searching for the right answer he would naturally not disclose his inmost thoughts, for in an oriental monarch this would be bound to result merely in polite acquiescence. He has also been called a hypocrite, pretending to revere the Muslim saints with outward displays of devotion. But surely this is all understandable. He was the monarch of a heterogeneous people, the framework of which was the Muslim element and one which had to be handled with due care. Whether he deceived them or not may be a matter of opinion, but that he needed to deal with the situation with care is beyond dispute, and this is all he attempted to do. Elizabeth of England was playing much the same game.

Intolerant in some respects Akbar was nevertheless an enlightened man. It is germane to recall that while, with patience and no little skill, he was uniting Muslims and Hindus in India, Elizabeth and Mary were beheading ·and burning Roman Catholics and Protestants for their beliefs, while in France there occurred the ghastly massacre on St Bartholomew's night in 1572.

Akbar the Great is the last of the outstanding figures of medieval Asiatic history. Such men sought and used power to gain their ends, some judiciously, some selfishly. But power and power politics are with us today. Intolerance is rampant. If the Christian Churches are no longer in open conflict, Jew and Arab certainly are in bloody confrontation. Communist and non-Communist countries are at war with one another and racial antagonism is splitting Africa. One might

[1] Father Daniel Bartoli, see Vincent A. Smith: *Akbar*.

well ask how much of this stems from genuine ideology and how much from the lust for and determination to retain power. The rule of Mao Tse-tung is virtually absolute, and the regime of the Colonels in Greece is as despotic as that of the kings of the past.

Historical perspective is or should be helpful for a consideration of the problems of today. One of our greatest statesmen, Winston Churchill, was always aware of this. The author recalls an occasion at which he was present when Churchill, confronted with a possible situation with Portugal during the war, as though waking from a dream, opened the discussion with the remark, 'Shades of Catherine de Braganza!' Here was vision and in these five simple words was an historical sweep which covered all the complexities raised by an apparently simple issue.

Perhaps there is a tendency in the West today to look at world affairs through Western eyes, and one might well query whether their sight is always clear. Philosophical thought in Asia and in the West is in many respects fundamentally different. The differences stem from racial character and religious beliefs. An understanding of these two factors is essential and the study of history undoubtedly helps in this. A good Muslim, Hindu or Buddhist is as good a man and as fit for ultimate salvation as any Christian. Perhaps it is we who are most intolerant. In a series of studies on comparative religions the Rev. P. Johanns, s.j., at the time Professor at the University College of St Francis Xavier, wrote: 'Hinduism may be called the most searching quest in the natural order of the Divine that the world has known. Notice how many conceptions it has in common, at least materially, with Christianity . . . We must say also that Hinduism in its better doctrines has not erred about the nature of God, but about the relation which the world has to God.'[1]

---

[1] Rev. P. Johanns, s.j.: *Hiduism.*

Bibliography

Abdul Fazh Allami, *Ain-i-Akbari* (tr. H. S. Jarrett).
Abdul Fazh Allami, *Akbarnama* (tr. H. Beveridge).
Ala-ad-Din Ata Malia, *A History of the World Conqueror.*
Archer, T. A. & Kingsford, C. L., *The Crusaders.*
Badaoni, *Tarakh-i-Badoni*, vol. II (tr. W. H. Lowe & C. R. Cowell).
Baha ad-Din Ibn Shadad, *Life of Saladin.*
Baldwin, M. W., *Raymond III of Tripoli and the Fall of Jerusalem.*
Barthold, W., *Formation of the Empire of Jenghiz Khan.*
Bretchneider, E., *Notes on Mediaeval Geography and History of Central
    Asia (R.A.S.).*
Bridge, E. A., *The Monks of Kublai Khan.*
Brion, M., *Tamerlane.*
Brown, G., *Literary History of Persia, The Tartar Dominion.*
Clavijo, R. Gonzalez de, *Narrative of the Embassy of Ruy Gonzalez de
    Clavijo.*
Conder, C. E., *The Latin Kingdom of Jerusalem.*
Curtin, J., *The Mongols.*
Czaplicka, M. A., *The Turks in Central Asia.*
Dawson, C., *The Mongol Mission.*
Dussand, R., *Topographical History of Ancient and Mediaeval Syria.*
Elliot, H. M., *History of India.*
Elphinstone, Lord, *History of India.*
Emperor Babur, *Memoirs of* (tr. F. G. Talbot).
Ferishta, *A History of the Rise of the Mohammadan Power in India* (tr.
    J. Briggs).
Fitch, R., *Ralph Fitch, England's Pioneer to India* (ed. J. H. Riley).
Fox, R., *Jenghiz Khan.*

Gibbon, E., *Decline and Fall of the Roman Empire*.

Gibbon, H. A., *Foundation of the Ottoman Empire*.

Glubb, J. B., *The Lost Centuries*.

Goldie, Father Francis, *The First Christian Mission to the Great Mogul*.

Gregor of Akani, *History of the Nature of the Archers (Mongols)* (tr. R. N. Fry and R. Blake).

Grousset, R., *Histoire d'Asie*.

Gulbadan, *History of Humayan* (tr. R. Lamb).

Haida, Mirza, *Tarigh-i-Rashidi* (tr. E. Dennison Ross).

Holden, E. S., *The Mogul Emperors of Hindustan*.

Hookham, H., *Tamerlane the Great*.

Howarth, H. H., *History of the Mongols*.

Hung, Wm., *The Transmission of the Book known as the Secret History of the Mongols* (H.J.A.S., XIV, 1951).

Jahangir, *Memoirs of Jahangir* (tr. A Rogers).

Jauhar, *Private Memoirs of the Mogul Emperor Humayan* (tr. C. Stewart).

Johanns, Rev. P., *Hinduism*.

John of Wurtzburg, *Description of the Holy Land*.

John, C. M., *The Crusaders' Attempt to Colonize Syria* (Journal R.C.A.S., vol. XXI).

Laet de, *Fragmentum Historiae Indicar* (tr. Lethbridge).

Lamb, R., *Tamerlane*.

Lamb, R., *Jenghiz Khan*.

Lamb, R., *From Men and Saints*.

Lane-Poole, S., *Life of Saladin*.

Lane-Poole, S., *Mediaeval India*.

Lane-Poole, S., *The Mohammedan Dynasties*.

Le Strange, G., *The Lands of the Eastern Caliphate*.

Leiden, *Histoires des Campaigns de Genghis Khan*.

Li Ch'ih-Ch'ang, *The Travels of an Alchemist, the Journey of the Taoist Monk Ch'ang-Ch'un from China to the Hindu Kush at the summons of Jenghiz Khan* (tr. Arthur Waley).

Marco Polo, *Travels* (tr. E. Latham).

Moer, Count von, *Kaiser Akbar* (tr. A. Heveridge).

Ockley, N., *History of the Saracens*.

Ohssar, D', *Histoire des Mongols*.

Pelliot, P., *Les Mongols et la Paupite*.

Prawden, M., *The Mongol Empire*.

Roe, T., *The Embassy of Sir Thomas Roe to the Court of the Great Moghul*.

Roose-Keppell, *Tarikh-i-Sultan Mahmud-i-Ghazni*.

Runciman, S., *A History of the Crusades*.

Runciman, S., *Byzantine Civilization*.

Schlumberger, C., *Renaud de Chatillon*.

Skrine and Dennison Ross, *The Heart of Asia*.

Smith, G. A., *The Historical Geography of the Holy Land.*
Smith, V. A., *Akbar.*
Steel, F. A., *India throughout the Ages.*
Stewart, C., *History of Bengal.*
Stubbs, W., *Chronicles and Memorials of the Reign of Richard I.*
Vinsauf, G., *Chronicles of Richard I Crusade.*

PAPERS

Letters of King Amalric, Master of the Temple, Officials of the Temple and other officials of Outremer, R.F.H., vols. II and XVI.
Palestine Pilgrims Trust Society Papers.
Turkistan at the time of the Mongol Invasion, Gibb Memorial Series.

Index